children's
british
history
encyclopedia

Authors: Nicola Barber and Andy Langley
Consultant: Andrew Robertshaw
Produced by Tall Tree Ltd, London

This edition published by Parragon in 2010
Parragon
Queen Street House
4 Queen Street
Bath BA1 1HE, UK

ISBN 978-1-4454-0891-0

Printed in Indonesia

children's
british
history
encyclopedia

step inside and discover our world

Bath · New York · Singapore · Hong Kong · Cologne · Delhi · Melbourne

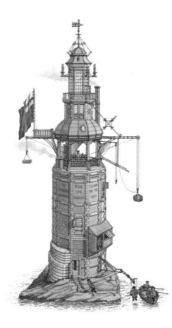

Contents

The History of Britain

The British Isles lie off the northwest corner of the European mainland. They are surrounded by sea, though only a narrow strip of water separates the southern coast from mainland Europe. The climate is mild, there are no really high mountains and the first people to settle here found plenty of wild animals to hunt in its forests and river valleys.

Britain was not always an island. Those first people arrived on foot, when the land was still part of the much bigger European landmass. Later, after water covered the 'land bridge' with Europe, new arrivals came across the sea in boats. Each group brought their own customs and skills. They included Celts, Romans, Anglo-Saxons, Vikings and Normans. Small and often warring kingdoms came together, until by a thousand years ago, the four main parts of the British Isles each had a distinct identity – England, Ireland, Scotland and Wales.

During the last thousand years, Britain steadily grew into one of the strongest and most influential countries in the world. The British people developed a system of government by parliament, which was later to be copied in many other countries. The great revolutions in farming and industry, that were to affect much of the world, began in Britain in the 18th century. In the 19th century, Britain ruled a vast worldwide empire, which brought power and wealth to the country and spread British ideas to other lands. From this empire grew today's Commonwealth.

In the 20th century, Britain played a key role in both world wars, and in the 21st century, although no longer a great power, it is still a leading force in trade, arts, sciences and world affairs. The British people of today, with their diverse origins, share a remarkable history.

Early Britain

The first part of this book covers a huge period of more than two million years. This is much more than any other section. Chapter Two covers about 500 years and Chapter Three just 200 years. The last chapter, about modern Britain, deals with little more than 100 years.

Why is there such a massive difference? For a start, we know very little about Britain in prehistoric times. Nobody wrote anything down, and all our information comes from fragments of fossil, bone, metal and other artefacts. From these, historians and scientists have built up a picture of early British life. But the picture is not complete or definite. It is like a giant jigsaw puzzle with most of the pieces missing.

The second reason for covering such an enormous period is that very little happened for most of that two million years.

p12 A flint spear head with chips removed to sharpen it.

p15 A carving of a bull shaped in stone.

p24 A golden torc or neck ring worn by Celtic men and women.

p18 A crescent-shaped necklace from the Bronze Age.

p29 A Celtic war trumpet with the horn end shaped as the head of a sacred animal.

p37 Coins made just before the Romans withdrew from the British Isles.

p13 Striking two flints together to create a spark and light a fire.

p28 A Celtic hillfort with a gateway protected by a small earthwork.

For the first million-and-a-half years, there were probably no human beings in the British Isles. Mammals crossed over a 'land bridge' that linked Britain to mainland Europe at the time and roamed the hills and valleys.

About half a million years ago, people began to arrive. They were hunters, pursuing the animals that they needed for food. At first, they simply wandered in small groups, sheltering in caves or crude shelters. They learned skills such as lighting fires, cooking food, gathering plants and making sharp flint tools. The most important change only occurred about 4,500 years ago. People learned how to be farmers. They herded livestock and grew special crops. This meant they could build more permanent homes and clear bigger patches of woodland. With more food and safer lives, the population of Britain began to increase.

p38 An Anglo-Saxon iron helmet reconstructed from pieces found at Sutton Hoo, Suffolk. The helmet had been buried with King Redwald of East Anglia in about AD 625, along with a collection of silver, bronze and gold items, in a large wooden ship.

p30 A Roman centurion commanded a 'century' of about 80 foot soldiers. The century was the Roman army's basic unit.

The First Britons

Half a million years ago, the world was in the grip of an Ice Age. Temperatures everywhere had fallen. In the coldest places – the north and the south – sheets of ice more than 200 metres thick in places covered land and sea. Only the area near the Equator remained warm.

Early Britons even had time to make jewellery. In this case, threading shells onto a thin strip of leather.

This was the middle of the most recent Ice Age. There have been many 'ice ages' throughout the world's long history, but each one has contained warmer periods, when part of the thick ice sheet has thawed. Scientists call these warmer times 'interglacial periods' and we are living in one now.

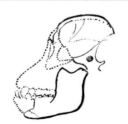

At its coldest, the freezing climate brought amazing changes. Most of Britain, except for the extreme south, disappeared beneath the ice. The seas froze over. In fact, so much water had turned to ice that the level of the sea was much lower than it is today. There was dry land connecting Britain with the mainland of Europe.

Across this 'land bridge' came people from Europe. They were probably different from us, as they belonged to an earlier type of human, called *Homo erectus* (upright man) in Latin.

Timeline (side column):

c.2 million BC Beginning of most recent Ice Age; first mammals probably arrive in Britain.

c.700,000 BC Early human, *homo erectus*, migrates to Europe from Africa.

c.500,000 BC *Homo erectus* crosses land bridge between Europe and Britain.

c.450,000 BC Settlers living in southern Britain use hand axes made of flint.

c.230,000 BC New type of human (Neanderthal) begins to displace *homo erectus*.

c.225,000 BC Flint toolmaking becomes a highly developed craft, especially in the Kent area.

c.120,000 BC Temperatures rise, thawing the worst of the glaciation; many more mammals migrate north to Britain.

c.70,000 BC Another period of glaciation begins.

c.30,000 BC First modern humans (*Homo sapiens sapiens*) in Britain displace Neanderthals.

c.23,000 BC Last period of most recent Ice Age begins.

Large animals such as early elephants and rhinos roamed prehistoric Britain and they were difficult to hunt. Plants and small birds were easier prey. But one elephant might provide enough meat to feed a group of people for a month. To catch these huge creatures, hunters drove them into marshy ground and killed them with stones and spears.

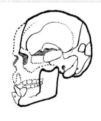

THE PILTDOWN HOAX

One day in 1912, a fossil hunter found the fragments of a human skull and flint tools, which seemed to be 250,000 years old, at Piltdown in Sussex. Scientists were thrilled to have discovered 'the first Briton', who had an ape-like jaw. But some were suspicious. They proved that the skull was a clever joke. The jawbone actually came from an orang-utan and had been stained to look old. The skull dated from the Middle Ages. Today, no one is certain who the hoaxer was.

Cleaning a deer skin with a flint tool. After the meat was eaten, the hunter pegged out the skin and scraped it to get rid of fat and hair. The skin was then sewn into simple clothing using other parts of the animal – its bone for the needle and sinews for the thread.

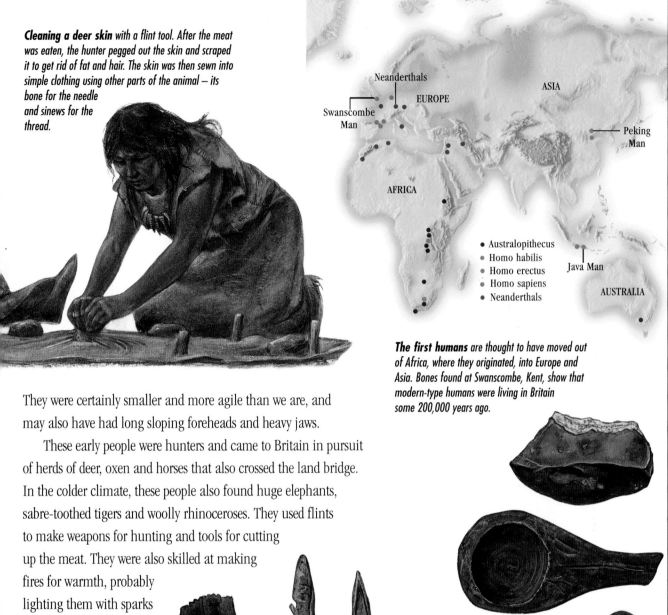

Neanderthals

EUROPE

ASIA

Swanscombe Man

Peking Man

AFRICA

● Australopithecus
● Homo habilis
● Homo erectus
● Homo sapiens
● Neanderthals

Java Man

AUSTRALIA

The first humans are thought to have moved out of Africa, where they originated, into Europe and Asia. Bones found at Swanscombe, Kent, show that modern-type humans were living in Britain some 200,000 years ago.

They were certainly smaller and more agile than we are, and may also have had long sloping foreheads and heavy jaws.

These early people were hunters and came to Britain in pursuit of herds of deer, oxen and horses that also crossed the land bridge. In the colder climate, these people also found huge elephants, sabre-toothed tigers and woolly rhinoceroses. They used flints to make weapons for hunting and tools for cutting up the meat. They were also skilled at making fires for warmth, probably lighting them with sparks created by striking two flints together.

Weapons and tools became more specialized as craftsmen grew more skilful at making them. They used longer and thinner pieces of flint to make pointed knives. They made heads for spears and harpoons out of bones or antlers, carving barbed hooks so that they were hard to dislodge. These heads of bone were fixed to wooden shafts.

The Ice Age

c.30,000 BC New cultures reach Britain from Europe; settlers bring new technology, using wood, bone and antler to make tools as well as stone.

c.23,000 BC Last glaciation of the most recent Ice Age begins; settlers have reached as far north as Derbyshire (the Creswell Crags).

c.18,000 BC Greatest extent of glaciation; ice covers everything north of the Severn Estuary.

c.16,000 BC Only larger mammals can survive the cold; very few humans remain living in Britain.

c.12,000 BC British climate grows slightly warmer; hunters return during the short summer months.

c.10,000 BC Thaw increases, and ice retreats; settlers reach as far north as Morecambe Bay.

c.8000 BC Floods force settlers to move to higher ground, such as the moors of North Yorkshire.

Woolly mammoths had thick skins to keep them warm in the icy climate. Plant-eating animals such as these were the first to move into new areas, looking for food. They were followed by the flesh-eaters, which fell into two main groups – dogs and cats, such as the sabre-toothed tiger.

Chips were broken off a flint to make a sharp spear point.

Over thousands of years, the climate slowly changed. After periods of intense cold, temperatures would rise and some of the ice sheet over Britain would thaw. At these times, more hunters would cross the land bridge and settle in the river valleys of the south. Then the great freeze would spread again, forcing people to retreat southwards to warmer regions.

All this time, people too were changing. The first *Homo erectus* people had been replaced by a more advanced kind of human, known as Neanderthals (a form of *Homo sapiens*). About 30,000 years ago, a new wave of people moved in; these were modern humans (*Homo sapiens sapiens*). They made tools from wood, bone and antler as well as stone, and were probably better organized for hunting and living together than the Neanderthals, who died out. To cope with the cold of Ice Age winters, some people built simple huts, with frames made from animal bones covered with skins.

Hunting game in about 25,000 BC. Our ancestors developed better hunting techniques than the Neanderthals. They made traps for animals, as well as fishing with lines, hooks and harpoons. They may even have used nets and boats. Unable to compete, the Neanderthals probably died out.

Striking a spark. Humans were the only animals that could make fire. This was important for many reasons. Fires kept people warm through long winter periods and were also used to cook meat. Fire could also scare away dangerous animals or frighten prey, such as deer or mammoths, into boggy ground where they could easily be killed.

EARLY BURIAL

One of the most important early sites in Britain is Goat's Cave in Paviland, Glamorgan. About 20,000 years ago, a young man was buried here. His corpse was hoisted up into the cave — which is nine metres from the ground. He was covered in red ochre and wore ivory bracelets and a necklace of wolves' teeth.

Many also made homes in caves, which sheltered them from the bitter winds and were better for keeping fires lit.

The last great freeze-up began in about 23,000 BC. Gradually, the climate grew colder again, and the ice sheet crept down from the north. Life for early humans in Britain slowly became harsher. The only ice-free region was the extreme south of England, and this was no more than a soggy wasteland where few plants could survive. Animals were scarce, so there was little to eat. Most people moved southwards into warmer mainland Europe to get away from the ice.

In about 12,000 BC temperatures began to rise again very slowly. The ice retreated northwards, and the thawing water drained away into lakes and rivers. The returning hunters were often forced to take refuge in hilltop caves to escape the floods of meltwater. They moved steadily to the north towards what is now Scotland.

People first discovered how to make fire whenever they wanted by striking sparks from flints. Later, special fire-making tools were developed using friction to make heat. Wrapping a bowstring round a rod, they drew the bow back and forth. This made the rod spin, its point rubbing on another piece of wood. The point grew hotter and hotter, which eventually produced a flame.

The First Settlements

Growing wheat and barley started in modern-day Iraq in a region called Mesopotamia.

By about 8500 BC, Britain was almost as warm as it is today. The ice had retreated everywhere, except for the tops of the mountains. The melting water formed rivers and lakes. The sea level rose, so that by 6500 BC the land bridge between southern England and Europe was under water. Britain and Ireland were now islands.

This brought problems for the groups of wandering hunters. They could no longer get back to Europe and were forced to settle in Britain. But the thaw made life easier too. The rising temperature and the moisture encouraged plants to grow. Trees began to cover the landscape. Increasing shelter and food attracted many animals, including deer and boar.

The hunting and gathering of food took up most of people's time. However, in about 4500 BC new people arrived, bringing with them seeds of wheat and barley for growing crops.

Spears and axes *were hard to use in thickly wooded areas. By 7000 BC, people were starting to use bows and arrows to hunt game. They were skilful enough to make thin blades of sharp flint for their arrow tips. Hunters also learned that their arrows flew straighter if they had feather flights fixed at the rear end.*

A fired clay pot. The farming people brought with them the skills to make pots of fired clay. Some were decorated with grooves and spirals, while others were smooth and shaped like bags. Pots like these were used to store grain or milk. Later, special pots were made for religious rituals.

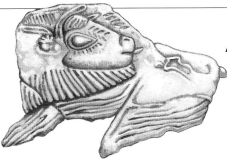

A carving of a bull made in stone. A large cattle herd was a symbol of a man's power and wealth. Herders seized areas of land from their neighbours for grazing their animals.

The new settlers also brought animals to rear for meat, including pigs, cattle and sheep, as well as tame guard dogs.

Instead of wandering in search of food, they settled in one area and grew their own. They chopped down trees with flint axes, sowed seeds and built fences to enclose their animals. In the autumn, they harvested the crops and butchered most of their livestock, but left enough alive to produce young for the next year.

Farming shaped a new way of life in Britain. People now needed to stay where their crops grew and their animals grazed. Gradually, they gave up their nomadic lives to build permanent buildings. Agriculture also speeded up the destruction of ancient woodland, as cattle and sheep chewed on the young shoots of new trees. Over the next 3,000 years, nearly half of Britain's woodland disappeared.

GATHERING FOOD

Wild foods formed an important part of early people's diet. Their favourites probably included hazel and pine nuts, the tender shoots of birch and willow, and mushrooms. They gathered nuts and seeds in autumn and stored them for the winter. When a patch of 'wildwood' was cleared by burning, there was room for young bushes and plants to grow. Their fruits were easier to gather than those of tall forest trees.

An early farming settlement. One-roomed houses were built of mud and timber, and roofed with pieces of turf or with straw thatch. Men and women prepared the cleared land for crops by digging it over with flint or wooden picks. Livestock was fenced into small fields just outside the settlement.

Tombs and Temples

c.4500 BC The Neolithic (New Stone) Age begins with the arrival of farming peoples from Europe; they introduce elaborate burial ceremonies.

c.3700–3400 BC Building of earliest long barrows and chambered tombs, such as Wayland's Smithy in Wiltshire, New Grange in County Meath and Pentre Ifan in Dyfed.

c.3500 BC First wooden 'henge' built at Stonehenge site in Wiltshire.

c.3300 BC Henge monuments built at Stenness and Brodgar in the Orkneys.

c.3100 BC Corpses buried singly in shaft graves in Yorkshire.

c.3000 BC Early stone circles erected in northern England, including Castlerigg in Cumbria.

c.2900 BC Corpses cremated and their remains buried beside other monuments in Dorchester and Oxfordshire.

c.2800 BC Complicated burial rituals in use at tombs of West Kennet, Wiltshire.

Circles of standing stones may have been used for human sacrifices and fertility rituals. The earliest circles were probably made by setting upright huge stones left behind by melting glaciers at the end of the Ice Age.

Trilithons *involve three standing stones where one enormous flat stone has been laid horizontally across two upright stones.*

Once they settled in their farming communities, early Britons learned how to live and work together. The richest among them owned the most cattle and people from the strongest or wealthiest families became leaders of the settlement. Warrior chieftains often led attacks on other groups, seizing land, livestock and grain.

But early Britons did not spend all their lives simply farming or fighting. After about 3600 BC, they began to build large monuments, some of which took an enormous amount of time and effort. The earliest of these were 'camps' on hilltops. Rings of ditches and banks were dug around a large open space, with causeways crossing them. No one knows exactly why these camps were made, but they may have been religious centres, where annual ceremonies were held, connected with nearby graves.

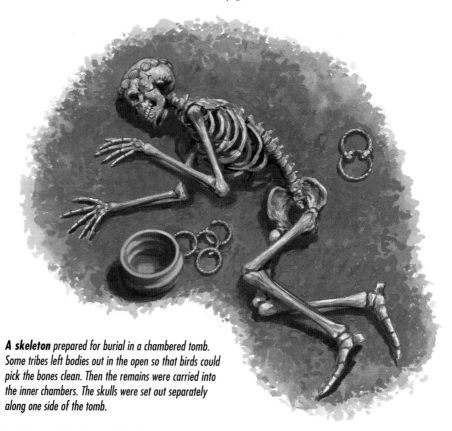

A skeleton *prepared for burial in a chambered tomb. Some tribes left bodies out in the open so that birds could pick the bones clean. Then the remains were carried into the inner chambers. The skulls were set out separately along one side of the tomb.*

Cutaway of the long barrow at West Kennet in Wiltshire. Over 100 metres long, this is one of the largest barrows in Britain. Inside is a passage with chambers on each side.

At the same time, grand tombs were being built to hold the bodies of chieftains and their families. Earlier peoples had buried their dead in simple graves, but these were the first tombs to be built up into field monuments. Some were rectangular mounds of earth called long barrows. Others, called chambered tombs, had stone spaces inside, with walls and roofs made of big slabs of rock.

Each tomb was the burial place for a family or group over many years. As many as 50 bodies might be buried in one long barrow. Tombs and barrows like these have been found all over the British Isles. Among the most famous are New Grange in Ireland, Belas Knap in Gloucestershire and Maes Howe in the Orkneys.

After about 3400 BC, people began to build larger centres for religious worship. The earliest of these were circles of wooden posts called 'henges', set inside round ditches and banks. By 3000 BC, the first circles of standing stones were being erected in Britain.

Grave goods found alongside the bodies of buried people included bronze daggers (left) and axes, as well as jewellery and other decorative goods.

GRAVE GOODS

Dead ancestors were honoured by most Neolithic people. Beside the bodies in the tombs, they placed 'grave goods' which the dead might need in the next world. These included tools, weapons (such as flint arrow heads), jewellery, pottery and food. The entrances to some tombs were later blocked off with stone slabs, perhaps to prevent grave robbers from ransacking these goods. The tombs often became the centre for elaborate rituals. On special days, such as solstices and equinoxes, people paid homage to their dead ancestors. Priests usually performed these rituals.

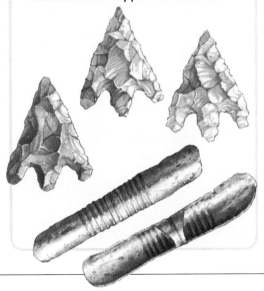

The Bronze Age

In about 2500 BC, a new wave of settlers began arriving on the east coast of Britain from mainland Europe. They were known as the Beaker people because of the bell-shaped decorated pottery cups they used. These people also brought with them a new and important skill – the making of metal tools and weapons.

A bronze pin used to hold a woman's hair in place.

Stone was still the most widely used material for axe-heads and knife blades. But the Beaker people knew how to make these things out of copper and how to make jewellery and ornaments from gold. They had also developed processes for mining the ore (the rock which contained the metal) and heating it to extract the copper.

Pure copper was too soft to make an effective tool. By about 2150 BC, metalworkers were adding tin to make a tough new alloy, or mixture, called bronze. It could be bent or moulded to exact shapes, and honed to give it a sharp cutting edge. At first, metal workers only used bronze to make small daggers and ornaments. These were not everyday tools, but were placed in tombs as grave goods. As craftsmen grew more skilful over the next 1,000 years, bronze replaced stone as the main material for the blades of tools such as axes, spears, arrows and knives.

A lunula, or crescent-shaped necklace, fashioned from a single sheet of beaten gold. As coppersmiths and goldsmiths grew more skilful, they could make more daring shapes such as this. Decorative patterns on these ornaments were often copied from pots made by the Beaker people.

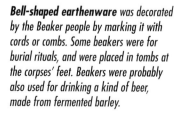

Bell-shaped earthenware was decorated by the Beaker people by marking it with cords or combs. Some beakers were for burial rituals, and were placed in tombs at the corpses' feet. Beakers were probably also used for drinking a kind of beer, made from fermented barley.

Bracelet

Dress pattern

People learned to spin *thread and weave woollen cloth during the Bronze Age. Wealthy people began to wear woollen clothes instead of animal skins. Women pinned their hair up tidily with pins made from bronze or bone.*

THE HORSE

The bones of horses have been unearthed in some tombs in southern England, such as West Kennet. People had always hunted herds of wild horses for their meat, but the Beaker people may have been the first to tame them for riding. These early horses were only the size of a small pony, so they could not be used for ploughing or other heavy work.

Britain had large supplies of copper ore in several regions. Tin ore was found only in Devon and Cornwall, and this area became an important centre of trade. Tin miners sent their products by sea all over the British Isles, as well as to mainland Europe. In this way a network of trading routes grew up, stretching as far as Spain. By 700 BC, Britons were exporting copper, tin and precious metals, as well as animal hides and fleeces.

In exchange, they got finished bronze ornaments and tools, as well as exotic materials such as amber and jet.

A Bronze Age hut. *Most dwellings were still simple, with thatched or brushwood roofs over scooped-out hollows in the ground. But in some areas, more permanent houses were built. One farming settlement on Dartmoor contained over 20 round huts with walls, benches and fireplaces made of granite.*

Circles of Stone

The greatest of the prehistoric monuments were the circles of standing stones. When the Beaker people arrived in Britain, several stone circles had already been erected. Built from about 3300 BC onwards, they stood in places as far apart as the Lake District, Orkney and southern Ireland.

Over the next thousand years, many more circles were completed. By about 1200 BC, more than 900 had been built. Some, such as Avebury in Wiltshire, cover a huge area and measure over a kilometre around. Others are much smaller.

The largest circles needed a vast amount of work over a long period of time. Some stones were transported over long distances, probably by boat, and then hauled on sledges by oxen. Hundreds of labourers dug the encircling ditches and the holes for the stones to rest in. The stones had to be shaped and trimmed, then pulled upright with ropes so that they stood firm.

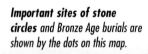

SCOTLAND

IRELAND

ENGLAND

WALES

Important sites of stone circles and Bronze Age burials are shown by the dots on this map.

- **zc.3300–3200 BC** Earliest stone circles built on northwest coast of Britain; also New Grange, County Meath.
- **c.3100 BC** The last long barrows are dug; circle at Ballynoe, County Down.
- **c.3000 BC** Circle at Stenness, Orkney.
- **c.2800 BC** First stage of Stonehenge, Wiltshire, made of timber is laid out.
- **c.2600 BC** Early copper working; circles at Avebury, Wiltshire.
- **c.2400 BC** Circle at Arbor Low, Derbyshire; also at Merry Maidens, in Cornwall.
- **c.2200 BC** Second stage of Stonehenge; first round barrows appear; erection of Druids' Circle, Gwynedd.
- **c.2100 BC** Third stage of Stonehenge; many smaller circles erected.
- **c.2000 BC** Circle at Callanish, Outer Hebrides.
- **c.1900 BC** Circle at Berrybrae, Grampian.
- **c.1700 BC** Circles at Beaghmore, County Tyrone.
- **c.1200 BC** Circle-building era ends.

Drums carved from chalk, unearthed at Folkton in Yorkshire. They had been buried next to a child in a round barrow. Among the designs are the face of a goddess, pairs of circles and patterns.

BURIAL URNS

People in northern Britain developed the burial customs of the Beaker people. By about 2200 BC, they were placing their dead in round barrows (circular mounds covered with turf or boulders). The bodies were laid on their sides, bent as if they were asleep. Some were cremated and the ashes placed in special urns (shown here). The urns were closed and buried in the barrows.

This carved golden square was found in Bush Barrow near Stonehenge. Inside the barrow was the body of a man who had obviously been rich or powerful. He had also been buried with a carved sceptre made of wood, stone and bone, as well as three daggers, a shield and an axe.

Druids were Celtic priests who worshipped in groves of oak trees. Some people believe that they also held ceremonies in stone circles such as Stonehenge.

Some circle sites changed greatly over the centuries. The most famous of all, Stonehenge in Wiltshire, went through several different phases. In about 2800 BC, a circular ditch and bank were constructed, with sarsen stones (sandstone boulders) at the entrance. Six centuries later, the Beaker people brought enormous 'bluestones' from South Wales and erected two rings, one inside the other. In about 2100 BC, bigger sarsens were set up as a series of 'trilithons' – two standing stones with another laid on top. In about 1550 BC, the original bluestones were raised in a circle inside the trilithons.

Nobody knows what these stone circles were for. They may have been temples where religious rituals took place. Some people believe the stones were set out so that people could watch the Sun's changing path and keep track of the seasons.

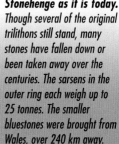

Stonehenge as it is today. Though several of the original trilithons still stand, many stones have fallen down or been taken away over the centuries. The sarsens in the outer ring each weigh up to 25 tonnes. The smaller bluestones were brought from Wales, over 240 km away.

Iron Age Farmers

Inside an Iron Age farmer's hut. Food was cooked in a metal pot hung over the central fire – the smoke escaped through a hole in the roof directly above. Everything had to be made on the farmstead, including woven cloth, pottery and iron tools.

In 750 BC, the population of the British Isles was only about 150,000. However, there were enough people to make a great change to the landscape. England, for example, had once been almost entirely covered with woodland. Now, nearly half of that woodland had disappeared: burned, or felled with axes, to make farmland.

Iron-tipped ploughs could be hooked to a team of oxen to plough through the heaviest of soils.

At about the same time, ironworking reached Britain from southern Europe. Smiths learned to extract iron from its ore, and to transform it into weapons and tools. Iron was better than bronze in many ways. It was much tougher and easier to work. Iron ore was also cheaper and more plentiful than copper, which is the main ingredient of bronze. Britain moved into what is known as the Iron Age. Using axes and picks with iron blades, farmers could clear land more quickly. More important still was the development of the iron-tipped plough. Drawn by a pair of oxen, this could churn up the soil more quickly and deeply than the old wooden plough or bronze hoe. Fields were also ploughed across at right angles, so many Iron Age fields were roughly square in shape.

CHARIOTS

Wheeled carts and chariots were used in the Iron Age. Warriors became very skilful in handling war chariots in battle. A soldier mounted behind the driver and two horses as they raced along enemy lines. He threw spears or shot arrows, then leapt off to fight on foot. Many important chieftains were buried with dismantled war chariots.

Harvested grain crops were stored under thatched shelters or in pits. Farmers took out the sheaves when needed and threshed them by beating or using oxen to trample them. This broke up the straw and released the grains from the ears.

Iron Age buildings were usually clustered together, surrounded by their well-fenced arable fields and perhaps an earth bank or timber fence, called a palisade. Beyond these was the rough grazing for livestock. The main crops were wheat and barley, which were harvested with iron sickles. The grain was either dried, using hot stones, and stored in pits, or stacked in huts raised from the ground away from rats. Besides cattle and pigs, farmers were now raising more sheep than ever before, mainly for their wool and milk.

The invention of the stone quern (handmill) for grinding grain produced finer flour which could be mixed with water and baked into a form of flat bread. Before this, most grains were boiled up into a porridge.

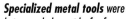

Specialized metal tools were being made by smiths for farmers. The bronze 'terret' was for attaching the yokes of carts to oxen. The iron reaping-hook with its bone handle was used to cut down grain crops at harvest time.

Celtic Times

All through the Iron Age, settlers from mainland Europe continued to flow into the British Isles. As trade increased across the Channel, there was greater contact between Britain and the continent. By about 500 BC, a new kind of culture was spreading across lowland Britain. This belonged to a people we now call the Celts.

The Celtic tribes probably came from central Europe and moved outwards into parts of Italy, France, Spain and Britain.

The Celts were farmers and lived – like other Iron Age people – in small village groups in the centre of their arable fields. These groups slowly collected together into larger tribes, living in their own special regions. Each tribe was ruled by a chieftain. There was an 'upper class' of warriors (who grew long moustaches) and a 'lower class' of slaves and labourers, who did most of the agricultural work.

The Celts were also a warlike people. The tribes often quarrelled with each other and fought savage battles. They could be a terrifying sight for the enemy. Many Celtic warriors were taller than southern Europeans, and some fought naked, with their long, fair hair stuck up into spikes whitened with lime. They screamed as they ran into battle, waving their iron swords and blowing horns and trumpets.

The Celts were fine craftsmen, who made splendidly decorated metal weapons and ornaments. This bronze shield was found in the river Thames. It was probably not meant to be used in battle, and may have been an offering to the god of the river.

This gold torc is typical of the kind of neck rings that both men and women liked to wear. It was probably made by craftsmen in East Anglia, who also produced beautiful brooches, weapons and mirrors.

A recreation of a round house on an Iron Age farm from about 300 BC. Experiments using Celtic farming methods show that their methods were very efficient, producing more than enough food to eat.

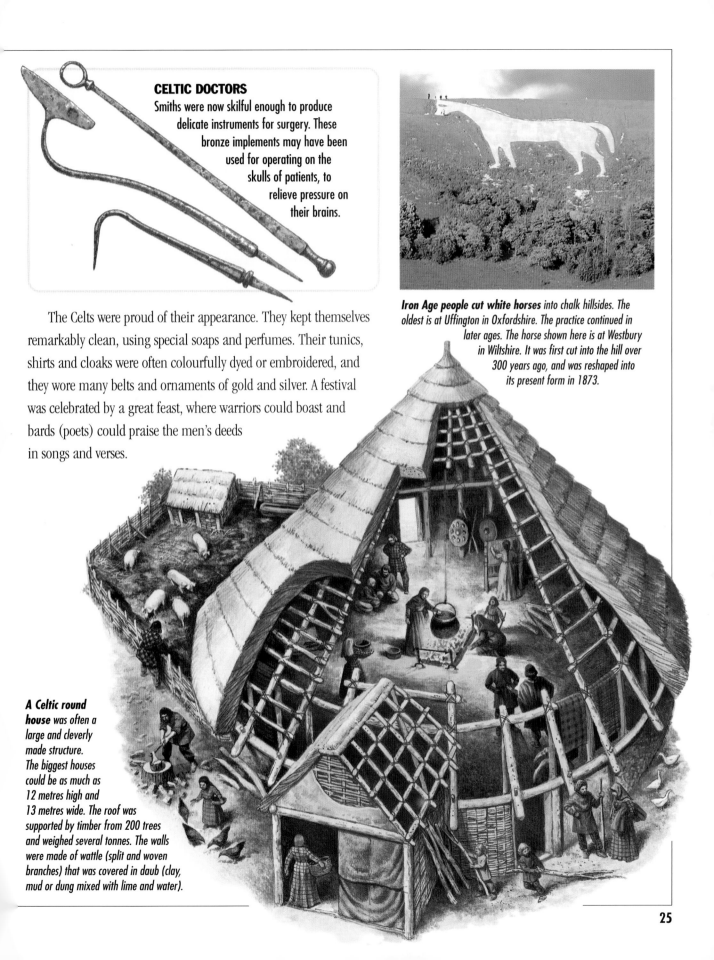

CELTIC DOCTORS

Smiths were now skilful enough to produce delicate instruments for surgery. These bronze implements may have been used for operating on the skulls of patients, to relieve pressure on their brains.

Iron Age people cut white horses into chalk hillsides. The oldest is at Uffington in Oxfordshire. The practice continued in later ages. The horse shown here is at Westbury in Wiltshire. It was first cut into the hill over 300 years ago, and was reshaped into its present form in 1873.

The Celts were proud of their appearance. They kept themselves remarkably clean, using special soaps and perfumes. Their tunics, shirts and cloaks were often colourfully dyed or embroidered, and they wore many belts and ornaments of gold and silver. A festival was celebrated by a great feast, where warriors could boast and bards (poets) could praise the men's deeds in songs and verses.

A Celtic round house was often a large and cleverly made structure. The biggest houses could be as much as 12 metres high and 13 metres wide. The roof was supported by timber from 200 trees and weighed several tonnes. The walls were made of wattle (split and woven branches) that was covered in daub (clay, mud or dung mixed with lime and water).

Religions and Ritual

A stone cross. Christianity swept away most Celtic religion during the late Roman times.

A bronze figure of a wild boar. The Celts believed that animals such as the boar, the stag and the bull were sacred, and were protected by their own god, Cernunnos, the Lord of the Beasts.

The Celts were ruled by chiefs and nobles, but there was another class which was almost as powerful. These were the priests, or Druids. They were in charge of religious rituals and settled arguments between tribes or individuals. They set the times for the annual festivals that marked key moments in the farming year, such as ploughing or harvest. They were also teachers, in charge of educating the sons of tribal leaders.

To become a Druid, you had to be born as part of the warrior class. You were chosen by a vote among your tribe, though sometimes candidates had to fight each other to decide who joined the priesthood. Then came the training, which might last as long as 20 years. Druids had many privileges. They did not have to take part in wars, yet they shared plunder gained in battle and they had great influence on decisions.

The main job of the Druids was to organize religious activities. The Celts believed in many gods and goddesses, as well as spirits and sacred animals. Among them were Sucellos, the sky god, whose hammer caused lightning, and Nodens, who made clouds and rain.

THE HORSE GODDESS

The goddess with a horse depicted by this statuette was called 'Epona'. Her name comes from the Celtic word *epos*, meaning 'horse'. There were several horse-goddesses in Celtic mythology, including Rhiannon, the Great Queen. Horses appear in many other legends, from Pegasus, the winged horse of Greek legend to Sleipnir, the eight-legged horse ridden by Odin, chief god of Norse mythology.

This bronze cauldron from Denmark is similar to metal vessels that would have been used in Britain. It shows animals, people and gods. The Celts used decoration on everything from iron and bronze shields and swords to pottery, metal mirrors and coins.

Other gods and spirits lived in sacred springs or in groves of trees in forests, and these places became magical sites, where ceremonies were held. Druids were the link between this supernatural world and everyday life. They even claimed to be able to predict the future, by interpreting the flight of birds or watching the death throes of sacrificial victims. Sacrifices of humans and animals were made to please the gods. The victims might be drowned, strangled or placed inside giant wicker basket figures and burned to death.

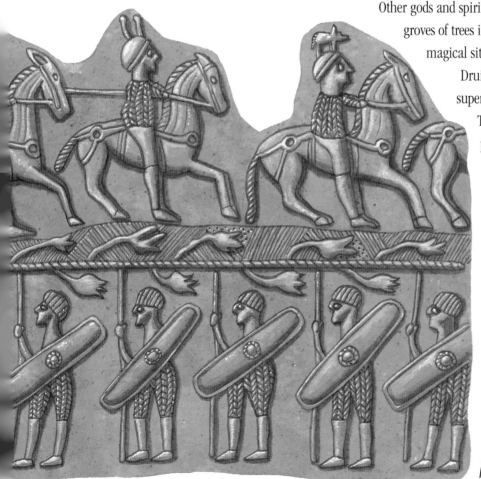

Human sacrifice played an important part in Celtic religion. The image on the left is a detail from the cauldron shown above. It features a figure on the left that may be a priest carrying out a ritual drowning or hurling a victim down a shaft. Each Celtic tribe had its own gods, customs, myths and legends.

Celts and Hillforts

Britons had been building forts on hilltops since before 1500 BC. These were places of refuge, which were difficult for an enemy to attack. Ringed with ditches and banks, they gave a good view of the land all around. Cattle and food stores could be kept inside, as well as supplies of weapons.

c.1500 BC Farmsteads and other communities make permanent settlements, protected against attackers by banks and ditches.

c.1300 BC Hilltop fort with timber palisade (fence of stakes) built in Derbyshire uplands.

c.1000 BC Hill settlement established at present-day Edinburgh on rocky outcrop above a loch.

c.850 BC Circular hillforts built in County Armagh and North Wales – a sign of more violent times.

c.700 BC Farmers settle on man-made islands on Loch Tay, Scotland.

c.500 BC Many hillforts are constructed in England and Wales as a rising population leads to a shortage of farmland and the outbreak of civil wars; several hillforts are attacked and burned.

c.400 BC Danebury hillfort, Hampshire, is rebuilt and strengthened.

c.100 BC Stone houses built on a mountain top in Gwynedd.

c.75 BC Danebury hillfort destroyed by fire and abandoned.

46 BC Central Irish tribes build earth wall along river Shannon to keep out enemies.

AD 43 Invasion by Romans under Claudius; Britons retreat to hillforts, which have to be taken by the Romans one by one.

A bronze war helmet made in about 100 BC. It is decorated with engraving, but the metal is too thin for it to have been much use in battle. It was probably intended as an offering for a Celtic god.

The earliest forts were probably farmsteads or villages with simple wooden stockades (barriers made of stakes) around them to keep out wild animals or human raiders. Then people began to choose sites on higher ground, which were easier to defend. As Britain's population grew, so did the threat of attack from other tribes. People needed strongholds to retreat to in dangerous times.

They dug ditches around the summit of a hill and heaped the earth into banks. Then they erected double stockades of timber and filled the spaces between them with rammed soil and rubble so that sentries could patrol along the top. Some large hillforts, such as Maiden Castle, in Dorset, had several rings of ditches and stockades.

CELTIC BATTLE

A Celtic war trumpet, or carynx. It consists of a long metal tube, which broadens out into a large horn end shaped with the head of a sacred animal. The trumpet was held upright when it was being blown. The Celts rushed into battle to the blare of instruments like this, as well as their own yells and screams. They often fought without armour, and painted their bodies in bright colours. They attacked with slings and stones, spears and long swords, and defended themselves with metal helmets and shields made of wood and leather.

Most hillfort sites were uneven. The ditches and ramparts had to follow the contours of the hills they were built on. A few had slopes on each side, making them almost perfect strongholds. Other forts were built on narrow cliff headlands which jutted out into the sea, so that an enemy could only approach along the narrow neck.

These hillforts gradually changed from being emergency places of safety into more permanent settlements. By about 100 BC, the larger ones had grown into towns, their streets lined with timber huts and grain stores. They became the headquarters for the local tribe and centres of trade.

SCOTLAND

IRELAND

WALES

ENGLAND

■ Hill forts
■ Smaller defended places

Hillforts in Celtic Britain were concentrated in the south and mid-west. But there were smaller fortified settlements in the far west and north, including Ireland, Scotland and Wales.

A Celtic hillfort. The gateway is protected by a small earthwork at the front, and by timber gatehouses on either side. The palisaded (fenced) walls around the settlement are built on top of earth banks. Inside, there are huts of wood and mud – some for living in, others for storing food or weapons. The tribal meeting hall is at the centre.

Roman Invasion

In 55 BC a fleet of 80 Roman ships landed on the coast of Kent. This was the first raid across the English Channel by Julius Caesar, the Roman leader in Gaul (France). But it was short-lived. The invaders were beaten back by storms and by resistance from local tribes.

55 BC Julius Caesar's first raid on southeast England.

54 BC Second Roman landing; Kentish tribes defeated.

AD 40 Roman emperor Caligula calls off invasion of Britain when his troops mutiny.

AD 42 Death of Cunobelinus, most powerful British leader.

AD 43 Major Roman invasion of Britain; Emperor Claudius visits the island.

AD 44 Claudius celebrates the invasion of Britain with a triumphal procession in Rome.

AD 47 Roman armies reach Devon and Cornwall in the southwest.

AD 51 Caratacus, last major leader of British resistance, is captured in Wales.

AD 60 Revolt of the Iceni tribe, led by Queen Boudicca, is suppressed.

AD 77 Agricola subdues the Welsh tribes.

Julius Caesar became one of Rome's three leaders in 60 BC. He conquered Gaul (France) in a brilliant campaign and then raided Britain. Back in Rome, he ousted his ruling colleagues and made himself dictator, but was assassinated five years later.

A Roman centurion commanded a 'century' of about 80 foot soldiers. Centurions wore plumed helmets and specially coloured cloaks. The century was the army's basic unit. A group of six centuries made a cohort, and ten cohorts made a legion. There were up to 30 legions in the whole army.

The next year, Caesar returned with 800 ships. This time he defeated the Kentish tribes, who agreed to give him hostages and pay a yearly sum of money, called a tribute. Soon, however, Caesar had more urgent business and returned to Gaul.

It was not until almost a century later that the Romans made a serious attempt to conquer Britain. Emperor Claudius wanted to secure trading links with the island and he also needed an easy victory to boost his standing in Rome. So in AD 43, a force of 40,000 Roman troops landed in Kent. They defeated the local leader Caratacus, who fled westwards. Claudius arrived to lead his army into Colchester, where ten tribal chiefs surrendered to him. Even the king of the Orkney islands, far to the north, sent a promise of loyalty.

The Roman army is shown in this carving defeating a German tribe; it was a ruthless and well-trained fighting machine. Few enemies could match the Romans' discipline and battle tactics.

The invaders then spread out to control lowland Britain. One legion marched to the southwest and two legions went north, establishing a series of forts. By AD 61, Roman rule reached the river Humber in the north and the river Severn in the west. The advance went on for the next 20 years. Under their governor, Agricola, Roman troops subdued Wales and northern England. Then they penetrated into Scotland, defeating the Caledonian tribes in the Grampian Hills in AD 84.

Britain lay at a corner of the enormous Roman Empire, and more than 1,200 kilometres from Rome. Many British tribes, such as the Caledonians and Brigantes of the north, threatened rebellion. How did the Romans control this remote province?

The answer was the army. Roman soldiers were the best armed and best trained in the world. After the invasion, there were over 50,000 troops in Britain — nearly 10 per cent of the Roman army. Most of these were in the highlands of the north and west, where peace was harder to maintain.

The soldiers were stationed in fortresses at key points such as Chester, York and Caerleon. There were also dozens of smaller bases, most of them spaced one day's march apart. Between the fortresses, the Romans built a network of roads, so that armies could travel swiftly across country.

They also organized Britain to make it easier to rule. They divided the land into regions, each one based on a tribal area. Much of the day-to-day governing of the regions and tax collecting was left to local chieftains. So the chieftains kept most of their power – but only if they remained loyal to Rome.

Roman strongholds, *around AD 100, and the road known as the Fosse Way are shown on this map of southern Britain. The names of powerful Celtic tribal areas in the region are shown in capital letters.*

The Roman footsoldier's sword *was a short, double-edged stabbing knife called a gladius. This sword, with its decorated scabbard and handle, would probably have belonged to an officer.*

Remains of Hadrian's Wall. *In AD 122, the Emperor Hadrian ordered a wall to be built from the Solway Firth to the North Sea, to separate the rebellious Brigantes from the northern tribes. In spite of their early victories, the Romans never conquered Scotland or the far north.*

Roman Towns

When the Romans arrived, nearly everyone in Britain still lived in the countryside. The Romans began to establish towns, which were an important part of their system for maintaining peace.

A carving showing Roman carpenters. Craftsmen had their workshops around the town's forum or in the narrow back streets. Most people (except slaves) worked only about six hours a day, from sunrise to noon.

Throughout the empire, they imposed the same system, moving people from their hillforts to settlements on the plains. In a town, people could be encouraged to live a more 'Roman' way of life and could be more easily controlled.

There were three main types of Roman towns in Britain. The *colonia* was only for Roman citizens who had full rights under Roman law. Next was the *municipium*, or free town, where only the ruling families were accepted as citizens.

Most women wore a tunic of wool or linen which reached down to the ankles. Only the rich could afford silk or cotton clothes. Women wore their hair piled high on their head in plaits and ringlets.

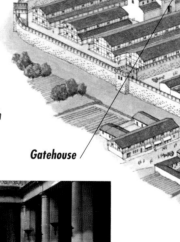

Stadium

Gatehouse

Cemetery

One of the grandest town buildings was at Bath, where natural hot water from a spring was piped into a swimming pool. People came to bathe, exercise and gossip.

AD **84** Agricola defeats Caledonian tribes in Scotland.

AD **87** Romans give up attempt to subdue the Scottish Highlands and withdraw south.

AD **105** Romans withdraw from Scottish Lowlands.

AD **118** Revolt by the Brigantes tribe in northern England.

c.AD **120** Major road-building programme begins.

AD **122** Building work begins on Hadrian's Wall.

c.AD **125** Britons join the Roman army.

AD **140** Romans advance north: work begins on the Antonine Wall.

c.AD **150** Britain and Ireland included in world map compiled by the Greek geographer Ptolemy.

AD **163** Romans withdraw from Antonine Wall.

AD **208** Emperor Septimius Severus divides Britain into two provinces.

c.AD **217** Most of Britain is now peaceful.

At the bottom was the *civitas* town, or capital of a tribal region, where no one had citizen's rights. By about AD 200, there were dozens of thriving towns stretching across the whole of southern Britain.

Many of the bigger towns were laid out in a grid pattern. At the centre was an open space called the forum. This had colonnades on three sides, behind which were shops, workshops and offices. On the fourth side stood the basilica, which contained the council chamber and the law courts. The forum's central space was used as a market place.

Roman builders took care to keep towns as healthy as possible. Pipes brought in clean water from lakes and rivers, while drains and sewers carried away dirty water. Most towns had at least one public bath.

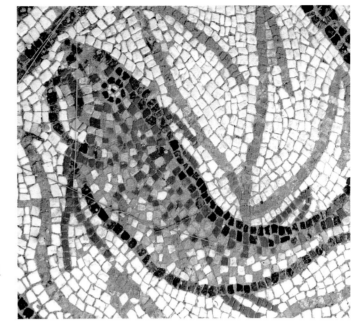

Mosaic patterns and pictures were made by craftsmen to decorate the walls or floors of fine houses. They used thousands of tiny cubes of coloured stone, clay or glass. Several preserved mosaics can be seen today.

Forum

Temple

Theatre

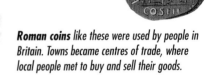

Roman coins like these were used by people in Britain. Towns became centres of trade, where local people met to buy and sell their goods.

A Roman town's grid system of streets divided the buildings into apartment blocks where most people lived. The main streets crossed at the central forum. Around the town was a high wall, with watchtowers and four gateways, which were locked at night.

Baths

Romano-British potters imitated Roman and Greek styles. Taller, pointed jars called amphorae were used for storing oil, grain and wine. The Romans planted vineyards for wine in southern Britain.

Life in Roman Britain

By AD 300, southern Britain was booming. 'Britain is a most wealthy island', wrote one Roman visitor. Farming had expanded, as the Romans ordered vast new areas to be ploughed for growing crops.

Gold jewellery was produced by smiths from their city workshops. Gold was mined in Wales and silver was extracted from lead deposits in Somerset and Derbyshire.

Well-organized factories, such as those in East Anglia and Oxfordshire, were producing large amounts of pottery. British woollen coats and rugs were very popular in Gaul. Gold, lead and silver were being mined in Wales and the west, and the iron industry was growing rapidly. Foundries have been found in the centres of towns such as Silchester in Hampshire.

There was plenty of work for people in these industries, as well as for house builders, road engineers, woodmen and carters or bargemen (who transported the goods).

c.AD 10 Even before the final invasion, tribal chiefs in southern Britain import luxuries from the Mediterranean.

c.AD 50 Lead mining begins in Somerset.

c.AD 85 Tribal leaders begin building villas in the south, including Fishbourne.

c.AD 135 Wetlands of East Anglia drained for farming.

c.AD 150 Romans make farming more efficient and increase harvests.

c.AD 160 Over 40 iron-smelting sites at work throughout Sussex.

c.AD 300 Pottery works flourish in Oxfordshire and East Anglia.

c.AD 320 British woollen textiles are popular on the continent.

AD 359 Surplus British grain shipped to Gaul to feed Roman troops.

c.AD 370 New boom in building villas.

Soldiers of a Roman legion, called legionaries, are shown here. They were the frontline of the army and were backed up by auxiliary troops. Britons were encouraged to join the auxiliary army and were granted citizenship.

There was also a much greater variety of food to eat. Farmers had been producing grain, cattle and pigs for several centuries, but the Romans introduced many new crops, including apples, grapes, onions and cabbages. Olive oil and wine were imported from Gaul and Spain.

British chieftains and powerful Romans lived very comfortably in grand palaces in the countryside. Besides these luxury buildings, there were hundreds of villas built in the Roman style and surrounded by an estate, with farmland and workshops for ironworking and pottery.

Meanwhile, in Hibernia (Ireland) life had scarcely changed. The Romans had never tried to conquer the island. As a result, the Irish tribal system remained as strong as ever.

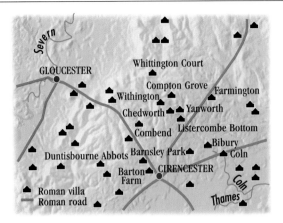

The Cotswold region of southern England was a popular area for villa-building. Most were working farms, built near roads or rivers along which produce could be taken to market.

A villa was both a farm and a place to live. It had comfortable living quarters for the owner and his family. On one side, the bedrooms opened onto a pillared veranda facing the private garden. On the other side was the courtyard, surrounded by farm buildings.

ROMAN SEWING KIT
All clothes had to be sewn by hand, using needles and a thimble made of bone or iron (shown here). The thread was usually linen, made from flax or wool — cotton, from Asia, was still scarce and costly. The fibres were spun into yarn, which was then woven into cloth. Spinning and weaving were part of the daily work of the women of a household.

Gods and Goddesses

The Romans had no single religion. Traditionally, they believed in a group of gods and goddesses, ruled by Jupiter, who took care of every part of their lives. Later, they worshipped their emperors, who proclaimed themselves to be gods as well!

c.AD **280** Chain of forts built on south coast to guard against Saxon raiders.

AD **312** Emperor Constantine recognizes Christianity as a state religion.

AD **321** Constantine makes Sunday a day of rest throughout Empire.

AD **367** Hadrian's Wall overrun by alliance of Picts, Scots and Saxons.

AD **395** Roman Empire divided into two parts: West and East.

c.AD **400** Irish settle on Britain's west coast.

AD **401** Roman troops begin withdrawal from Britain.

c.AD **408** More Saxons settle in Britain.

AD **410** Emperor Honorius tells Britons to defend themselves: the city of Rome is sacked by Visigoths.

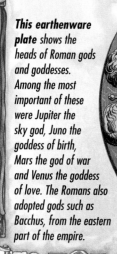

Vesta was goddess of fire and the hearth. She was worshipped in nearly every Roman home and a symbolic fire was kept alight in her special temple in Rome throughout the year.

The Romans were generally tolerant of other people's beliefs, often adding foreign gods to their own. In Britain, however, they saw the Druids, with their human sacrifice rituals, as a threat and set about destroying Druid power. The Romans brought their own gods to Britain and built temples in their honour, with altars where they made offerings of food and wine. In their homes, families had small shrines, where they placed gifts for the household gods who, they believed, watched over them. By about AD 200, the Romans in Britain had adopted several Celtic gods, such as Sulis the water goddess and Nodens, the god of health.

Now, however, another powerful religion was taking hold: Christianity. At first, the Roman emperors banned the new faith, because Christians only believed in one God, and refused to worship the old gods. But Constantine, emperor from AD 306 to 337, made Christianity the religion of the Roman Empire.

This earthenware plate shows the heads of Roman gods and goddesses. Among the most important of these were Jupiter the sky god, Juno the goddess of birth, Mars the god of war and Venus the goddess of love. The Romans also adopted gods such as Bacchus, from the eastern part of the empire.

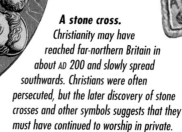

A stone cross.
Christianity may have reached far-northern Britain in about AD 200 and slowly spread southwards. Christians were often persecuted, but the later discovery of stone crosses and other symbols suggests that they must have continued to worship in private.

End of the Empire

By AD 300, the vast Roman Empire was in trouble. Large numbers of Huns, Goths and Vandals from northeast Europe were on the move. They threatened the borders of Rome's provinces and the imperial army was not strong enough to defend them properly. In Rome, there were food shortages and civil war.

The Romans continued to make a profit from British trade, but this could not stop their empire from collapsing.

The Romans decided to abandon their most remote provinces first. Despite the profits from British trade, the cost of keeping a large garrison on the island was very high. There were frequent attacks from the north. In AD 367, an alliance of Picts, Scots and other tribes ravaged much of northern Britain. At the same time, Saxon pirates from Germany raided the southeast coast, and Irish tribes attacked in the west.

To meet these dangers, the Romans sent fresh troops and built new forts. But in AD 401, Roman troops were called home to defend northern Italy. By AD 407, almost the entire army had left the island. When the Britons begged the Emperor Honorius for help against their enemies, he refused. Roman rule in Britain was at an end.

Roman legionaries on the march. Troops in Britain felt cut off from Rome and in AD 383 they elected their own emperor, Magnus Maximus. He weakened the island's garrison by taking an army to invade Italy, and was killed.

The god Mithras was the Persian god of light and truth. One temple of Mithras was built in AD 205 at Carrawburgh on Hadrian's Wall. Many Mithran temples were built underground, to look like caves.

This cavalry parade helmet from Ribchester in Lancashire probably belonged to a Sarmatian horseman, a member of an army of 5,000 brought by the Romans from the Danube region in central Europe. By AD 200, the Romans were enlisting many foreign soldiers from the countries within their empire.

Anglo-Saxons

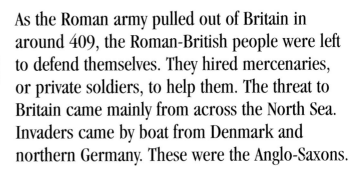

Anglo-Saxons were skilled at working with gold as shown by this brooch made with finely woven gold threads.

c.409 Roman soldiers and officials leave Britain.

c.420 Saxon settlers land on East Anglian coast.

c.430 King Vortigern hires Saxon mercenaries to defend Britain against other invaders.

c.450 Scots from Ireland establish Dalriada, a colony on Scottish west coast.

c.491 Saxons gain control of south coast.

c.500 Britons win important victory against Saxons at Mount Badon.

577 Saxon victory at Dyrham, Gloucestershire, pushes remaining Britons back into Wales and Cornwall.

c.625 Lavish burial of Redwald at Sutton Hoo.

632 Kings of Mercia and Gwynedd unite to defeat Northumbria.

672 Egfrith of Northumbria defeats the Picts in Scotland.

736 Ethelbald of Mercia proclaims himself King of all Saxon kingdoms.

757–796 Offa rules Mercia and builds dyke between his kingdom and Wales.

This warrior's iron helmet was reconstructed using pieces found at Sutton Hoo, Suffolk. The helmet was part of a hoard buried with King Redwald of East Anglia in about 625. His body was placed in a wooden ship which was then buried.

As the Roman army pulled out of Britain in around 409, the Roman-British people were left to defend themselves. They hired mercenaries, or private soldiers, to help them. The threat to Britain came mainly from across the North Sea. Invaders came by boat from Denmark and northern Germany. These were the Anglo-Saxons.

There were other invaders, such as Scots from Ireland, who set up colonies on what is now the west coast of Scotland. But the Anglo-Saxons were more numerous and chose to move into the richest parts of Roman Britain, the south and east. The newcomers were looking for land to farm and build homes on.

The Celtic Britons were unable to stop this invasion, though under a powerful leader, who may have been the King Arthur of later legend, they won several victories, including a famous battle at a place known as Mount Badon in about 500.

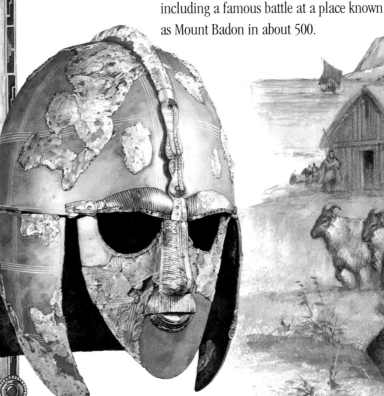

Celtic Britons were forced westwards, into Wales, Cornwall and Cumbria, and some even went to Gaul, settling in what is now Brittany in France.

The Anglo-Saxons did not settle in the Roman towns, but in villages close to their newly-ploughed farmland. They remained warriors, and were led by lords or chieftains. Powerful chieftains became local kings, fighting one another to gain more land. By the 600s the strongest kingdoms were Kent, East Anglia, Sussex ('land of the South Saxons'), Mercia ('people of the Marches'), Wessex ('West Saxons') and Northumbria.

The strongest kings were named Bretwalda or 'Ruler of Britain'. They included Ethelbert of Kent (died 616), Redwald of East Anglia (died about 625), Edwin of Northumbria (died about 633) and Offa of Mercia (died 796). Offa claimed to be king of all the 'English', and ordered the building of an earth wall (now called Offa's Dyke) to keep out Welsh raiders. By the 800s, Anglo-Saxon kings were Christian lawmakers who encouraged trade and contacts across Europe.

This is a map of the Saxon kingdoms in about AD 700. In the far north, present-day Scotland was occupied by the Celtic Picts and Scots. Bernicia and Deira were absorbed into the much larger kingdom of Northumbria. Britons were now confined to Wales and Cornwall, while much of southern Britain had been settled by Saxons.

Saxon farmers harvesting grain. They grew rye, barley, wheat and oats, as well as vegetables. A good harvest meant food for the winter. Bad weather might ruin the crops and leave families facing starvation during the cold winter months.

Viking Invasions

In the ninth century, the Anglo-Saxons or 'English' themselves faced invasion from across the North Sea. The threat came from Vikings, fierce fighters who set sail in their longships, bound for Britain.

VIKING LONGSHIP

The longship was the Viking raiding ship. Though up to 25 metres long, it was only 2 metres wide. Slim and strongly built of timber, it slid easily through the waves powered by a big square sail or long oars. A longship could carry between 40 and 60 men. There was no deck or keel, so the boat rocked wildly in stormy seas. For this reason, most raids were in spring and summer, and the boats were hauled up on shore for winter.

The Vikings came from Denmark, Norway and Sweden. Like the Anglo-Saxons 400 years earlier, they were looking for land to settle, but they were also looking for loot. The first skirmish with the invaders was in Dorset in 789, but the north suffered the first serious blow, when Viking raiders attacked the monastery at Lindisfarne in Northumbria in 793 and two years later ravaged Iona off Scotland.

By the mid 800s, fleets of up to 350 longships were attacking the British isles, and Viking armies sacked London and seized York. King Edmund of East Anglia was killed by Vikings in 869.

Vikings settled in Ireland, Scotland and along the east coast. Only in Wessex was there much resistance. Here, King Alfred organized an army and a navy, and in 878 he defeated the Vikings at Edington in Wiltshire.

A Viking warrior was equally at home in a ship at sea as on horseback or on foot ashore. Viking sailors crossed the Atlantic, even landing in North America, and Viking traders travelled as far east as Constantinople (now called Istanbul).

A Saxon and Viking in battle. More assaults on the British isles began at the end of the 900s. King Ethelred tried to pay the Vikings off with Danegeld (money), but they kept returning. In 1013, the Danish king Sweyn Forkbeard led a full-scale invasion and Ethelred fled to France.

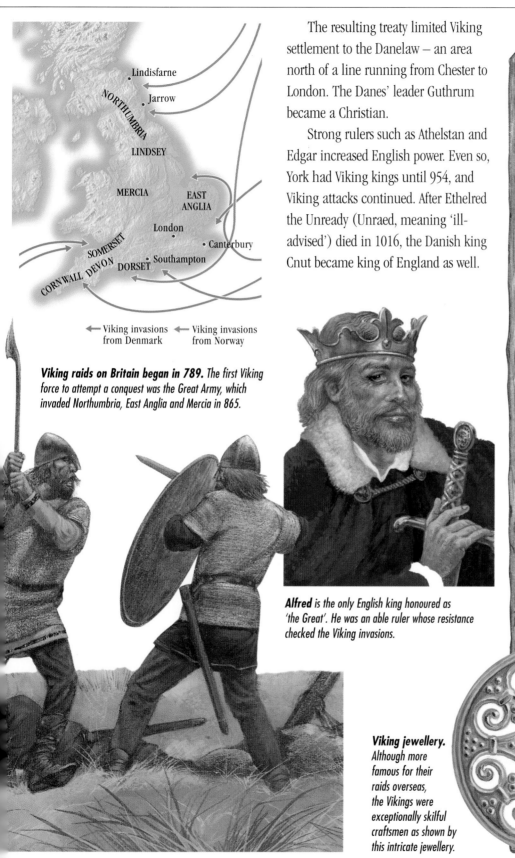

The resulting treaty limited Viking settlement to the Danelaw – an area north of a line running from Chester to London. The Danes' leader Guthrum became a Christian.

Strong rulers such as Athelstan and Edgar increased English power. Even so, York had Viking kings until 954, and Viking attacks continued. After Ethelred the Unready (Unraed, meaning 'ill-advised') died in 1016, the Danish king Cnut became king of England as well.

Viking invasions from Denmark

Viking invasions from Norway

Viking raids on Britain began in 789. The first Viking force to attempt a conquest was the Great Army, which invaded Northumbria, East Anglia and Mercia in 865.

Alfred is the only English king honoured as 'the Great'. He was an able ruler whose resistance checked the Viking invasions.

789 The *Anglo-Saxon Chronicle* reports the first Viking raid on the English coast.

793 Vikings loot the monastery at Lindisfarne.

795 Devastating raid on Iona, in which 68 monks and laymen are killed, and the abbey is burned to the ground.

c.837 Viking fleets sail up the rivers Boyne and Liffey, Ireland.

841 Vikings establish base at Dublin and dominate shipping in the Irish sea.

865 Scandinavian 'Great Army' overruns East Anglia.

878 Alfred defeats the Danes at Edington and forces their surrender; treaty agreed at Wedmore, Somerset.

902 The Danes are expelled from Dublin.

c.943 Much of Wales united under Hywel Dda 'the Good'.

c.991 Major new Viking attacks on Britain.

1017 Cnut accepted as king of all England.

Viking jewellery. Although more famous for their raids overseas, the Vikings were exceptionally skilful craftsmen as shown by this intricate jewellery.

The Middle Ages

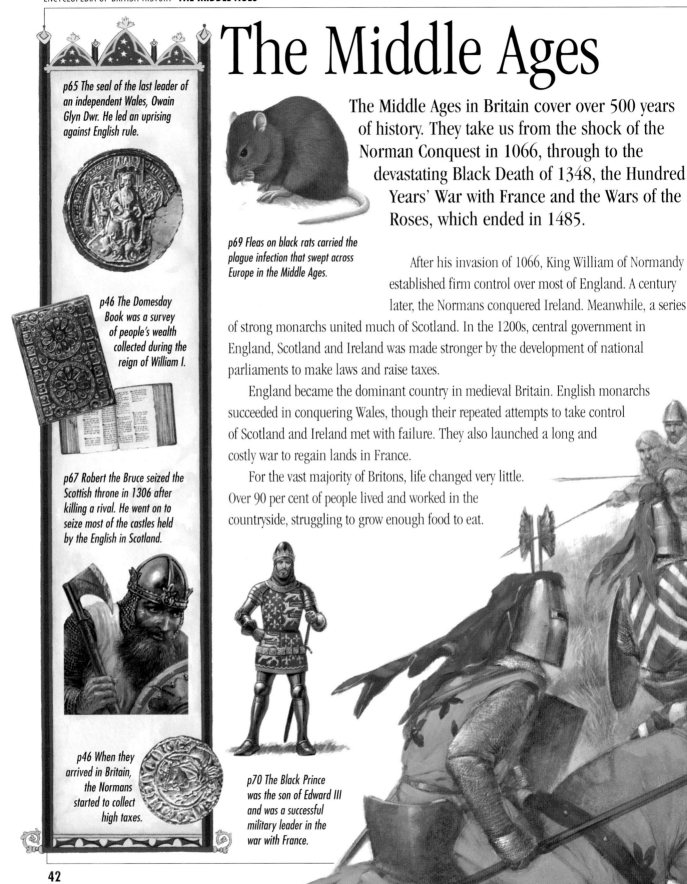

The Middle Ages in Britain cover over 500 years of history. They take us from the shock of the Norman Conquest in 1066, through to the devastating Black Death of 1348, the Hundred Years' War with France and the Wars of the Roses, which ended in 1485.

After his invasion of 1066, King William of Normandy established firm control over most of England. A century later, the Normans conquered Ireland. Meanwhile, a series of strong monarchs united much of Scotland. In the 1200s, central government in England, Scotland and Ireland was made stronger by the development of national parliaments to make laws and raise taxes.

England became the dominant country in medieval Britain. English monarchs succeeded in conquering Wales, though their repeated attempts to take control of Scotland and Ireland met with failure. They also launched a long and costly war to regain lands in France.

For the vast majority of Britons, life changed very little. Over 90 per cent of people lived and worked in the countryside, struggling to grow enough food to eat.

p65 The seal of the last leader of an independent Wales, Owain Glyn Dwr. He led an uprising against English rule.

p69 Fleas on black rats carried the plague infection that swept across Europe in the Middle Ages.

p46 The Domesday Book was a survey of people's wealth collected during the reign of William I.

p67 Robert the Bruce seized the Scottish throne in 1306 after killing a rival. He went on to seize most of the castles held by the English in Scotland.

p46 When they arrived in Britain, the Normans started to collect high taxes.

p70 The Black Prince was the son of Edward III and was a successful military leader in the war with France.

p61 Crusaders travelled to the Middle East in an attempt to capture the holy city of Jerusalem.

Towns were very small and travel between them was slow and difficult. Trade only began to grow in the 1330s, when the wool industry developed.

However, the Middle Ages also saw the first great period of British architecture. Kings and noblemen built massive stone castles as centres of power. The Christian Church grew stronger, too, and the landscape was dotted with splendid cathedrals, abbeys and parish churches. Many of these buildings can still be seen today.

p57 Jesters and other court entertainers would keep the guests at a medieval castle amused during a banquet.

p66 The Battle of Bannockburn in 1314, when Scottish forces defeated the English army under Edward II.

Norman Conquest

When King Edward 'the Confessor' died in January 1066, he was childless. Who was going to be the new English monarch? There were two candidates – Duke William of Normandy, and Harold, the son of Earl Godwin of Wessex. William claimed that the throne had been promised to him by Edward. But the Witan, or royal council, did not want a foreign ruler and recognized Harold as the new king.

Harold's first problem lay in the north, where a Norwegian army had landed and seized York. He marched swiftly north and defeated the invaders at Stamford Bridge. Almost immediately came news of another, even bigger, threat: Duke William's army had landed on the south coast.

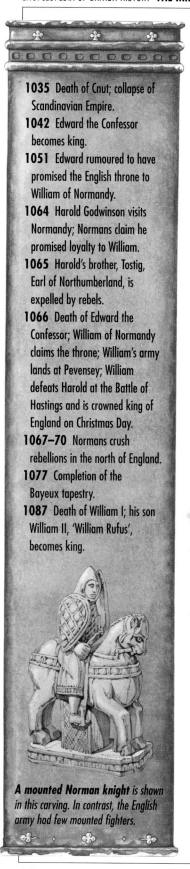

1035 Death of Cnut; collapse of Scandinavian Empire.

1042 Edward the Confessor becomes king.

1051 Edward rumoured to have promised the English throne to William of Normandy.

1064 Harold Godwinson visits Normandy; Normans claim he promised loyalty to William.

1065 Harold's brother, Tostig, Earl of Northumberland, is expelled by rebels.

1066 Death of Edward the Confessor; William of Normandy claims the throne; William's army lands at Pevensey; William defeats Harold at the Battle of Hastings and is crowned king of England on Christmas Day.

1067–70 Normans crush rebellions in the north of England.

1077 Completion of the Bayeux tapestry.

1087 Death of William I; his son William II, 'William Rufus', becomes king.

A mounted Norman knight is shown in this carving. In contrast, the English army had few mounted fighters.

Turning his weary troops around, Harold hurried to face the Normans at Hastings. The battle was even at first, with the English lines standing firm on a hilltop. Then William's footsoldiers pretended to retreat and the defenders rushed down after them. This was fatal. The Norman cavalry closed in on both sides and butchered the English, and Harold himself was killed.

After his victory, William captured the ports of Romney and Dover, then advanced towards London. At Berkhamsted, he was met by the last remaining English leaders, who surrendered and promised loyalty to him. William the Conqueror was crowned on Christmas Day 1066 as king of England, in Westminster Abbey.

The Norman army crossed the English Channel to Sussex and, deciding against scaling the chalk cliffs at Beachy Head, landed slightly to the east, at Pevensey. In their ships, they brought with them cavalry horses and timber forts, ready to assemble. Their heavily armoured cavalry and skilled archers played a key part in the battle at Hastings.

The map shows England and Wales after the Norman invasion. The major castles throughout the land served as bases for imposing control or conquering the surrounding areas.

Castles
Route taken by William in 1066

Newcastle
Durham
York
Nottingham
Norwich
The Border Castles
Worcester
Cambridge
Oxford
London
Canterbury
Salisbury
Lewes
Deal
Dover
Exeter
Lewes
Hastings

The Bayeux tapestry was made, probably in England, after the conquest. The embroidered linen strip, 69 metres long, tells the story of the invasion, from Harold's visit to William in 1064 to his defeat at Hastings.

William I was a strong, though just, ruler. He died in 1087, after being hurt when his horse stumbled. His son William Rufus succeeded him.

Norman Rule

William I's system of taxation was very unpopular with the poor and led to several uprisings against his power.

"The king set a heavy tribute (tax) on poor folk, though he still let his men harry (harrass) all that they went over." This entry from the *Anglo-Saxon Chronicle* for 1067 shows that William was ruthless in exerting power over his new kingdom.

His army of no more than 10,000 men was faced with a hostile British population of over two million. The early years of his reign saw major rebellions against the Normans in areas as far apart as Kent, the West Country, Wales, northern England and the Fens of East Anglia. These were put down violently.

The most famous resistance to William came in the Fens. In 1070, a band of outlaws led by Hereward the Wake ('the Watchful') made a stand on the Isle of Ely. They beat off fierce attacks by the Normans, but were eventually betrayed by local monks. Hereward himself escaped and was never captured.

William built a series of castles at key points, to guard important roads, ports, river crossings and towns. These early castles had to be erected quickly, so they were made of timber and sited on top of an earth mound, surrounded by a ditch and a bank. Later castles were built of stone.

The style of dress worn by ladies of the Norman ruling class had developed from long tunics. These dresses had wide sleeves and were laced closely on the upper body. Men wore shorter tunics, with breeches or leggings beneath. Most clothes at this time were made of linen or wool: only the wealthy could afford to wear cotton or silk.

DOMESDAY BOOK

In January 1086, William launched a remarkable survey of England. He sent commissioners to almost every area to collect details about the size and value of landholdings, who held them and what livestock they kept. The king's aim was to find out how much tax he could draw from different regions. But the Domesday survey also gives an amazingly thorough picture of life in over 13,000 settlements. It shows that farmland covered about 65 per cent of the country, but woodland only about 15 per cent.

Most people in England were villeins (villagers), who held small areas of land, or they were humbler cottars, who had even less. They served the local lord by working his land. The lord himself was granted the land by the king, in return for promising to raise troops when needed. This system, called feudalism, was made stricter during Norman times.

SCOTLAND

Areas of uncertainty

1080s

1070
1071

1070–80

WALES

ENGLAND

LONDON

1068–70

1067–8

Norman rule was extended north and west over England between 1066 and 1087. William divided up the land among his supporters.

Normans playing an early form of cricket. One man wields a stave called a 'cric', an Anglo-Saxon word meaning 'shepherd's crook'. The word umpire comes from the Norman French 'non-pair', meaning 'odd man out'.

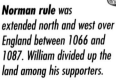

The king also rewarded his followers by giving them important positions in the Church, and land seized from the owners. This meant that he would have loyal barons to govern England in his place whenever he returned to Normandy. By 1086, the Domesday survey showed that only two English noblemen were still major landholders.

The Norman barons formed a brand-new ruling class, which spoke French and had French customs. French replaced English as the main language at court and in matters of law, and French words were absorbed into English speech. The influence was permanent; today thousands of common words, such as parliament, royal, city, soldier and prince have French origins.

At least 500 castles were spread throughout England and Wales by 1100. Stone castles, with a tower or keep at the centre, were much more expensive than timber, but were far stronger.

Scotland United

1057 Malcolm III kills Macbeth and becomes king.

1070 Malcolm makes link with England by marrying Margaret, sister of Edgar, who is heir to the English throne.

1072 Malcolm attempts to invade Northumbria, but is forced to submit to William I of England.

1074 Malcolm begins to fortify city of Edinburgh.

1091 William II forces Malcolm to submit again after crushing his invasion of Northumbria.

1112 King Alexander invites Norman barons to settle in Scotland.

1121 First royal burgh founded in Scotland at Berwick-upon-Tweed.

1124 David I becomes king; grants land to more Norman knights, including Robert de Brus (Bruce).

1139 Treaty with England allows Scots to retain conquered area south of the border.

1149–57 Scots seize Northumbria.

1153 Death of David I: his 12-year-old grandson Malcolm becomes king.

1160 Malcolm IV subdues Argyll, Dumfries and Galloway.

1165 Death of Malcolm; William I of Scotland becomes king.

1173–74 William invades northern England and is taken prisoner; he is released after signing treaty and handing over castles and lands.

1176 Pope allows Scottish Church to remain independent of England.

1214 Death of William I of Scotland.

The Normans never tried to conquer the Scots people. When they took power in England, Scotland was still divided into small provinces, which did not pose a threat. Nor was the land rich enough to attract invaders. Besides, the centre of English power was far to the south, making a full-scale invasion expensive and difficult.

In the 1100s, Scotland remained mostly at peace. It also grew more united under a succession of strong and wise kings. They extended the kingdom northwards from the south and east. In 1266, the Western Isles were added.

However, Norman influence on Scotland was very strong. In 1112, the Scots ruler Alexander invited Norman knights to settle in his country. This was a clever way to show friendship and avoid full-scale war.

King David I of Scotland was brought up at the English court. He was a deeply religious man, who reformed the Church in Scotland and used his wealth to build ten large monasteries.

When his brother David became king in 1124, he also encouraged Norman barons by granting them estates in southern Scotland.

The arrival of the Normans brought feudalism to Scotland. King David gave land in return for an oath of loyalty and a promise to provide troops. The barons pledged to be the king's vassals (servants). Each one then shared out his estate among his own vassals and supporters. In this way, feudalism stretched from top to bottom of society – from king to peasant.

David and his successors also copied the Norman methods of government. They founded cathedrals, built castles and appointed sheriffs to keep order and collect taxes. As a result, Scotland became a stable and wealthy nation.

THE SCOTTISH FLAG

The lion rampant (standing with its forepaws in the air) became the emblem of the Scots kingdom in the 1100s. It was later replaced by the St Andrew's Cross, a diagonal white cross on a blue background. King Richard I of England put three lions on his Royal Standard in 1195.

Castles were built as strongholds for bodies of troops, as kings asserted their growing control over this wild region from King David I's reign onwards. Good building stone was hard to find, so these castles were often simple in design.

Plantagenets

The broom plant was the symbol of the Plantagenets, whose name comes from the plant's Latin name: Planta Genista. Henry II's father, Geoffrey of Anjou, is said to have worn a sprig in his cap.

Henry Plantagenet was not just King of England. He was also Duke of Normandy and Count of Anjou and through his wife, Eleanor, he was Duke of Aquitaine. This made him the richest and most powerful ruler in France, and brought him many rivals and enemies.

Henry II's wife, Eleanor, was a powerful woman. Before marrying Henry, she had been married to the king of France and had travelled on the Crusades.

In the British Isles, Henry II quickly established firm control after the chaos and civil war during the reign of his predecessor, Stephen. In 1157, Henry forced Malcolm IV of Scotland to give back the territory he had seized in northern England.

He tore down the 'adulterine' castles, which the barons had built without royal permission. He reformed the legal system and introduced trial by jury and circuit courts.

Henry also conquered Ireland. The Normans had left the Irish chieftains to fight among themselves. But in 1166, the king of Leinster asked Henry for help against his enemies. A band of knights was sent to recover his lands and soon began to build themselves a kingdom in the southeast.

Thomas Becket was promoted by his friend Henry II to be Archbishop of Canterbury in 1162. But Henry was enraged when Becket opposed many of his reforms for the Church. The Archbishop was forced to flee to France, but foolishly returned in 1170. "Will no one rid me of this turbulent priest?" asked Henry angrily. Eager to impress the king, four knights rode to Canterbury and killed Becket in the cathedral.

Alarmed at their power, Henry gathered a large army and seized Dublin, forcing the Irish kings to submit to him.

Strong and energetic as he was, Henry made some disastrous mistakes. He quarrelled with his wife, Eleanor of Aquitaine, who urged his sons to turn against him. When he died in France in 1189, he was at war with his third son, Richard. It was Richard who took his place on the English throne.

The extent of the Angevin Empire in about 1200. It stretched from the east coast of Ireland down to Gascony on the border between France and Spain.

Canterbury Cathedral. Soon after Thomas Becket's death, people claimed to have seen miracles performed at his tomb in the cathedral. It became a holy shrine visited by many pilgrims. Thomas Becket was made a saint by the Pope in 1173.

Henry II spent well over half of his reign outside Britain, governing his lands in France. His Angevin (meaning 'from Anjou') Empire was a flourishing centre of learning, art, music and poetry. The English court was crude by comparison.

Medieval Britain

A procession of penitents during the Black Death. Many people believed that the plague was God's punishment for human wickedness. They walked in religious processions, praying for forgiveness. Some even whipped themselves to show their penitence. Death was regarded as a way of making all people equal, because it came to rich and poor alike.

1166 Henry II curbs the power of barons and destroys adulterine castles.

1170 Population of London exceeds 30,000.

c.1180 Henry II reforms local government and introduces system of common law.

c.1200 Norman settlement brings greater prosperity to Ireland.

1215 King John signs Magna Carta, which restricts power of the English monarch.

1245 Rebuilding of Westminster Abbey begins; many churches built in England and Scotland.

1315–18 Poor harvests; famine in England and Wales.

1348 The Black Death reaches southern England.

1351 With fewer peasants to work the land following the plague, wages rise.

1381 Peasants' Revolt in London, sparked by a new poll tax.

c.1400 London prospers; many new trading wharves built on the Thames.

1479 New outbreak of the Black Death in England.

Market-day in a medieval town. Most big towns held a weekly market. Merchants, pedlars and craftsmen set up their stalls. Villagers sold the cheese, vegetables and eggs they could spare. Drovers brought in cattle and other livestock.

Britain in the High Middle Ages was a dangerous place. In England, the three centuries between 1189 and 1485 saw countless uprisings, attempted invasions, civil wars and riots. Several rulers met violent ends, including kings Edward II, Richard II and Richard III.

In Wales, people lived in constant fear of conquest by the English. In Ireland, the chieftains fought against each other and against the might of the Normans. Even Scotland, the most peaceful region, faced threats from Scandinavian and Irish raiders and, in the end, invasion by the English.

Violence was not the only danger. For most people, getting enough to eat was the biggest difficulty. By 1300, the population of the British Isles had increased to five million. Farmers, using methods which had hardly changed since Roman times, could not grow enough food for everyone. The resulting famine killed nearly 15 per cent of the population by 1318.

The problem of famine was solved by something far worse – disease. The plague (now known as the Black Death) reached southern England from Europe in 1348 and spread to Scotland and Ireland a year later.

Since the fourth century, Christians had gone on pilgrimage to visit holy places and the shrines of saints. In spite of the hardships and the dangers of robbers on the road, bands of pilgrims travelled long distances. The most popular shrines in Britain included Canterbury, where the bones of Thomas Becket were kept, Durham and St David's in West Wales.

Chapel

Dormitory

Cloister

The Black Death killed almost half of the British population. However, this meant that there were fewer mouths to feed, and food became more plentiful.

In the meantime, the Church became the centre of medieval life. Catholicism was the only religion in Britain and few people questioned it. Even the poorest peasant went to mass every Sunday. The Church had power – not just over people's minds, but also over scholarship, the production of books and schooling. It raised its own tithes (taxes), made its own laws and owned huge areas of land. Groups of Christians lived in communities where they could work and pray. When the Normans arrived, there were about 45 of these monasteries (for men) and nunneries (for women) in Britain.

Herb and vegetable garden

Refectory

Kitchens

In the private world of a monastery, one side was taken up with the large abbey church, where eight daily services were performed. The other three sides housed the living and eating quarters, and important buildings such as the chapter house, where meetings were held. At the centre was an open space, surrounded by a covered walkway called the cloister, where the monks worked and read. Monasteries were usually located near a stream to provide drinking water and power for a mill.

FEUDAL SYSTEM

After Saxon times, feudalism grew more complicated. Kings rewarded their nobles with fiefs (grants) of land, in return for military service. The nobles rented fields to peasant-farmers, also in exchange for service. After about 1300, the system declined as towns grew; people began to pay rent in cash, and kings hired professional soldiers to fight wars.

Farming the Land

1086 Domesday survey catalogues farmland of England, who holds it and what crops are grown.

c.1180 First windmills built in Norfolk to grind corn.

c.1200 There are six million sheep in England; their wool accounts for about half the country's wealth.

1272 The menu for the coronation banquet of King Edward I includes 60 oxen and cattle, 100 pigs and 3,000 fowls, as well as swans, rabbits and fish.

1300 Sheep population of England has risen to 18 million; wages fall, with a labourer earning one old penny a day and a carpenter three pence.

1315–16 Disastrous harvests in England and Wales due to torrential rain; also epidemics of disease which wipe out cattle.

1348–51 Black Death depletes workforce of peasants; the survivors have to travel to find work and demand higher wages.

1381 The Peasants' Revolt led by Wat Tyler; there is rioting in Essex and Kent.

1397 A nobleman in Wales complains that his villagers refuse to perform their feudal services – a frequent complaint.

Wheat was a major crop for medieval farmers. However, they lacked pesticides and fertilisers that allow modern farmers to produce so much.

As the population grew between 1100 and 1300, more food was needed. Nearly all of this had to be grown at home – very little was imported from abroad. To increase the harvest, more land than ever before had to be cleared for farming. Woodland was destroyed, marshes and fens drained and livestock put to graze on moorland.

Most peasant farmers in England lived on a manor – the estate organized around a lord's residence. It usually contained a village, the central house or castle, a church and surrounding farmland. The lord of the manor and his officials governed the community, making sure that rents were paid and services performed.

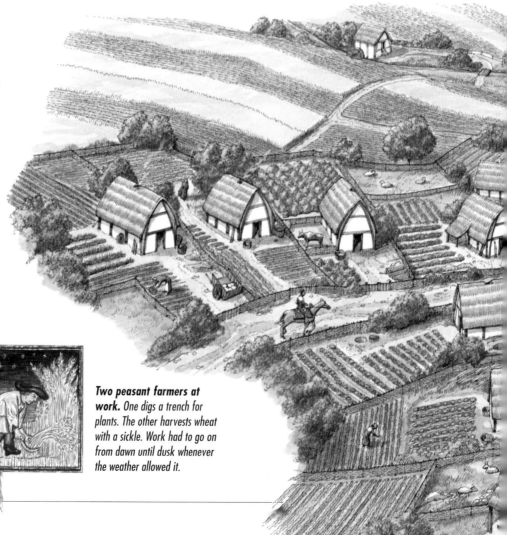

Two peasant farmers at work. One digs a trench for plants. The other harvests wheat with a sickle. Work had to go on from dawn until dusk whenever the weather allowed it.

There were three or four large arable fields around the village. These were divided into strips and shared out among the families. The peasants often helped each other to plough and harvest their strips, but did the rest of their fieldwork separately. Besides this, they were also bound to take their turn at working on the lord's own *demesne* (private land) as part of their feudal duty.

In summer, villagers drove their cattle and sheep out to graze on the unfenced common land around the arable fields. In autumn, the lord allowed them to let their pigs loose in his woodland to feed on acorns and beechnuts. This food was vital, because there was only enough food for a few animals in winter. The rest were slaughtered and their meat was preserved by smoking or salting, so that it would keep for several months.

Medieval farming tools.
The saw (right) was useful for pruning hedges and fruit trees. The long-handled scythe (left) was used for mowing grass in the village's hay-meadow. Everyone helped with the hay harvest in midsummer. Straw and hay were important materials — not only for animal feed in winter, but also for thatching roofs and stuffing mattresses.

A typical medieval village in the English Midlands. Cottages and workshops were built of timber and thatch. Only the church and the lord's house were made of stone. Peasants knew little about crop rotation or manuring the land. In their 'three-course' system, they grew crops on a field for two years, then left it fallow (unploughed) for one year so that it regained some fertility.

Peasants usually had a very hard life. Those at the bottom of the scale (the serfs) owned nothing — not even their clothes or animals. Serfs were not allowed to leave the manor without permission. There were only two ways for a serf to gain his or her freedom: by marrying a 'free' peasant, or by saving money to buy a piece of land. However, few achieved this. A poor diet and hard work meant that the average peasant in 1300 would not live past the age of 25.

Castles

If a king or chieftain wanted to keep control of an area of land, he needed soldiers and a fortified base for them to live in. From this base, they could patrol the district for about 16 kilometres around – the distance they could ride out and back in a day.

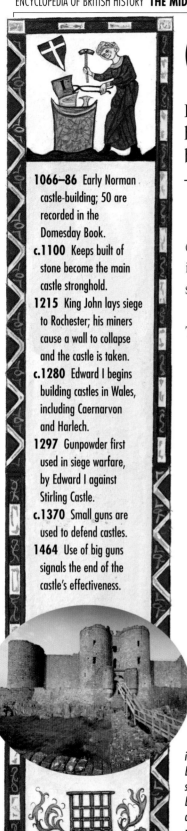

1066–86 Early Norman castle-building; 50 are recorded in the Domesday Book.

c.1100 Keeps built of stone become the main castle stronghold.

1215 King John lays siege to Rochester; his miners cause a wall to collapse and the castle is taken.

c.1280 Edward I begins building castles in Wales, including Caernarvon and Harlech.

1297 Gunpowder first used in siege warfare, by Edward I against Stirling Castle.

c.1370 Small guns are used to defend castles.

1464 Use of big guns signals the end of the castle's effectiveness.

There had been hilltop forts in Britain since Iron Age times, but the Norman kings deliberately built a chain of castles to impose order on their conquered land, and to guard important sites. These castles developed from timber towers on earth mounds to massive stone keeps surrounded by curtain walls.

By the 1300s, more than 1,500 castles dotted the countryside of Britain and Ireland. They were now so strongly built that only a long siege could force the garrisons of soldiers inside to surrender. The castles had water-filled moats, two sets of curtain walls, strong gates and portcullises. From the towers, archers could shoot down at anyone below the walls, or drop stones or burning pitch. An attacking army was equipped with plenty of special weapons too.

Harlech Castle in Gwynedd was started in 1283 as part of King Edward I's programme to subdue northern Wales. Edward's castles had no central keep, but several rings of high walls, studded with round towers.

This giant catapult was called a 'trebuchet'. It had a long wooden beam with a heavy weight on one end and a sling on the other. The sling was loaded with a stone and then released. Weapons such as this were put together at the site of the siege and were hard to move. Other missiles included balls of flaming oil, severed heads and the rotting bodies of animals.

Giant siege machines hurled stones to shatter the walls and battering rams thudded at the timber gates. Miners dug tunnels beneath the walls, then lit fires. As the props burned, the tunnel fell in, making the castle wall above collapse. Attackers could also climb over the walls using tall scaling ladders. However, the best weapon was starvation. A besieging army could stop food supplies from going into a castle, and could also dam up or poison the water supply.

Baron's bedroom

Great hall

Kitchen and store rooms

CASTLE LIFE
By about 1200, a castle was really a fortified home for a king or lord. He lived there with his wife, children and servants for at least part of the year. The lord and his family were the only people to have a private room, called a 'solar'. Everyone else slept in the castle's great hall.

The keep was a castle's central stronghold. *It was a tall tower with thick stone walls. The single entrance, through the gatehouse, could be reached only when the gate and portcullis were open and the drawbridge let down over the moat.*

Jesters, acrobats, musicians or jugglers might entertain the lord of the castle and his guests at supper. Sometimes a knight would sing songs about love and brave deeds.

Knights and Chivalry

c.500 Heavily armoured mounted Frankish soldiers become successful in Europe.

c.1000 Beginnings of feudal system, in which knights serve local lord and are in turn served by serfs.

1066 Norman knights lead conquest of southern Britain

c.1100 Knights wear more extensive mail armour, covering arms and legs as well as the body.

c.1150 5,000 knights recorded in Britain.

c.1300 The number has declined to about 2,500 knights; many families do not take up knighthood due to the expense of armour and equipment.

c.1300 Knights' armour strengthened with steel plates covering the limbs.

1314 Scots' triumph at Bannockburn is a significant reverse for mounted knights; Scots spearmen halt charges by English cavalry.

c.1400 Knights begin to wear full suits of plate armour.

1415 British longbowmen destroy French mounted knights at Agincourt.

c.1450 Only a few hundred knights now recorded.

c.1550 Plate armour reaches its decorative peak, but armoured knights are by now made obsolete by firearms.

A mounted knight was a terrifying sight on the battlefield. He remained the most powerful weapon on the battlefield until the arrival of gunpowder.

When William I swept into Britain in 1066, his army was headed by mounted horsemen. Norman knights used the fighting methods of the Frankish warriors who had dominated warfare in Europe for three centuries. The knight had many advantages over the poor footsoldier. He could move faster on horseback, and was better protected with his coat of mail.

By about 1300, the descendants of these knights had become part of Britain's ruling class, numbering around 2,500. They had to promise to serve the king in battle, in return for grants of land. Only boys who were born into this noble class were usually trained as knights.

A knight's career began at about the age of seven, when he was sent to live in a lord's household. Here he was taught good manners, how to ride and even how to sing ballads.

This shield shows the sign of a lion standing on one leg, in a pose known as rampant. Shields in the 1300s were usually made of wood and covered with leather. Later shields were specially shaped for jousting, with a curved edge to rest the lance on.

A knight and his lady might live on the produce of their land or manor. They lived in castles or fortified manor houses and their land was worked by peasants who owed them service. The lord's wife, the lady of the manor, ran the kitchens and living quarters and was responsible for the house when the knight was away.

CHIVALRY

There was more to knighthood than fighting. Knights were expected to follow a strict code of conduct, called chivalry. This demanded not only courage and fighting skill, but loyalty, generosity and courtesy (good manners – especially towards women).

These two knights *are meeting at a joust. The joust, when knights scored points by hitting their opponent, was often part of a tournament. Tournaments began around AD 1000 as a way to practise for battle.*

At the age of 14, he became a squire, working as a servant for another knight. He learned all the fighting skills, from wrestling and archery to swordplay and putting on armour.

At last, aged about 21, the squire became a full knight. He was 'dubbed', kneeling before the king, his father or his master, who tapped his neck with a sword. He made the vows of chivalry – promises to protect the weak and poor and to punish evildoers. Finally, he was presented with spurs, a sword and – sometimes – a full suit of armour.

Some knights had their own lands to look after in times of peace. Others hired themselves out to fight for someone else. A knight in full armour was hard to recognize in battle. In the 1100s, they began to display their own special signs, called arms, on their shield or armour.

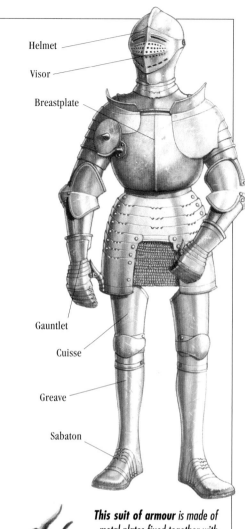

Helmet

Visor

Breastplate

Gauntlet

Cuisse

Greave

Sabaton

This suit of armour *is made of metal plates fixed together with rivets, or leather straps. Underneath, he wears a tunic of mail or a padded jerkin.*

Crusades

King Richard I of England preferred fighting for his religion overseas to governing his kingdom. For three years after his coronation in 1189, he was not even in Europe. He was leading a Crusader army against Muslim forces in Palestine.

c.660 Arab Muslims conquer much of the Near and Middle East, including Palestine; Christian pilgrims are allowed to visit sacred sites.

c.1050 Seljuk Turks invade the Near East and make access for pilgrims harder.

1095 Pope calls on Christians to recapture Holy Land.

1096 First Crusade: Jerusalem is retaken.

1147 Second Crusade: Christians defeated and forced to retreat.

1187 Muslims under Saladin take Jerusalem again.

1189–91 Third Crusade: Christians fail to recapture Jerusalem.

1202–54 Four more Crusades to Holy Land achieve little.

1271 Prince Edward joins Eighth Crusade in Palestine.

1272 Edward forced to return home on death of his father, Henry III.

1291 European interest in Crusades begins to fade.

The Crusades had begun as a noble idea nearly a century before. In about AD 1000, the Seljuk Turks (who were Muslims) had advanced from their homeland in Central Asia and conquered a large area of the Byzantine Empire in Asia Minor. This included the city of Jerusalem and other places in Palestine which Christians believed were important holy sites.

A Crusader knight. The armies of the Crusades were huge forces. The Third Crusade, which set out in 1189, was made up of more than 50,000 men. However, it failed in its goal of capturing the holy city of Jerusalem.

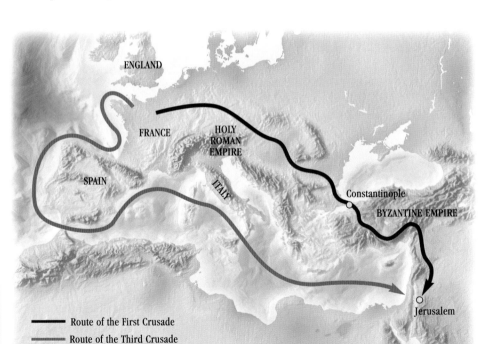

Crusader armies used two routes to reach the Middle East. They either travelled by sea through the Mediterranean or over land through modern-day Turkey and the city of Constantinople (now called Istanbul).

Saladin, Sultan of Egypt and Syria, was the greatest of the Muslim leaders, not only defeating the Crusaders, but ruling wisely and efficiently.

A **Crusader castle.** *The Crusaders took over Muslim castles, or built new ones, to defend the states they had conquered. Several of these castles were on ideal sites, protected on two or three sides by water or sheer rock cliffs.*

The Byzantine emperor had begged for help from the Christian monarchs of Europe. The pope supported him by promising that God would forgive the sins of those who took part in this Holy War. So in 1096, the armies of the First Crusade set off to drive the Seljuks out of the Holy Land. At first they were successful – Jerusalem was recaptured, and a Christian army was left to guard it.

However, the Second Crusade of 1147 was a disaster, and by 1189 the Muslim forces, led by Saladin, had taken Jerusalem once again. King Richard swiftly gathered soldiers for a Third Crusade. The Christian army – including English, French and German troops – landed in Palestine in 1191.

With Richard at their head, the Crusaders quickly captured the town of Acre. However, they failed to retake Jerusalem. Their leaders quarrelled amongst themselves, and Richard was left behind to make a treaty with Saladin. The Muslims kept Jerusalem, but allowed visits from Christian pilgrims. There were to be five more crusades to the Holy Land, most of which ended in failure. One, in 1204, ended disastrously when the crusading army turned on the Byzantine emperor, sacking his capital, Constantinople.

A **Crusader knight.** *Crusaders found the climate of Palestine unbearably hot. Many soon copied the Turks, wearing loose airy surcoats over their mail armour and protecting their heads from the strong sun.*

61

Kings and Parliament

After the death of Henry II, England became an even more difficult place to govern. The new king, Richard I, spent most of his reign in France or on crusade. He made sure that leading barons and churchmen kept strict control while he was away, but they could not prevent a rebellion by his brother John in 1194. Nor could the barons prevent the French king Philip from seizing part of Normandy.

1189 Richard I becomes King of England.

1193 Richard imprisoned in Germany; John tries to seize power in England, but later flees to France.

1199 Death of Richard; John is crowned king.

1203 John's nephew Arthur disappears.

1203–04 Philip of France conquers Anjou and Normandy.

1214 John's allies defeated at Bouvines in France; most land on continent lost to French.

1215 Civil war in England; barons force John to put seal to Magna Carta.

1216 Louis of France invades England (leaves 1217).

1216–32 England is ruled by council.

1258 Barons seize power.

1264 Henry captured at Battle of Lewes.

1265 De Montfort calls enlarged parliament; de Montfort killed.

1272 Death of Henry III; Edward I becomes king.

Things quickly grew worse after Richard's death in 1199. John was the new ruler of England and the Angevin Empire. The barons in Anjou did not like this: they wanted John's young nephew, Arthur, as king. But in 1203, Arthur mysteriously disappeared, and many suspected that John had murdered him.

King Philip of France took the opportunity to invade Anjou and Normandy, and soon John had scarcely any empire left. He scurried back to the safety of England and tried to prepare an army to regain his lands. This meant raising taxes, which made him very unpopular. Then in 1214, there was yet another defeat in France.

The English barons had had enough. They rebelled against the king and seized London. In June 1215, they forced John to accept the terms in the Magna Carta, meaning 'Great Charter'.

Simon de Montfort was born in France. He married Henry III's sister and governed Gascony for him until 1252. However, he turned against the king and led the rebellious barons who published the provisions of Oxford in 1258. These demanded that the king should govern through a council. After defeating Henry, de Montfort became virtual ruler of England and summoned the first representative English parliament in 1265.

Parliament today. In Saxon times the king had been advised by a witan (council) of the most powerful men in the realm — noblemen and churchmen. These became known as parliaments (discussions). It was only in 1265 that the first community representatives, or 'commons', were invited to parliament.

The 'Magna Carta' contained 63 clauses, most of which were aimed at protecting the feudal rights of the barons and churchmen. Among the most important demands was that the king should allow justice for everyone, and should not imprison anyone without a legal process. John later ignored the charter, but in 1225 Henry III confirmed it as a bill of his subjects' rights and it became a vital part of English law.

In the Magna Carta, King John agreed to respect the rights of the Church and nobles, and to set up a committee of elected men to safeguard the law.

John died a year later without acting on any of these conditions. The new king, Henry III, was only nine years old, and the country was governed by a council until 1232. Henry was a quiet, religious man who was happier building palaces and churches than dealing with the growing discontent that was felt among his barons.

In 1264, this discontent exploded into civil war. The barons, led by Simon de Montfort, wanted to restrict the king's power, and demanded that he must consult a council of noblemen three times a year.

The barons defeated Henry at the Battle of Lewes and imprisoned him. In 1265, de Montfort called together the promised council, consisting not just of barons, but also of men who were elected from the shires and cities. This was the first time that an English parliament had represented anyone other than noblemen. But it did not last long. Within a few months, de Montfort had been defeated and Henry had restored royal power.

King Henry III made only weak attempts to win back the lost parts of the Angevin Empire, and renounced them altogether in the Treaty of Paris in 1259. He also angered the English barons by having many French relatives as close advisers.

King John's great seal on Magna Carta. The barons set up a tent in a meadow called Runnymede by the Thames in Surrey. The king arrived and the Archbishop of Canterbury read out the articles of Magna Carta. King John did not 'sign' the charter, but set his mark, or seal, in wax which was attached to it.

Ireland and Wales

1171 Henry takes army to Ireland and receives homage from the king of Leinster.

1198 Death of the Ruaidri of Connacht, last of the Irish High Kings.

1204 King John imposes English laws concerning Irish property and inheritance.

1219–31 Llywelyn I 'the Great' overruns Dyfed and Gwent in Wales.

1243 Henry III sends out commissioners to extend English landholdings in Ireland.

1256–57 Llywelyn II 'the Last' controls most of Wales.

1257 Treaty of Montgomery; Henry III acknowledges Llywelyn as Prince of Wales.

1264 First recorded meeting of the Irish Parliament.

1277 Edward I invades Gwynedd; English forces invade the south; Llywelyn keeps some lands.

1282 Edward begins castle-building programme in Wales.

1283 Llywelyn rebels, is captured and executed.

1301 Prince Edward, son of Edward I, given title of Prince of Wales.

1315 Invasion of Ireland by Scots, led by Edward Bruce.

1318 Bruce killed in battle at Faughart near Dundalk.

1394 Richard II's army re-conquers Leinster.

1399 Richard's second expedition to Ireland cut short by rebellion at home.

A Celtic harp, similar to the famous harp of Brian Boru. Brian was king of Munster in about AD 1000, and became Irish High King after conquering most of southern Ireland.

The Normans had first landed in Ireland in 1169. Two years later, King Henry II led a major expedition here and received vows of loyalty from the king of Leinster. He seized Dublin, and the Irish kings submitted to his rule, agreeing to pay him tribute (taxes). By 1183, the last of the High Kings had been forced to give up his throne. Henry made his son, Prince John, Lord of Ireland.

Over the next century, the English invaders gradually established themselves, seizing land and settling in many areas. By 1300, the English controlled most of Ireland. New cathedrals, parish churches and castles were built. Trade and farming flourished and there was a demand for imported luxuries. Ireland eventually had its own parliament, which first met in 1264.

In 1315, a Scottish army landed in Ireland, invited by a local chieftain who wanted to expel the English. The Scots were led by Edward Bruce, brother of King Robert. Within a year they had invaded Meath and Edward had been crowned king of Ireland.

The English kings Edward III and Richard II tried to re-establish their grip on Ireland. In 1399, Richard II invaded, but with little success. By the early 1400s, English power in Ireland had shrunk to a small area around Dublin. This was called the Pale, and had to be defended with castles, beacons and ditches.

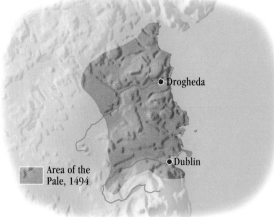

• Drogheda

• Dublin

Area of the Pale, 1494

An Irish footsoldier. From the late 13th century, Irish armies were strengthened by 'gallowglasses' hired from Scotland. These heavily armed infantrymen got their name from the Gaelic 'galloglaigh', meaning 'foreign soldier'.

Some Norman settlers in Ireland married into Irish families and took Irish names. In 1315, Scottish settlers moved into the northeast area of Ulster. By the 1400s, the English controlled only the Pale, a small region on the east coast.

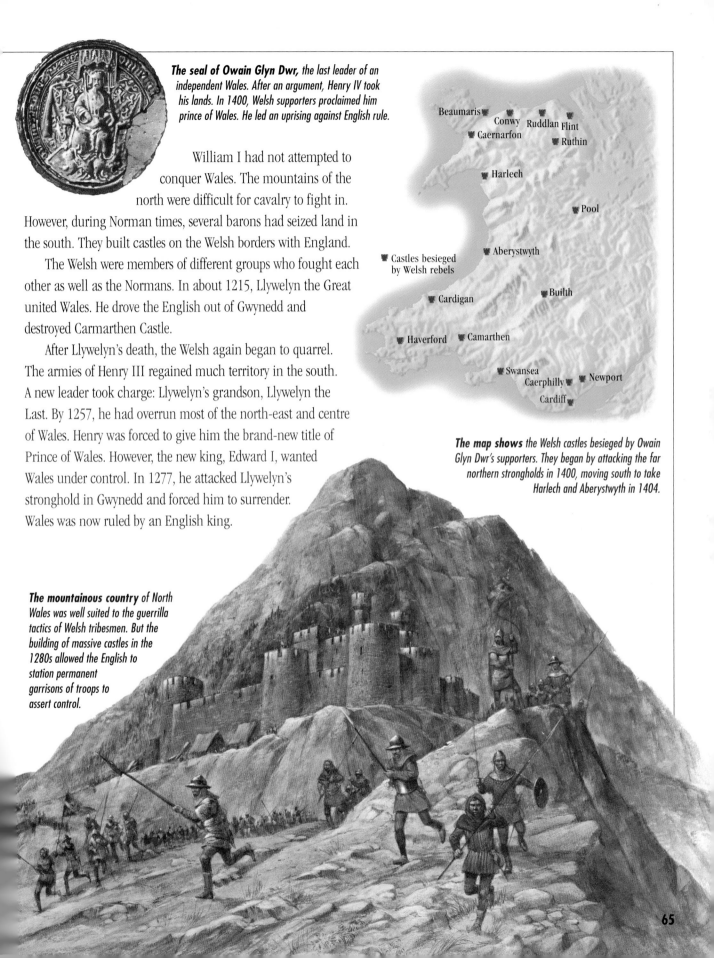

William I had not attempted to conquer Wales. The mountains of the north were difficult for cavalry to fight in. However, during Norman times, several barons had seized land in the south. They built castles on the Welsh borders with England.

The Welsh were members of different groups who fought each other as well as the Normans. In about 1215, Llywelyn the Great united Wales. He drove the English out of Gwynedd and destroyed Carmarthen Castle.

After Llywelyn's death, the Welsh again began to quarrel. The armies of Henry III regained much territory in the south. A new leader took charge: Llywelyn's grandson, Llywelyn the Last. By 1257, he had overrun most of the north-east and centre of Wales. Henry was forced to give him the brand-new title of Prince of Wales. However, the new king, Edward I, wanted Wales under control. In 1277, he attacked Llywelyn's stronghold in Gwynedd and forced him to surrender. Wales was now ruled by an English king.

Beaumaris
Conwy Ruddlan Flint
Caernarfon Ruthin
Harlech
Pool
Castles besieged by Welsh rebels
Aberystwyth
Cardigan
Builth
Haverford Camarthen
Swansea
Caerphilly Newport
Cardiff

The map shows the Welsh castles besieged by Owain Glyn Dwr's supporters. They began by attacking the far northern strongholds in 1400, moving south to take Harlech and Aberystwyth in 1404.

The mountainous country of North Wales was well suited to the guerrilla tactics of Welsh tribesmen. But the building of massive castles in the 1280s allowed the English to station permanent garrisons of troops to assert control.

Wallace and Bruce

For most of the 1200s, Scotland was a strong and stable country. The Scots were ruled by the Canmore dynasty of kings, who extended control into Argyll and Caithness and drove the Norwegians out of the Western Isles. In 1251, King Alexander III forged a link with England when he married Margaret, the daughter of Henry III.

The seal of John Balliol. Most Scots accepted him as their king in 1292. But Edward I bullied him, demanding that Scottish nobles fight for him against France.

1214 Death of William the Lion; Alexander II becomes king of Scotland.

1230 Alexander extends rule and repels Norse invasion.

1249 Death of Alexander II; Alexander III is king.

1266 Treaty of Perth; Scots gain the Western Isles from the Norse.

1296 Edward I invades Scotland; Scots defeated at Dunbar.

1297 William Wallace defeats the English.

1305 Wallace captured.

1306 Robert Bruce is crowned king.

1307 Edward II becomes the English king.

1314 Bruce defeats English at Bannockburn.

1327 Edward III becomes the English king.

1328 Treaty of Northampton; English recognize Scottish independence.

However, disaster soon struck. Alexander died in 1286, and he was the last male of the Canmore line. The only heir was his infant granddaughter Margaret, who also died, while travelling across the sea to her new realm in 1290. Suddenly, Scotland was adrift without a clear leader.

The Scots asked Edward I of England to decide who should be their new king. He chose John Balliol, a relative of David I, hoping that he would help in an English takeover of Scotland. Balliol, however, rebelled against Edward and in 1296 the English king invaded and Balliol surrendered.

It seemed that Scotland was about to fall. The only resistance came from William Wallace who won a victory over the English at Stirling in 1297. A year later, he too had been defeated. In 1305, he was captured and killed and Edward began to gain control of southern Scotland.

At the Battle of Bannockburn in June 1314, Robert Bruce chose to face the English on marshy ground, where his smaller army of men had dug pits. The English cavalry charge failed and the knights were cut down by Scots pikemen. King Edward II was forced to flee from the battlefield.

According to legend, Robert Bruce watched a spider while he was in hiding after a defeat. As the spider tried to swing from one beam to another, he was encouraged by its determination and went on to win his next battle.

Two events saved the country. The first was the death of Edward I in 1307 – his successor, Edward II, was weaker and a poor military leader. The other was the rise of Robert Bruce, who seized the throne in 1306. He was supported by many Scots, who hated the English occupation. Things at first were desperate. Robert was twice defeated by the English, but in 1314 his army routed Edward's troops at Bannockburn, near Stirling. Robert went on to capture Berwick Castle and even raided northern England. Edward's grip on Scotland was broken. In 1328, his son, Edward III, recognized Robert as king.

Robert Bruce in armour. *Robert's grandfather had claimed the Scottish throne in 1290, but had been passed over for John Balliol. Robert himself seized the throne in 1306 after the murder of a rival baron, John Comyn. He went on to recapture most of the castles held by the English in Scotland.*

The Black Death

The blacksmith was one of the most important tradesmen in a village, responsible for making and repairing tools and horseshoes.

The 14th century was full of disasters. The population grew rapidly, but farmers could not grow enough food to keep up with the increase. Many people starved, especially when bad weather destroyed crops and disease killed livestock during the famine of 1315–17. Then the Black Death arrived, which wiped out a third of Britain's population between 1348 and 1351. After this, kings raised crippling taxes to pay for the long and futile war against France.

Landowners began to look for an easier way of farming. The solution was simple – sheep. Huge flocks of sheep could be kept on grassland, which did not need ploughing or harvesting. Their fleeces could be sold for a large profit. By 1400, there were as many as 18 million sheep in England alone.

The wool from sheep, woven into cloth, became England's most important product. Huge amounts of cloth were exported to Europe. Weaving centres, such as Leeds, Halifax and Bury St Edmunds, quickly developed into thriving new towns. British ports, such as Bristol and Southampton, grew rapidly as more and more trade arrived from Europe. London was the most important city in the land. It was the chief port and trading centre, and had the biggest population.

TALLY STICKS

During the 13th century, deals between two traders were recorded with tally sticks. The amount owed was marked on the stick with notches – thick ones for pounds, thinner ones for shillings and thinnest of all for pennies. Then the stick was split in two, and each trader kept half. The amount of the debt could be checked by putting the two halves together again, so that they 'tallied'. When the debt was paid off, the whole stick might be kept as a record. By the 14th century, business methods were more complicated, and merchants used paper bills instead. The amount of paperwork grew rapidly and tally sticks were no longer used.

Merchants extended their businesses as the economy grew. Land carriers brought goods along a network of trading routes which linked the cities of Europe with those in the Near East. Ships brought silks and precious metals from the Mediterranean, returning with British wool.

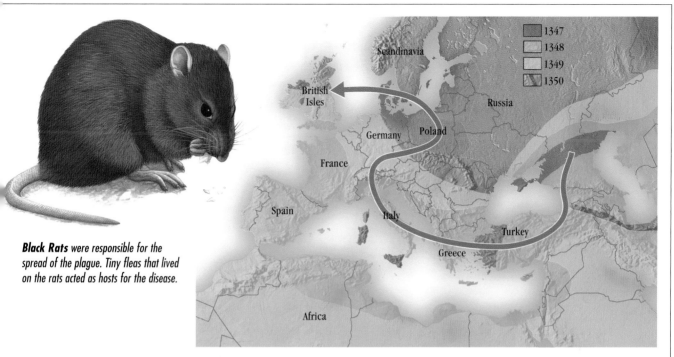

Black Rats were responsible for the spread of the plague. Tiny fleas that lived on the rats acted as hosts for the disease.

Map legend: 1347, 1348, 1349, 1350

Scandinavia
British Isles
Russia
Germany
Poland
France
Spain
Italy
Turkey
Greece
Africa

In June 1348, a fleet of Gascon ships from Bordeaux sailed into the Dorset port of Melcombe Regis. The ships carried wine – and bubonic plague. This deadly disease had already swept across Europe from the plains of Asia, killing millions in its path.

The plague, or Black Death as it was later called, spread with terrifying speed. The first sign was a black swelling in the armpit or the groin. Death was almost certain and very quick but agonizing. So many perished that the graveyards were soon full and corpses had to be buried in fields. Within a year, about one third of the population of England and Wales had died. By 1349, the Black Death had reached all of Scotland except the far north. Ireland had also been ravaged.

This was the greatest disaster in British history. The population plunged from about five million to three million. It kept falling, as the plague broke out again several times. Whole villages were abandoned and some towns were almost deserted. By 1450, there were barely two-and-a-half million people left in England and Wales.

From East Asia, the plague swept into the north and west of Europe.

Medieval towns made ideal places for disease to spread. The streets were filthy, with open gutters in the middle where townsfolk threw all their waste. In the crowded houses, people rarely had clean water for washing.

Hundred Years' War

The Hundred Years' War actually lasted from 1337 to 1453. It covered the reigns of five English kings, each of whom tried in vain to gain control of France.

1328 Charles IV of France dies leaving no male heir.

1337 Philip of France seizes Gascony; Edward III claims French throne and declares war.

1346 English forces win the Battle of Crécy.

1347 Calais falls to Edward III after long siege.

1356 English win Battle of Poitiers; French king captured.

1360 Treaty of Bretigny brings brief peace.

1369 War resumes; England lose territory.

1375 One-year truce agreed at Bruges.

1377 Richard II becomes king.

1399 Richard II deposed and murdered; Henry IV becomes English king.

1413 Death of Henry IV: his son Henry V becomes king.

1415 Henry defeats French at Agincourt.

1419 Henry captures Rouen after long siege and seizes Normandy.

1420 Treaty of Troyes; Henry is heir to French throne.

1422 Death of Henry V; Henry VI becomes king at only nine months old.

1429 Joan of Arc leads French to defeat English.

1451 French capture Bordeaux and Bayonne.

1453 English driven out of Gascony; end of the war.

Flexible mail or padded leather jerkins were worn by footsoldiers and bowmen. By the 1400s, knights fought in suits of plate armour.

The Black Prince, son of Edward III, was a successful battle commander in France.

The conflict began with the death of Charles IV of France, who left no male heir. Edward III of England claimed the throne because he was grandson of an earlier French king. Also, England ruled Gascony in France and the French were trying to seize power there. France angered Edward by supporting the Scots in their struggle against England and by interfering with England's wool trade in Flanders.

The first stage of the war lasted until 1360. Edward defeated the French in two battles, at Crécy and Poitiers. He also captured King John of France and seized the important port of Calais.

JOAN OF ARC
Believing that God had called her to save France, a peasant girl called Joan inspired the French army to rescue Orléans. She then led troops to Rheims so that France's new king could be crowned. However, Joan fell into the hands of the English and she was tried and burned as a witch.

This map shows sites of major battles of the Hundred Years' War. The English victories came mostly in the early stages.

A Welsh longbowman at the Battle of Agincourt. The power and rapid shooting of the longbow (up to ten arrows per minute) made it a devastating weapon. At Agincourt, these archers shattered the French cavalry charge and opened the way for victory over a larger force by a small English army.

⊗ Sluis (1340)

⊗

Calais (1347)
⊗ Agincourt (1415)
⊗ Crécy (1346)

Harfleur (1415)
⊗
⊗ Rouen (1419)
Formigny (1450) ⊗ Rouen (1449)

⊗ Melun (1420)

⊗ Palay (1429)
⊗ Orléans (1428)

⊗ Poitiers (1356)

⊗ La Rochelle (1415)

⊗ Auberoche (1356)

⊗ Bergerac (1450)
Bordeaux (1451)

⊗ French victories
⊗ English victories

After this Edward agreed to give up his claim to the French throne, in return for rights over Gascony, Calais and other territories.

However, war broke out again in 1369. This time Edward lost much of what he had gained before. When Henry V became king in 1413 the next phase of war began. Henry's victory at Agincourt led to his ruling much of northern France. But by the 1430s these gains were being swept away by the French army, inspired by Joan of Arc. By 1453, England had lost all except for Calais.

Henry VI came to the throne as a baby. Unlike his father Henry V, he was no soldier but a scholarly, religious man. His reign saw England lose most of its territory in France, and civil war begin at home.

Wars of the Roses

1453 King Henry VI declared insane; York appointed Protector.

1455 King recovers; York dismissed, but defeats Lancastrians at St Albans.

1460 Lancastrians defeat and kill Duke of York at Wakefield.

1461 Edward of York defeats Lancastrians; deposes Henry.

1470 Lancastrians and Yorkist rebels restore Henry to the throne; Edward flees.

1471 Edward returns and takes the throne; Henry murdered.

1483 Edward V becomes king under Protector, Richard of Gloucester, who seizes throne.

1485 Henry Tudor defeats and kills Richard III at Bosworth; becomes Henry VII.

War with France ended in 1453. Soon a series of civil wars began in England which lasted until 1485. These were fought between rival branches of the Plantagenets – the Houses of York (whose symbol was the white rose) and of Lancaster (whose symbol was the red rose). Henry VI was from the Lancastrian branch. He was a weak ruler who suffered fits of madness.

While Henry was ill, Richard, Duke of York governed as Protector. But when the king recovered, York was dismissed. With an army of supporters, York defeated the royal army at St Albans in 1455 and became Protector again. In 1460, a Lancastrian army under Henry's wife, Margaret, defeated the Yorkists at Wakefield, and the Duke of York was killed.

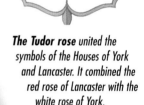

The Tudor rose united the symbols of the Houses of York and Lancaster. It combined the red rose of Lancaster with the white rose of York.

This map shows the principal battles of the Wars of the Roses of 1455–85, which ended with the Lancastrian-Tudor triumph at Bosworth Field.

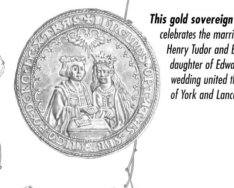

This gold sovereign celebrates the marriage of Henry Tudor and Elizabeth, daughter of Edward IV. The wedding united the Houses of York and Lancaster.

Hexham (1461)

Towton (1461)

Wakefield (1460)

Blore Heath (1469)

Bosworth Field (1485)

Stamford (1470)

Mortimer's Cross (1461)

Northampton (1471)

Tewkesbury (1471)

St Albans (1455)

St Albans (1461)

Barnet (1471)

◎ Yorkist victory
⬣ Lancastrian victory

Richard's son, Edward of York, took on the cause and had himself proclaimed King Edward IV of England in 1461. He went on to crush Margaret's forces and depose Henry. In 1470, Margaret forced Edward to flee and Henry became king once again. Edward returned in 1471 and reclaimed the throne. He ruled until his death in 1483, when civil war broke out yet again. The king's son, Edward V, was only 12 years old, so his uncle Richard became protector. Richard locked Edward in the Tower of London and had himself crowned King Richard III. The last Lancastrian claimant, Henry Tudor, defeated Richard at the Battle of Bosworth in 1485.

HENRY VI

King Henry VI's weak and indecisive reign was marked by periods of mental illness when he had to be looked after like a child. It came to a halt altogether in 1465 when he was captured by the Yorkists and imprisoned in the Tower of London. He was freed in 1470 and restored to the throne, but was too ill to rule. When his only heir, the Prince of Wales, was killed in battle, Henry's supporters melted away. He was murdered in 1471.

Henry Tudor, the new king, kneels after the battle at Bosworth. Many of the king's supporters changed sides, helping Henry to victory. Richard was killed as he fought on foot.

Tudors and Stuarts

The age of the Tudor and Stuart monarchs was a turning point in British history. Over the course of just over 200 years, the country saw tremendous changes, with the growth of parliamentary power and a united kingdom emerging from what had been separate nations. The new Britain grew stronger, laying the foundations for an overseas empire.

In 1485, when Henry VII seized the English throne, the British Isles were still emerging from the Middle Ages. Scotland, Ireland, Wales and England were still separate nations, ruled by ancient laws. They were looked on as poor and uncivilized countries in a remote corner of Europe. The vast majority of British people lived in the countryside, working on the land. There were few big towns, and little organized industry.

p82 The first 'Great Bible' was introduced to British churches in 1538.

p78 An executioner's axe. Henry VIII executed two of his six wives.

p90 Ships sailed vast distances so that explorers could find new sea routes for trade.

p79 A 'lira da braccio', an early kind of violin. Music was one of Henry VIII's loves.

p77 Henry VII's coat of arms with a dragon and dog.

By 1714, when Queen Anne died, the picture was vastly different. There was a United Kingdom of Great Britain after the union of Scotland with England and Wales in 1707. Two great European powers, France and Spain, had been defeated and the British navy ruled the oceans. Britain was the most successful trading nation in Europe, with the beginnings of an empire which stretched from North America to the coast of India. The industrial age was beginning, and people were starting to migrate from the countryside to the developing factory towns.

In between, crucial influences had been at work. The Renaissance had reached Britain from southern Europe, producing some of the greatest writers, musicians and artists in history. The Reformation had brought religious divisions, and the power of parliament had increased hugely, following the shocks of the Wars of the Roses.

p84 Portraits of Elizabeth I were painted to stress her power.

p87 The streets of an Elizabethan town would be crowded with stalls, shoppers, carts, horsemen and people bringing in their goods to sell.

p88 Ornate glassware and pottery, decorated with engraving or with designs in silver and gilt, were produced by craftsmen. Many precious metals and gemstones came from the Americas.

The Age of the Tudors

1485 Richard III defeated and killed at Bosworth; Henry VII becomes first Tudor monarch.

1509 Death of Henry VII; his son Henry VIII is king.

1512 Scotland and France at war with England.

1533 Henry divorces Catherine of Aragon and marries Anne Boleyn; English Reformation begins.

1536 Dissolution of the monasteries.

1547 Henry VIII dies; his nine year-old son Edward VI becomes king; English victory over Scotland at Pinkie.

1553 Death of Edward VI; his sister Mary becomes queen.

1555 Mary begins persecution of Protestants.

1558 Death of Mary; her sister Elizabeth I becomes queen.

1564 Birth of William Shakespeare.

1585 War begins between England and Spain.

1587 Execution of Mary, Queen of Scots.

1588 Defeat of Armada.

1603 Death of Elizabeth I; James VI of Scotland becomes King James I of England.

The period before the accession of Henry VII was very unstable. In the 50 years prior to 1485, there had been six changes of ruler.

The age of the Tudor and Stuart monarchs was a turning point in British history. Over the course of just over 200 years, the country saw tremendous changes, with the growth of parliamentary power and a united kingdom emerging from what had been separate nations. The new Britain grew stronger, laying the foundations for an overseas empire.

For many, Britain became a more prosperous place. Industry and farming expanded, and there was an explosion in overseas trade. British explorers and merchants opened up new sea routes across the Atlantic and Indian Oceans. The boldest of them all, Francis Drake, became the first Briton to lead an expedition around the world.

The Tudor age also saw England growing much stronger than her neighbours. Wales was formally placed under English rule by Henry VIII. His armies also inflicted severe defeats on Scotland. This was in spite of French military support for the Scots.

Tudor Britain saw a boom in new building, from great palaces to humbler town houses. Many of these dwellings were half-timbered, with wooden frames, clay or brick walls and thatched roofs.

TUDOR COSTUME

Clothes were a means of displaying wealth. Rich women could afford clothing made from fine wool, linen or silk. They wore padded skirts held up with loops. Over these went bodices and colourful floor-length gowns. These might have all sorts of fashionable features – puffed sleeves, high collars or starched ruffs around the neck. Silk stockings were also a great luxury. Middle-class women wore knitted woollen stockings and white aprons to protect their gowns.

Henry VII's coat of arms.
At the centre is a shield quartered with lions (representing England). The French motto underneath means 'God and My Right'.

The crowns of Scotland and England were united in 1603. By that time, too, Ireland was ruled by England.

However, the most far-reaching change was to divide Britain from other parts of Europe. The Reformation separated the English Church from the control of the Roman Catholic Church. This caused conflict with Catholic nations such as Spain, but it also spurred a feeling of independence. Britain's growing sense of itself as a nation was reflected in many ways, from the plays of William Shakespeare to the victory over the Armada – a fleet sent by King Philip II of Spain to invade Britain.

__The map shows__ how the power of the early Tudor monarchs depended on support from noblemen in the English counties. Without it, the monarchs might have found it impossible to rule.

__King Henry VII__ married Elizabeth of York. By marrying Elizabeth, he united the warring Houses of York and Lancaster. Henry's most important task was to found a dynasty and leave a strong son to succeed him. But his eldest child Arthur tragically died of disease in 1502, and Arthur's ten-year-old brother Henry became heir to the throne.

Northumberland

Cumberland   Durham

Westmorland

Yorkshire

Lancashire

Cheshire — Derby   Lincoln
                Nottingham

Stafford — Rutland

Shropshire   Leicester   Norfolk
                Hunts
            Warwick   Northampton
    Worcester   Bedford   Cambridge
  Hereford   Suffolk
                        Herts   Essex
    Gloucester   Oxford
                Bucks   Middlesex
                Berks   • London

Wiltshire   Surrey   Kent

Somerset   Hampshire   Sussex

Devon

    Dorset

Cornwall

Number of Gentlemen of the Privy Chamber of Henry VIII coming from the county

Number of court knights from the county accompanying Henry VIII to the Field of the Cloth of Gold in 1520

Henry VIII

1509 Henry VIII takes the throne; marries Catherine of Aragon.

1512–13 War against France; Henry leads troops to Calais.

1513 Scots defeated at Battle of Flodden.

1520 Henry meets king of France at the 'Field of the Cloth of Gold'.

1522–25 War with France again.

1527 Henry asks the pope to annul his marriage; papal court set up in London to decide.

1531 Henry declares himself Supreme Head of the English Church.

1533 Henry divorces Catherine and marries Anne Boleyn.

1536 Henry divorces Anne and has her executed, marries Jane Seymour. Dissolution of smaller monasteries.

1539 Dissolution of larger religious houses.

1539–40 Henry marries and divorces Anne of Cleves and then marries Catherine Howard.

1542 Catherine Howard executed.

1543 Henry marries Catherine Parr.

Henry VII was an unpopular king because he taxed his people heavily. When he died in 1509, there was general rejoicing. The new king, Henry VIII, was very different from his father. He was tall, handsome and full of energy. He had a large appetite and was immensely fond of both food and drink.

Yet Henry only became king by accident. His elder brother Arthur had been heir to the throne, but he had died young. So Prince Henry took Arthur's place, and married his widow, the Spanish princess Catherine of Aragon.

Henry was determined to win glory in war. In 1513, he led an army to France. The expedition wasted a lot of money and gained little. Meanwhile another English army stopped an invasion by the Scots at the Battle of Flodden. Bored by the daily running of government, Henry left most of this work to his Lord Chancellor, Thomas Wolsey. The king preferred to spend his time hunting, jousting and playing music.

There was one thing that Henry desperately wanted – a son to become king after him. Queen Catherine of Aragon became pregnant four times; all the babies were boys but none survived more than a few weeks. In 1516, Catherine bore a daughter, who was named Mary. In 1526, Henry fell in love with Anne Boleyn, who had recently come to his court. But Anne would not become his mistress – she wanted Henry to divorce Catherine first. The king ordered his chancellor, Thomas Wolsey, to arrange for the pope to agree to the divorce.

Henry VIII in his thirties was still strong and athletic. He spent many hours practising single combat or jousting in full armour, and was a fine marksman with the bow. However, though he led his army in France, he did not take part in any battles.

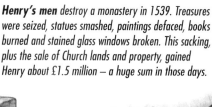

An executioner's axe. Henry sentenced to death many who opposed him. Sir Thomas More, one of the king's chancellors, and John Fisher, Bishop of Rochester were beheaded in 1535.

Henry's men destroy a monastery in 1539. Treasures were seized, statues smashed, paintings defaced, books burned and stained glass windows broken. This sacking, plus the sale of Church lands and property, gained Henry about £1.5 million – a huge sum in those days.

Months slipped by without a judgement, for the pope disapproved of the divorce. Henry blamed Wolsey for the delay and in 1529 he sacked him.

When the pope would not allow Henry VIII to divorce Catherine of Aragon, Henry decided that he would defy the pope, and take charge of the English Church himself. In 1532, Henry forced priests to recognise him as head of the English Church. A year later, he appointed a new archbishop, Thomas Cranmer, who granted him a divorce from Catherine. He and Anne were secretly married, and Anne was crowned queen. She gave birth to a girl, Princess Elizabeth, in September 1533. No sons came, and by 1536 Henry wanted to be rid of Anne. She was accused of adultery and executed. Only days later, the king married Jane Seymour. She produced a male heir for Henry – Prince Edward. Soon after Edward's birth Jane died of fever. Henry now had a son at last, but no wife.

In 1536, Parliament passed an act to 'dissolve', or close down, many of the smaller monasteries. Later, the larger ones were dissolved as well. Their treasures were plundered and seized by the monarch.

Henry was to marry three more times. In 1539, he agreed to marry a German princess, Anne of Cleves. This would give him a useful ally in Europe. But he found Anne dull and quickly divorced her. Next was Catherine Howard, who became queen in 1540 and was beheaded for adultery in 1542. A year later, Henry married Catherine Parr, who looked after his children and nursed him through his final illness.

THE MARY ROSE
In July 1545, Henry VIII travelled to watch his naval fleet assemble in Portsmouth harbour. But he witnessed a tragedy. His flagship, the *Mary Rose*, keeled over in the strong wind, filled with water and sank with the loss of over 500 men. In 1982, the ship's hull was raised from the seabed. During the recovery, thousands of everyday Tudor objects were found, including coins, weapons, board games, boots and shoes.

A 'lira da braccio', an early kind of violin. Music was one of Henry's greatest loves. He composed several songs, played the organ and the lute, and sang to his own accompaniment. He even sang with the choirs in his royal chapels.

Scotland and the Tudors

During the first half of the Tudor period, Scotland was still independent and thriving. Scottish kings were determined not to come under English control. They turned for help to England's most powerful rivals – the French. The alliance between Scotland and France was renewed in 1512.

The thistle is the Scottish national symbol. Its origins are unclear, but one story tells of how a group of Scots were woken by the cries of a Viking raider who stepped on a thistle in his bare feet. In gratitude for this warning, the thistle was adopted as the nation's national symbol.

1513 King James IV killed at Flodden; his heir is 18-month-old James V.

1537 James marries Madeleine of France.

1541 James uses Scots Parliament to protect the authority of the pope.

1542 English army defeats Scots at Solway Moss, Cumberland; death of James V, whose heir is the one-week-old Mary (later Mary, Queen of Scots).

1543–49 English attacks on southern Scotland.

1547 English victory at Battle of Pinkie.

1558 Mary marries Francis, heir to the French throne.

1560 The 'Reformation Parliament' scraps papal authority and bans Mass; death of Francis.

1561 Mary returns to Scotland.

1567–68 Mary flees to England; her son James VI (later James I of England) becomes yet another infant king.

A year later, war broke out between England and France. The Scottish king, James IV, seized the chance to help his European ally and invaded northern England. Near the village of Flodden in Northumberland, the Scots were brutally defeated by a smaller English force, and King James was killed.

After this there was peace for a while. The new king, James V, was horrified by Henry's split with Rome, and tried to prevent the same thing happening in Scotland. He passed laws to ensure obedience to the pope. This pleased his allies in France, a Catholic country.

Pikes, axes and swords were some of the battle weapons used at Flodden. The Scots were poorly trained and this probably led to their defeat, despite their enthusiasm.

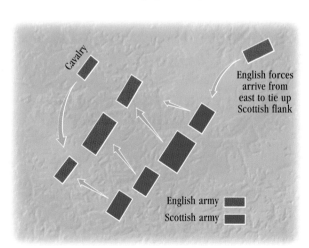

Cavalry

English forces arrive from east to tie up Scottish flank

English army
Scottish army

During the Battle of Flodden in 1513, the Scottish army were cut off by an outflanking manoeuvre by English forces to the north. Despite initial success on the field, the Scots were defeated.

At Flodden, the Scottish troops charged downhill armed with long pikes. They were easily beaten by the English, who had shorter and more handy 'bills' which could smash through armour. The English killed anyone they caught. The Scots lost 10,000 men, including King James himself.

MARY STUART

Mary, Queen of Scots, had a strong claim to the English throne. Henry VIII had been her great uncle. When she married the French dauphin Francis in 1558, she posed an even greater threat to the English monarch.

Peace came to an end in 1542. The ageing Henry VIII was now very fat and could scarcely walk. All the same, he planned one last attempt to conquer France. But first, he had to stop Scottish forces attacking him from the rear. His army defeated the Scots at Solway Moss. After Henry's death in 1547, the Scottish army was once again battered to defeat at Pinkie, in Lothian.

By this time James V was also dead. Scotland's new monarch was his infant daughter, Mary. When she grew up, she strengthened the ties between Scotland and France by marrying the dauphin, or heir to the French throne. But he died in 1560, and Mary returned to Scotland. She found that things had changed. The Protestant faith had grown very popular, and she could not keep control. Mary, Queen of Scots, was forced to give up her throne in 1567 and take refuge in England.

Tartan cloth had been worn by the Scots since at least the 13th century. There was a different pattern of stripes for each district or clan. At this time, a single length of tartan plaid was worn over the shoulder and held at the waist with a belt.

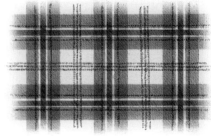

Edward VI and Mary

1547 Death of Henry VIII; Edward VI becomes king, under the Protectorate of the Duke of Somerset.

1548 The king's council orders all religious images to be destroyed.

1549 Book of Common Prayer authorized by parliament; riots in Devon, Cornwall and East Anglia in protest at rising prices and high rents.

1550 Somerset replaced by the Duke of Northumberland.

1551 Mary refuses to accept new Protestant services; she holds Catholic Mass.

1553 Death of Edward VI; Lady Jane Grey reigns for nine days before being ousted by Mary Tudor.

1554 Reunion with Rome; Mary marries Philip of Spain; rebellion in Kent led by Sir Thomas Wyatt.

1555 Persecution of Protestants begins; two Protestant bishops burned at the stake.

1556 Thomas Cranmer, once Archbishop of Canterbury, burned.

1557 England joins Spain in war against France.

1558 England forced to surrender Calais to the French; death of Mary; Elizabeth becomes queen.

Henry VIII died in 1547. He was hugely fat and in great pain from ulcers. His long reign had ended sadly, with the terrible waste of men and money in his last expedition to France. As he lay dying, the old king had written his will. He stated that his children Edward, Mary and Elizabeth should succeed him. Within the next 11 years, they all came to the throne.

The death of Henry VIII left England in a state of religious turmoil between Catholics and Protestants.

The new king, Edward, was only nine years old, so England and Wales were governed by a 'protector', the Duke of Somerset. But Somerset was a poor leader. His rule led to riots in the western counties, and conflict between powerful nobles. In 1550, he was replaced by the Duke of Northumberland.

Meanwhile, the English Reformation was gathering pace. More religious houses were dissolved, and their treasures seized by the Crown. The first English Prayer Book became the official text for religious services. Edward VI was a keen Protestant, and hated his sister Mary, who remained Catholic. He made a will declaring that the next monarch should be Jane Grey, a relative of the Tudors.

PROTESTANT MARTYRS

Condemned Protestants suffered a nasty death during Mary's reign. They were tied to stakes and surrounded with bundles of firewood, which were then lit. At least 275 people met this slow and agonizing end. These victims were later commemorated by the Protestant writer John Foxe, whose *Book of Martyrs* contained many grisly pictures and descriptions. It was a huge bestseller during Elizabeth's reign, and helped to exaggerate Mary's brutality.

The first 'Great Bible' was placed in all churches after 1538. Books were still scarce and expensive, so many Bibles were attached to the lecterns with chains.

PHILIP OF SPAIN

Philip became king of Spain in 1556 and was also, briefly, the only Spanish king of England while he was married to Queen Mary. After her death, he also offered to marry the new queen, Elizabeth I, but she refused.

When the teenage king died in 1553, there was almost civil war. Jane ruled for just nine days before Mary displaced her as queen and condemned her to death.

It soon became clear that Mary was determined to reverse the Reformation and stamp out the Protestant faith in England. Her aim was to reunite the English Church with the Catholic Church in Rome. In 1554, the pope sent a cardinal to London to restore his power. Parliament repealed (cancelled) the religious laws of Edward's reign and at least 275 leading Protestants were condemned to death and burnt at the stake.

Mary made herself even more unpopular by marrying her cousin Philip, the heir to the throne of Spain. Philip became joint ruler, so now England was allied with a leading Catholic power. There was an uprising in Kent, and England was forced to join Spain in a war against France. During this conflict, the French captured Calais, the last English stronghold in Europe.

Edward VI ruled for just six years. During his reign he held little power. Instead, two dukes, Somerset and Northumberland, acted as regent and wielded almost absolute control of the English government.

Mary Tudor had a tragic and loveless upbringing. She was separated from her mother, rejected and declared a bastard by her father, and scorned by her brother. Even marriage to Philip of Spain brought little relief, as he abandoned her shortly afterwards.

Elizabeth I

On 17 November, 1558, Princess Elizabeth sat beneath an oak tree at Hatfield House in Hertfordshire. She had spent much of her adult life here, away from the royal court. Her sister Queen Mary did not trust her, because she was not only popular but a Protestant as well. In 1554, Mary had even imprisoned her in the Tower of London for two months.

1533 Elizabeth born in Greenwich Palace, London, to Henry VIII and Anne Boleyn.

1536 Anne Boleyn beheaded.

1554 Elizabeth arrested on Mary's orders and accused of involvement with rebellions; she is held in the Tower of London and released after two months.

1558 Death of Mary; Elizabeth becomes the new queen.

1559 Laws confirming the Protestant faith in England; Elizabeth rejects offer of marriage from son of Holy Roman Emperor.

1562 Elizabeth nearly dies of smallpox; parliament urges her to marry.

1569 Anti-Protestant rebellion in northern England.

1570 Pope excommunicates Elizabeth.

1571 Ridolfi Plot to assassinate Elizabeth discovered.

1572 Treaty signed between England and France.

But now news arrived that Mary was dead and Elizabeth was the new queen. She travelled to London, where she was crowned eight weeks later. It was a time of great uncertainty. Many people feared that a young female monarch would not be strong enough to rule the country. There were two major problems to be solved at once: religion and marriage.

Mary's attempt to turn England back into a Catholic country had caused turmoil. In 1559, Elizabeth framed new religious laws with the help of her chief minister, William Cecil. These established England as a Protestant country. The queen became Supreme Governor (rather than head) of the Church, and priests had to use the English Prayer Book.

The problem of Elizabeth's marriage was never settled. Many kings and princes were keen to marry her, and her ministers wanted her to produce an heir to the throne.

Sir Walter Raleigh was a talented poet, soldier and explorer. He was one of Elizabeth's favourites in court, and had many rivals. He fell from favour when the queen discovered that he had secretly married one of her maids.

Portraits of Elizabeth I were painted to stress her grandeur. They were not meant to be accurate likenesses. Here, she wears a sumptuous costume and jewels. Her left hand touches the globe, as a symbol of her subjects' explorations and conquests. Portraits also had to flatter her, and those she did not like were destroyed.

THE ROYAL COAT OF ARMS

Queen Elizabeth's coat of arms showed a shield quartered with the lions of England and the feathers of Wales. Above was a helmet and crest, and around it was a French motto which means 'Evil Be To Him Who Thinks Evil'. Underneath was another motto in Latin, which means 'Always the Same'. The supporters on either side were the lion of England and the dragon of Wales. Henry VIII's Parliament had passed the Acts of Union between 1536 and 1543, bringing Wales officially under English rule. It also became a Protestant country, and a Welsh translation of the New Testament appeared in 1567.

SEMPER EADEM

The Tower of London acted as Elizabeth's prison for two months prior to her reign. Once she became queen, it served as the prison for several traitors who were intent on overthrowing the Protestant queen and returning the country to Catholicism.

But Elizabeth realized that a foreign husband would make her unpopular and lessen her own power.

England now needed friends abroad. After the queen's new Protestant laws, many Catholic countries became enemies. The pope 'excommunicated' Elizabeth, cutting her off from the Catholic Church and declaring that she had no right to rule. But the queen found an ally in the French. In 1572, England and France made a treaty promising to help each other if they were attacked by another power.

Elizabethan ladies of fashion. Clothes for the wealthy grew more ornate throughout Elizabeth's reign. Both sexes wore clothes which were padded, quilted, embroidered or stiffened with whalebone. The sleeves on women's dresses were separate and tied or pinned to the bodice, with padded pieces to disguise the join.

Dozens of grand houses were built in Elizabeth's time. Some retained features of the old fortified castles, such as the moat, but this was more for decoration than for defence. Others were huge palaces, or 'prodigy houses', with many windows and interiors adorned with tapestries, carvings and stone staircases.

Elizabeth signed Mary's death warrant. She took a long time to agree because she was unwilling to execute someone who was not just of royal blood but her own cousin. Elizabeth also realized that Mary's death might give Catholic plotters overseas a better excuse to assassinate her.

Elizabethan Life

At the beginning of the Tudor Age, Britain's population increased for the first time since the Black Death. That growth continued (in spite of outbreaks of famine and disease) through Elizabeth's reign. By 1603, the population of England and Wales had risen from 3 million to 4.25 million.

More people meant greater demand for food and goods. Industry began to prosper and more land was cultivated to grow crops. But this was not good for everyone. As farmland became more valuable, landowners enclosed more fields for their sheep and cattle to graze. Villagers had less space to grow crops and feed their own animals. Rents and prices rose, as well — much faster than workers' wages. The old feudal system of the Middle Ages had broken down by the 1570s, leaving many labourers without jobs or land. This caused a massive increase in begging. Parliament passed a series of Poor Laws to try to deal with them. In 1572, each parish was made responsible for providing jobs for the poor.

1558 Thousands perish in epidemic of influenza and famine caused by bad harvests.

1559 Protestants, led by John Knox, occupy Edinburgh.

1560 Scotland breaks with Rome and formally becomes Protestant.

1563 New laws fix hours of work for labourers.

1565 Sweet potatoes brought to England from the New World.

1572 New Poor Law gives parishes the duty of providing for poor and old people.

1574 Scots pass law to control wandering beggars.

1580 Longleat House in Wiltshire completed.

1587 Burghley House in Lincolnshire completed.

1588 First complete Welsh translation of the Bible.

1589 First flushing lavatory built by Sir John Harington.

1596 Food riots in Kent; protesters against land enclosures march from Oxfordshire to London.

Coins were made of pure gold or silver in early Tudor times. But Henry VIII debased (spoiled) the coinage by mixing it with base metals such as lead. In 1561, Elizabeth restored coins to their proper purity.

Meals, for most people, consisted mainly of bread, soup and boiled meat. Rich people could afford luxuries such as sugar, wine, spices and bread made from white flour.

WORKING CLOTHES

Ordinary people could not afford to copy the fantastic and colourful costumes of the wealthy. They wore clothes that were more comfortable and practical, but very drab. Men wore a loose-fitting shirt and breeches of coarse woollen cloth. Women wore a kirtle (dress) and apron of the same material. These were usually coloured brown or blue with simple vegetable dyes. The clothes would rarely get washed, and in winter underclothes were never removed at all. Outer garments and boots were made of leather.

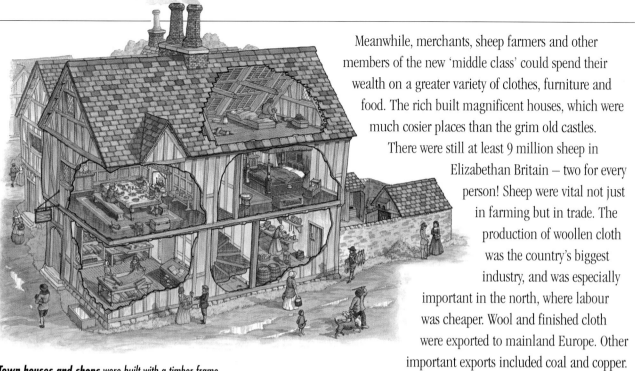

Meanwhile, merchants, sheep farmers and other members of the new 'middle class' could spend their wealth on a greater variety of clothes, furniture and food. The rich built magnificent houses, which were much cosier places than the grim old castles.

There were still at least 9 million sheep in Elizabethan Britain – two for every person! Sheep were vital not just in farming but in trade. The production of woollen cloth was the country's biggest industry, and was especially important in the north, where labour was cheaper. Wool and finished cloth were exported to mainland Europe. Other important exports included coal and copper.

London, Britain's biggest city, had a population of over 200,000 in 1600. It was overcrowded, noisy and smelly. One visitor described the city as 'the filthiest in the world'. Queen Elizabeth feared that London would grow so large that it would become a focus of riots. She tried to limit the number of new buildings and inhabitants.

Over 90 per cent of Britons still lived in the countryside and depended on townspeople to buy their produce. However, the state of the roads was a barrier to trade. They were little better than muddy tracks. Traders sent their cargo by river or sea whenever they could.

Town houses and shops were built with a timber frame covered with bricks and plaster, and roofed with clay tiles. Servants slept in the attic. The family living room and bedrooms were on the first floor, and the kitchen and storerooms on the ground floor.

The streets of an Elizabethan town would be crowded with street stalls, shoppers, carts carrying goods, horsemen and country people bringing in their goods to sell. Shops of craftsmen such as metalworkers and cobblers were on the ground floor of houses. Each workshop or inn had its own sign, as many people were still unable to read. Pickpockets looked for victims in the crowd.

The Renaissance in Britain

1491 Death of William Caxton, printing pioneer.

1564 William Shakespeare born in Stratford-upon-Avon, Warwickshire.

1567 Opening of London's first proper theatre, the Red Lion.

1575 Tallis and Byrd publish a collection of their musical settings.

1580–1600 Nicholas Hilliard paints series of miniatures.

1589–91 Shakespeare's first plays written and performed.

1590 Edmund Spenser begins writing his poem *The Faerie Queene*, which glorifies Queen Elizabeth.

1591 William Smythson designs Hardwick Hall, Derbyshire.

1599 The Globe playhouse opens in London.

1616 Death of Shakespeare.

During the Elizabethan age, only men were allowed to act on stage. They played all the parts in a play, even the female roles.

The Globe playhouse was where Shakespeare's company performed plays. Spectators could pay one penny to stand as 'groundlings' below the stage, or two pennies to sit in the sheltered galleries.

Ornate glassware and pottery, decorated with engraving or with designs in silver and gilt, were produced by craftsmen. A lot of precious metal and gemstones came from the Americas.

Since about 1500, Britain had felt the effects of the Renaissance. This 'rebirth' had seen an outburst of fresh creativity throughout Europe. Starting in Italy in the 14th century, it had spread. Painters, writers, sculptors and scholars began to look at the world in new ways, and use new techniques and theories.

In Britain, the painter Nicholas Hilliard produced exquisite miniature portraits of courtiers and monarchy, including Elizabeth herself. Thomas Tallis and William Byrd composed beautiful choral music and Robert Smythson designed stunning palaces. Writers, such as Christopher Marlowe and Ben Jonson drew huge audiences to new city playhouses.

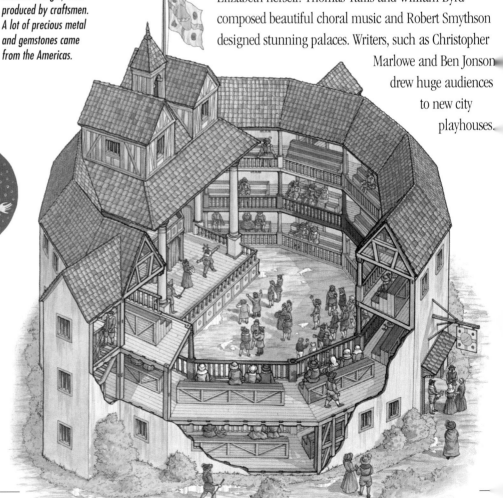

Shakespeare was born in Stratford-upon-Avon, Warwickshire, in 1564. He left the town as a young man to work in London, but returned as a rich and successful playwright when he retired. His birthplace can be visited today.

William Shakespeare, the most famous playwright of all, created a new type of verse drama, which gave a vivid picture of the Elizabethan world. In comedies such as *Twelfth Night* and tragedies such as *King Lear*, he explored the range of human feelings. Until late Tudor times, actors worked as travelling bands. But by 1600 several playhouses had been built in London, notably the Globe, where most of Shakespeare's greatest plays were first seen. These theatres boasted music and special effects.

The spread of Renaissance ideas was made easier by the development of printing. Until the 1470s there had been few books in Britain. Each one had to be copied out by hand. In 1476, William Caxton produced the first printed book in Britain, using techniques invented in Germany. Soon, new printing presses were set up, turning out quantities of cheap books and pamphlets. For the first time, information and ideas were available to anyone who could read. The printed word became an important way of forming public opinion.

WILLIAM CAXTON

Caxton was a cloth merchant who learned the new craft of printing. He used single pieces of type for each letter. These were put together to form a page of print, then broken up and used again. Caxton published over 100 titles, covering history, religion and adventure. Among them were the life of St Jerome (above), Chaucer's *Canterbury Tales* and Malory's stories of King Arthur.

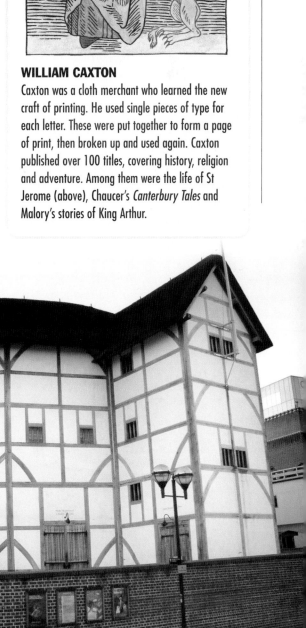

This reconstruction of the Globe theatre was completed in 1997 and sits next to the river Thames just 200 metres from the site of the original Elizabethan theatre.

Explorers, Pirates and Armadas

1497 John Cabot reaches coast of Newfoundland.

1555 The Muscovy Company founded to trade with Russia.

1562 John Hawkins begins carrying slaves from West Africa to the Caribbean.

1568 Revolt in Netherlands against Spanish rule; Elizabeth sends help to rebels.

1570 Pope excommunicates Elizabeth.

1576–83 Attempts by Frobisher and Gilbert to find a northwest passage.

1577–80 Drake circumnavigates the world.

1585 First, unsuccessful New World colony founded on Roanoke Island.

1586 Spanish finalize plans to invade England; Babington Plot against Elizabeth is uncovered; Mary Queen of Scots is sentenced to death.

1588 Spanish Armada sets sail and is attacked in the English Channel; the Spanish retreat northwards; 60 ships survive.

1595 Raleigh's trip in search of El Dorado fails.

1600 East India Company founded to trade with Asia.

1607 Colony of Virginia founded.

Ships sailed vast distances so that explorers could find new sea routes for trade. Some explorers aimed to reach the Far East, by sailing westwards across the Atlantic – but they found the American continents in the way!

When the Tudor Age began, Europeans were on the brink of amazing discoveries about their world. Merchants were eager to expand their business, and find new sea routes. But the sea was also one of the greatest threats to Britain's safety.

There was one place above all that merchants wanted to reach – the Far East. In Cathay (China) they could buy wonderful silks, gold and porcelain. In the Spice Islands (the Moluccas) they could buy precious cloves and nutmegs. The trouble was, nobody knew the way. Then, in 1487, Portuguese ships rounded the southern tip of Africa. This opened up an easterly sea route to India and the Far East. In 1492, Spanish ships under Christopher Columbus set out for China in the opposite direction — westwards. To Columbus's surprise, he found the vast continents of the Americas instead.

Plundered treasure. *Drake's piratical expeditions made him very rich. On his round-the-world voyage, he captured treasure worth £25 million from one galleon alone!*

FINDING YOUR WAY
Navigating a Tudor sailing ship was a mixture of experience and guesswork. The captain could find out his latitude (how far north or south he was) by using an astrolabe or a backstaff. By looking at the Sun through these, he could measure its angle above the horizon. However, working out longitude (how far east or west), without reliable clocks, was much more difficult.

Britain joined in the adventure. In 1497, John Cabot sailed westwards from Bristol in search of silks and spices. He landed on the coast of Newfoundland. There were no exotic goods to buy, but something that was just as valuable – fish. North America and the Caribbean became a crucial part of Britain's trading empire.

Meanwhile, other explorers were trying to find other ways to the Far East. In 1577, Francis Drake set off to lead the second expedition to circumnavigate the world, following in the footsteps of the Portuguese explorer Ferdinand Magellan. Drake returned three years later in 1580.

In the meantime, trouble had been brewing between Britain and Spain, who wanted to return Britain back to Catholic rule. In July 1588, an invasion fleet, or Armada, of 130 Spanish ships reached the English Channel. The English fleet harassed the invasion force all the way up the narrow Channel. The Armada anchored off the Dutch coast for safety.

Then the English commander Lord Howard sent in eight blazing 'fireships'. The terrified Spaniards were forced away from the shore and the two fleets clashed in a battle off Gravelines. The Spaniards suffered terrible losses and gave up the invasion. They headed for Spain, round the north of Scotland, but fierce storms scattered the fleet and many were wrecked – only 60 ships made it to Spain.

The Armada was first sighted off the Isles of Scilly, to the west of Cornwall. A chain of beacon fires relayed the news along the south coast. The English fleet gathered to attack. It was bigger in number than the Armada, with 197 ships, but had fewer men.

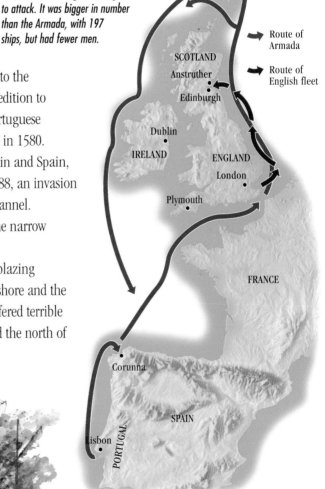

→ Route of Armada

→ Route of English fleet

The eight fireships were stuffed with anything which would burn – including tubs of butter! The guns were loaded with double shot, and went off when the fire reached them. The ships were released at night, under full sail, to be blown towards the tightly packed Spanish fleet.

The route taken by the Spanish Armada. After the Battle of Gravelines, it escaped northwards because that was the way the wind blew. Many Spaniards were washed up on the Irish coast.

91

The Stuarts

This coin, depicting James VI as a mounted knight, marks the king's accession to the throne of England.

When Elizabeth I died in 1603, she left no son or daughter to succeed her. Her successor was James VI of Scotland and he became the first Stuart king of England. The Stuarts were to reign over both England and Scotland for over 100 years, but not always peacefully.

As James travelled south in 1603, he was welcomed by his new English subjects: later he remembered 'their eyes flaming with nothing but sparkles of affection, their mouths and tongues uttering nothing but sounds of joy'. This enthusiasm was not to last.

The Stuarts had ruled Scotland since 1371. James was the son of Mary, Queen of Scots, put to death as a possible rival by Elizabeth. Yet he had been the only real choice to succeed the old queen. When he arrived in London, James was already a skilled and experienced ruler. He brought with him many Scottish courtiers, but he was also careful to appoint English ministers to advise him. Nevertheless, many people at the English court remained deeply suspicious of this new Scottish king.

The early years of James I's reign were successful in many ways. He ended the war with Spain, and he managed to achieve a balance between the different religious groups – Catholics, Anglicans and Puritans. But he spent money extravagantly, and his court gained a reputation for scandal and intrigue. Later in his reign, James fell under the spell of one of his courtiers, George Villiers, lavishing money on him and making him Duke of Buckingham. The Duke quickly became powerful in the English court. He also became a friend of James's son, Prince Charles, and in the last year of the old king's life Charles and Buckingham took control of all political decisions.

1603 James VI of Scotland (1566–1625) becomes James I.

1605 Gunpowder Plot to blow up Parliament fails.

1609 'Plantation of Ulster' Protestant settlers move on to land taken from Irish Catholics.

1611 Publication of the Authorized Version of the Bible, known as the King James Bible.

1620 The Pilgrims set sail from Plymouth, England, on 16 September. They sign the Mayflower Compact on 11 November. They land at Plymouth Colony, New England, on 21 December.

1621 Protestation of House of Commons stating their right to free speech.

1621 William Bradford succeeds John Carver as governor of the American colony. He serves as governor until 1656. He negotiates a treaty with the Wampanoag people.

1623 Prince Charles and George Villiers (later Duke of Buckingham) travel to Spain and try to secure marriage between Charles and the daughter of King Philip IV.

1625 Death of James I.

This is the lantern that belonged to Guy Fawkes. It was Fawkes who put at least 20 barrels of gunpowder in a cellar beneath the Houses of Parliament. But the plot was discovered and he was captured and tortured to reveal the names of the other conspirators.

JAMES I
James I did not receive a warm reception from the English court. Many English contemporaries were rude and snobbish about the king's appearance and behaviour. They said that he was ugly and coarse, that he drank too much, was difficult to understand, and that he dribbled!

In November 1620, a three-masted sailing ship called the *Mayflower* dropped anchor off the coast, near present-day Provincetown, Massachusetts. The ship carried 102 passengers from England. Many of the people on board the *Mayflower* were dissenters. They belonged to a group of English Protestants called Puritans who disagreed with many of the practices of the Church of England. Their leader was William Brewster (1567–1644), who, in 1606, had broken away from the Church of England to form a separate congregation. At this time, it was illegal to set up an independent congregation in England, and Brewster and his followers, known as Separatists, were persecuted. To escape arrest, Brewster and members of his congregation fled to the Netherlands.

In 1619, Brewster and another Separatist called William Bradford (1590–1657) returned to England. The Separatists were dissatisfied with life in the Netherlands and their thoughts turned to the promise of the 'New World' far across the Atlantic Ocean. Brewster and Bradford negotiated with the Virginia Company for some land, and found merchants willing to back their venture.

On 16 September, 1620, the would-be colonists boarded the *Mayflower* at Plymouth and set sail for the 'New World'. They reached Cape Cod in November. Before landing, 41 of the male passengers signed a document which became known as the Mayflower Compact. This document was an agreement for cooperation that became the foundation of the government of the new colony. The first settlers became known as Founders, Forefathers, or – after a term used by William Bradford himself – Pilgrims.

The land on which the Pilgrim Fathers settled was already occupied by Native Americans of the Wampanoag people. The newcomers and the Native Americans negotiated trade agreements. The Native Americans also showed the settlers ways of growing food, hunting and fishing that were an essential part of their survival in this new colony.

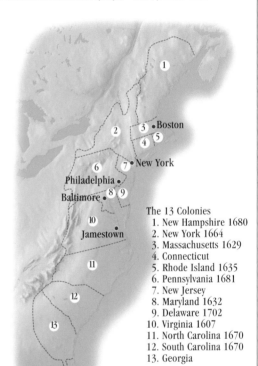

The 13 Colonies
1. New Hampshire 1680
2. New York 1664
3. Massachusetts 1629
4. Connecticut
5. Rhode Island 1635
6. Pennsylvania 1681
7. New Jersey
8. Maryland 1632
9. Delaware 1702
10. Virginia 1607
11. North Carolina 1670
12. South Carolina 1670
13. Georgia

This map shows the 13 original British colonies on the east coast of North America. Plymouth Colony, in Massachusetts, was the second permanent British settlement after Virginia.

In 1605, a group of English Catholics plotted to blow up the Houses of Parliament and with it King James I, his wife and his eldest son. The plotters were led by Robert Catesby (second from right), but the most famous of them all is Guy Fawkes (third from right). The plotters hoped that in the confusion after the explosion and murder of the king, English Catholics would be able to take over the country.

Charles I and War with Scotland

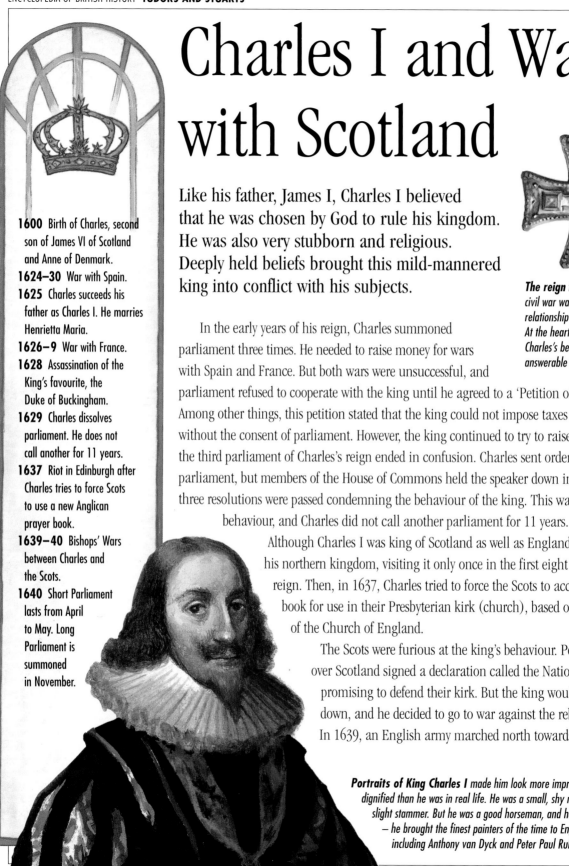

Like his father, James I, Charles I believed that he was chosen by God to rule his kingdom. He was also very stubborn and religious. Deeply held beliefs brought this mild-mannered king into conflict with his subjects.

1600 Birth of Charles, second son of James VI of Scotland and Anne of Denmark.

1624–30 War with Spain.

1625 Charles succeeds his father as Charles I. He marries Henrietta Maria.

1626–9 War with France.

1628 Assassination of the King's favourite, the Duke of Buckingham.

1629 Charles dissolves parliament. He does not call another for 11 years.

1637 Riot in Edinburgh after Charles tries to force Scots to use a new Anglican prayer book.

1639–40 Bishops' Wars between Charles and the Scots.

1640 Short Parliament lasts from April to May. Long Parliament is summoned in November.

The reign that led England to civil war was marked by a stormy relationship with parliament. At the heart of the problem was Charles's belief that he was answerable to no one but God.

In the early years of his reign, Charles summoned parliament three times. He needed to raise money for wars with Spain and France. But both wars were unsuccessful, and parliament refused to cooperate with the king until he agreed to a 'Petition of Right' in 1628. Among other things, this petition stated that the king could not impose taxes on his subjects without the consent of parliament. However, the king continued to try to raise taxes. In 1629, the third parliament of Charles's reign ended in confusion. Charles sent orders to dissolve parliament, but members of the House of Commons held the speaker down in his chair until three resolutions were passed condemning the behaviour of the king. This was revolutionary behaviour, and Charles did not call another parliament for 11 years.

Although Charles I was king of Scotland as well as England he neglected his northern kingdom, visiting it only once in the first eight years of his reign. Then, in 1637, Charles tried to force the Scots to accept a new prayer book for use in their Presbyterian kirk (church), based on the practices of the Church of England.

The Scots were furious at the king's behaviour. People from all over Scotland signed a declaration called the National Covenant promising to defend their kirk. But the king would not back down, and he decided to go to war against the rebellious Scots. In 1639, an English army marched north towards Scotland.

Portraits of King Charles I made him look more impressive and dignified than he was in real life. He was a small, shy man, with a slight stammer. But he was a good horseman, and he loved art — he brought the finest painters of the time to England, including Anthony van Dyck and Peter Paul Rubens.

The official introduction of the new prayer book in Scotland was on 23 July, 1637. A protest was organised at a service in St Giles's Cathedral in Edinburgh. The congregation planned to stage a walk-out, but as the minister began to speak the first words of the service, a more violent reaction erupted. A woman stood up and hurled her three-legged stool across the cathedral. The rest of the congregation joined in and soon the riot had spilled out on to the streets.

However, Charles lacked confidence in his troops — and enough money to pay for them — and he was forced to make peace. The first Bishops' War ended before a shot was fired.

The king desperately needed money to raise a bigger army. For the first time in 11 years he called parliament, but MPs were unwilling to grant the king the funds he needed. The parliament lasted only three weeks and became known as the 'Short Parliament'. Meanwhile, Scottish armies marched into the north of England and seized Northumberland and Durham. And so the second Bishops' War ended with victory for the Scots. They knew that Charles had little choice but to agree to their demands. In 1640 he called parliament once again.

A Scottish nobleman presents King Charles I with a petition. The Scots wanted the king to give up his attempt to force a new prayer book upon them. Charles was advised and backed by William Laud, his Archbishop of Canterbury. Laud disapproved of traditional Scottish practices in the Presbyterian kirk where there was no set form of service or prayer book.

HENRIETTA MARIA
In 1625, Charles I married Henrietta Maria, daughter of Henry IV of France and Marie de Medici. The first years of the marriage were difficult as Charles was still deeply under the influence of the Duke of Buckingham. But after the Duke's death, Charles came to love and rely on his wife.

Civil War

Supporters of the king were known as Royalists. This officer wears a buff coat – a thick leather jacket – and a metal breastplate. In the early battles of the civil war, Royalists also wore red sashes around their waists to distinguish themselves from Roundheads, who wore orange sashes.

Parliament met in November 1640. This was the beginning of the 'Long Parliament', so called because it was not officially dismissed for 20 years. Once again, MPs condemned the king for his actions. They also removed William Laud and another of the king's most powerful advisers, the Earl of Strafford, from office. Charles was powerless to prevent the execution of Strafford in 1641. Laud was executed in 1645.

This map shows the main battles of the English Civil Wars. The pink shading shows the areas held by the Royalists after the Battle of Marston Moor (1644).

The king was forced to agree to other parliamentary reforms, too. These included a requirement that parliament should meet every three years, and that it should be dismissed only by its own, and not the king's, consent. MPs also tried to force Charles to hand over command of the army. Charles refused and, on 4 January 1642, he went with 400 men to the House of Commons to arrest five MPs for treason. But the MPs were warned and they escaped. Both sides began to prepare for war. The king's followers, known as Royalists, were initially based in York. Parliamentarians controlled London and the southeast.

The king formally declared war by raising his standard at Nottingham on 22 August 1642.

The first objective for King Charles was to regain control of the capital, London. The Royalist and Parliamentarian armies met at Edgehill in Warwickshire in October 1642, but the fighting ended inconclusively. Then the Royalists marched towards London, but they got only as far as Turnham Green before being forced to turn back. This was the closest the Royalist army came to capturing London.

Parliamentarian soldiers were nicknamed 'Roundheads' partly because of the short haircuts worn by their supporters, but the name was also a term of political abuse. The peak of their helmet was hinged to allow it to be taken on and off.

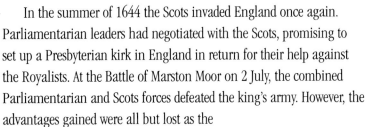

In the summer of 1644 the Scots invaded England once again. Parliamentarian leaders had negotiated with the Scots, promising to set up a Presbyterian kirk in England in return for their help against the Royalists. At the Battle of Marston Moor on 2 July, the combined Parliamentarian and Scots forces defeated the king's army. However, the advantages gained were all but lost as the Parliamentarians quarrelled among themselves about how to continue the campaign against the king. In parliament, MPs listened to the arguments of Oliver Cromwell, the Puritan MP for Cambridge. He said that the only way to end the war was to improve the military training and resources of the Roundhead armies. And so the Roundheads set up the 'New Model Army'.

The highly trained and well-disciplined New Model Army defeated the Royalist forces at Naseby on 14 June, 1645. This was the first of a series of Roundhead victories that led to the surrender of the Royalist headquarters in Oxford in 1646. Charles escaped, but was quickly handed over to parliament. However, the victorious Roundheads were still deeply divided. Parliament was suspicious and fearful of the New Model Army – particularly after the army kidnapped the king and held him under guard at Hampton Court.

During 1648, there were Royalist uprisings across the country, but they were not co-ordinated and were easily put down by the army. The king's final hope of a military solution was dashed when the Scots were defeated by the New Model Army at the Battle of Preston in August.

The king was brought to trial in January 1649. He stood accused of making war on his own people. The trial lasted for five days, and Charles was sentenced to death as a tyrant, traitor, murderer and public enemy.

Oliver Cromwell was born on 25 April 1599 in Huntingdon. He was first elected as an MP in 1628. He was a Puritan, but he preached 'liberty of conscience', believing that people should be allowed to follow their own faiths and beliefs.

Charles I left London on 10 January, 1642. He headed for Hull where there were large stores of military supplies, but he was unsuccessful in his attempt to take the city. At the same time, Queen Henrietta Maria went to the Netherlands to raise money for the Royalist cause by pawning the crown jewels.

Ireland and Scotland

Despite the defeat of Royalist forces in England, supporters of the monarchy were still active in both Ireland and Scotland. It was vital for the new Commonwealth in England that these rebels should be subdued. In August 1649, Oliver Cromwell and the New Model Army landed in Ireland.

The Royalists in Ireland were supported by the Irish Catholics. Cromwell fought a very harsh campaign in Ireland – he held the rebels responsible for the horrors of earlier massacres. The English army attacked and killed the inhabitants of Drogheda, a garrison town north of Dublin, when they failed to surrender. Cromwell reported to parliament that such actions were justified because they would '... tend to prevent the effusion [shedding] of blood for the future...' A similar massacre took place at Wexford in the south of Ireland.

Next, Cromwell turned his attention to Scotland. After the execution of Charles I, his son was proclaimed Charles II of Scotland. In 1650, Charles II landed in Scotland and gathered together an army of loyal followers. Cromwell marched northwards with the New Model Army and inflicted a crushing defeat on the Scots at Dunbar in September. Nevertheless, the fighting dragged on for another year. Charles II fled south in a last desperate attempt to raise more support. His army was finally defeated at Worcester in September 1651.

A Pikeman. *Pikes were up to 5.5 metres long. Pikemen were carefully trained to handle their weapons when marching and attacking.*

1649 Cromwell lands in Ireland (August) and prepares to attack combined Royalist and Catholic opposition. Massacres at Drogheda and Wexford.

1650 Charles II makes an agreement with Scots to accept Presbyterianism in return for their support to restore him to English crown. Cromwell leads an army to Scotland (July). Cromwell defeats Scottish army at Dunbar (September).

1651 Scottish armies defeated at Stirling. Charles II enters England but is defeated at Worcester (3 September).

Oliver Cromwell *leads the New Model Army outside Edinburgh. In 1650, Cromwell was appointed captain-general of the army in place of Sir Thomas Fairfax who refused to invade Scotland. Even Cromwell was unwilling to fight the Scots, who were fellow Puritans. But when forced to fight he defeated the Scots at Dunbar, east of Edinburgh.*

Cromwell's route in 1649 following Catholic rebellion of 1641

✕ Stormed by Cromwell and garrisons and priests massacred

ULSTER

• Castlebar

CONNAUGHT

Drogheda ✕

• Tuan

• Dublin

LEINSTER

Kilkenny

• Limerick ✕

MUNSTER ✕ Ross ✕

Clonmel ✕ Carrick ✕ Wexford

• Killarney

• Cork

This map shows the main areas of conflict between Irish Catholics and the Cromwellian army, leading to the Battle of Drogheda in 1649.

DROGHEDA

On 11 September 1649, Cromwell's army attacked the garrison town of Drogheda. When the inhabitants rejected the terms of surrender offered to them the Parliamentarian troops killed all the soldiers in the garrison and many of the townspeople too. The massacre at Drogheda and Cromwell's brutality soon became infamous in Ireland.

Charles barely escaped with his life and he was hunted by the Parliamentarians for 40 days before he escaped to France and safety.

The Scots were not treated as harshly as the Irish by Cromwell. Nevertheless, both Scotland and Ireland were now unwillingly part of a united Britain under Cromwell's leadership.

The Commonwealth

1652 Act of Settlement – six Irish counties are cleared of Catholic landholders and settled by English Protestants.
1653 Cromwell forcibly dismisses the Rump Parliament (20 April). 'Nominated Parliament' hands back power to Cromwell (12 December). Cromwell becomes Lord Protector.
1654 End of war with the Netherlands. First Parliament of the Protectorate (3 September).
1655 Royalist uprising in the West Country led by Colonel John Penruddock is put down by New Model Army. Military leaders, called major-generals, are appointed to each region to keep the peace.
1656 Second Parliament of the Protectorate.
1658 Death of Oliver Cromwell.

A Puritan family in typical sombre dress. The Puritan movement began in the late 1500s and gathered strength through the 1600s. Puritans wished to purify the Church of England from Catholic ways.

On 20 April, 1653, Cromwell called his musketeers into the chamber of the House of Commons. He declared to the astonished MPs that they were 'corrupt and unjust men' before removing the Speaker. The Rump Parliament was dismissed.

Cromwell's anger with the MPs of the Rump Parliament was caused by their unwillingness to act on the many reforms he and the army considered necessary. Cromwell ordered a new parliament to be chosen from a list drawn up by church representatives but this 'Nominated Parliament' did little better than its predecessor. In December, its members handed back power to Cromwell and a new plan was drawn up, in which Cromwell became 'Lord Protector' of England, Scotland and Ireland.

Many people remained suspicious of Cromwell and fearful of the power of the army. After an unsuccessful Royalist uprising in the West Country, Cromwell divided the country into 11 districts and appointed military leaders to run them. Some were strict Puritans who were unpopular because they closed down alehouses and stopped popular pastimes and sports. Nevertheless, this was a time of relative religious tolerance and prosperity after the strife of the Civil War. In 1658, on his deathbed, Cromwell named his son Richard as his rightful successor.

After the horrors of the Civil Wars, the Commonwealth was a time of peace for most ordinary people. Trade flourished in coastal towns such as this. However, Puritan rule was strict – theatres were closed, and Christmas was a fast-day.

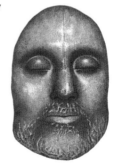

The death mask of Oliver Cromwell who died on 3 September, 1658. He was buried in Westminster Abbey. In 1661, after King Charles II was restored to the throne, Cromwell's remains were dug up and hung at Tyburn where criminals were executed. His head was stuck on a pole on top of Westminster Hall.

LORD PROTECTOR

The first parliament of the Protectorate was held in 1654. Cromwell had several aims. He wanted to set up a Puritan Church, but wished to allow freedom of worship. He was very interested in education and wanted to reform the legal system. He believed that capital punishment (execution) should be used only for major crimes such as murder, treason and rebellion.

Cromwell dismisses the Rump Parliament. 'You are no parliament; I will put an end to your sitting...' he told the MPs. The Rump was unwilling to pass reforms required by Cromwell and the army.

Charles II

1630 Birth of Charles II, eldest son of Charles I and Henrietta Maria.

1649 Execution of Charles I. Charles II is proclaimed king of Scotland.

1651 Defeat of Royalist troops at Worcester. Charles escapes to France.

1659 Declaration of Breda sets out terms of restoration of king.

1660 End of Long Parliament. Restoration of King Charles II (May). By now coffee houses are becoming fashionable meeting places in cities.

1662 Charles marries Catherine of Braganza, daughter of the king of Portugal.

1665 Great Plague causes thousands of deaths. War with the Netherlands (until 1667).

1666 Great Fire of London (3–6 September).

1678 So called 'Popish plot' to murder the king results in persecution of Catholics.

1684 London experiences a freezing winter; a 'Frost Fair' is held on the iced-over River Thames.

1685 Death of Charles II (6 February).

On 25 May, 1660, King Charles II landed at Dover. After 15 years in exile the king was returning to his kingdom.

It had soon become apparent that Richard Cromwell was not capable of running the country. 'Tumbledown Dick' was quickly removed from office, and parliament invited Charles to return and take up his crown. People across the country rejoiced that the strict Puritan regime of the Commonwealth was at an end.

During the Commonwealth, the Puritans had banned many festivals and pastimes that they considered frivolous. For example, in 1652 Christmas was abolished and in 1654 cock-fighting, a popular sport in town and country, was banned. In the towns, theatres were closed down and alehouses shut.

After the restoration of Charles II, it is little wonder that people greeted the return of merriment with relief. Sports such as football and cricket were very popular. In London there were many colourful pageants on the River Thames, such as the Lord Mayor's Show, and many celebrations were held. Once again, Christmas, May Day and harvest time became important festivals and were enjoyed by both rich and poor. In the relaxed atmosphere of Charles's court, French fashions and music became all the rage.

The policies of the Restoration were established between 1660 and 1662. The Church of England became more powerful. Charles himself wished for religious tolerance, particularly towards Roman Catholics – he himself was a Protestant but the rest of his family were Catholics, including his wife.

Louis XIV, shown here, and the court of France were great influences on Charles II, so much so that he tried to emulate their splendour in his own court.

This horn book was used to teach children the letters of the alphabet. Sons of the nobility and the gentry were usually sent to public or grammar schools. Girls were mostly educated at home.

Coffee was introduced from Arabia into Europe in the 16th and 17th centuries. Together with tea and chocolate, coffee changed the drinking habits of many British people, replacing beer as the main beverage. Coffee drinking became a craze for the well to do, and after the 1650s coffee houses opened all over London and in many other cities and towns.

But there was still deep suspicion of Roman Catholic 'popery' in parliament and across the country. In 1662 parliament passed an act banning any religious services except those of the Church of England.

As the years passed, the king and his wife failed to produce any children. This meant that the legitimate heir to the throne was Charles's brother, James. He was a devout Catholic and, although his daughters from his first marriage were brought up as Protestants, he had since remarried a Catholic princess. In 1678, two conspirators named Israel Tonge and Titus Oates came forward with accusations about a Catholic plot to murder Charles and put James on the throne. The accusations were untrue, but hysteria about 'popish' plots overran the country and many Catholics were persecuted and killed. Some MPs tried to force the king to agree to an 'Exclusion Act' which would prevent James succeeding him. But Charles refused and when he died in 1685, James II was proclaimed as his successor. As he lay dying, Charles allegedly accepted the Catholic faith.

The Restoration ended a period of great turmoil in Britain: a raging civil war, a king beheaded and a time of strict Puritan rule. The war had had a devastating effect on many areas of the country and on many ordinary people. The Restoration was a peaceful time in which the country and people prospered once more.

Between 1660 and 1669, Samuel Pepys kept a detailed diary of his life. Among other things, he recorded the effects of the Great Plague and the Great Fire in London. He wrote of the plague: 'But Lord, what a sad time it is, to see no boats upon the River – and grass grow all up and down Whitehall-court – and nobody but poor wretches in the streets.'

Charles II arrives in London to an enthusiastic welcome. The diarist Samuel Pepys was one of those who travelled across the Channel to bring the king back. The crowds who greeted Charles were enthusiastic in their welcome. Pepys wrote: 'The shouting and joy expressed by all is past imagination.'

1633 Birth of James, second son of Charles I and Henrietta Maria.

1634 Created Duke of York.

1642–6 Lives in Oxford during Civil War.

1648 Escapes to Netherlands.

1660 Restoration of brother Charles I. Marries Anne, daughter of Earl of Clarendon. They have two daughters, Mary and Anne.

1668–9 James is admitted to Roman Catholic Church.

1673 Marries Catholic princess Mary of Modena.

1677 Eldest daughter, Mary, marries William of Orange.

1685 Succeeds his brother as James II (6 February).

1688 'Glorious Revolution'. James II is allowed to escape.

1689 Parliament declares abdication of James II (12 February).

1690 James lands in Ireland. James defeated at Battle of Boyne.

1701 Death of James II.

The young William III of Orange. *William was born in The Hague, the Netherlands, on 14 November, 1650, eight days after his father's death. He was trained to be a ruler from his earliest years.*

The Glorious Revolution

When James II came to the throne in 1685, memories of the horrors of civil war were still present in people's minds. No one wanted more conflict. But the new king was a Roman Catholic and many feared the outcome if he tried to impose his religion on his subjects. In the end, his reign was short, brought to an abrupt conclusion by the events of the 'Glorious Revolution'.

Shortly after he became king, James was faced with a rebellion by the Duke of Monmouth, the eldest of the illegitimate children of Charles II. However, the rebellion was short-lived and the Duke and his followers were punished with great ferocity.

The main hope for Protestant leaders lay in the fact that James's heir was his eldest daughter, Mary, borne by his first wife. She was a Protestant and was married to William III of Orange, ruler of the Dutch Protestants. However, even this hope faded when it was announced that James's second wife was pregnant. In June 1688, she gave birth to a son – the new heir to the throne who would undoubtedly be brought up in the Catholic faith.

William began to make preparations for an attack by sea using the Dutch fleet. James could not believe that his own daughter and son-in-law would attack him and invade Britain.

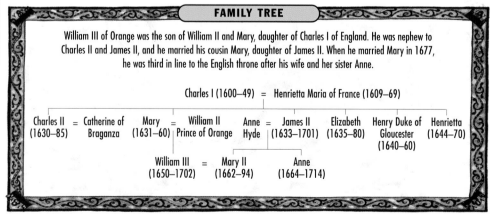

FAMILY TREE

William III of Orange was the son of William II and Mary, daughter of Charles I of England. He was nephew to Charles II and James II, and he married his cousin Mary, daughter of James II. When he married Mary in 1677, he was third in line to the English throne after his wife and her sister Anne.

Charles I (1600–49) = Henrietta Maria of France (1609–69)

Charles II (1630–85) = Catherine of Braganza

Mary (1631–60) = William II Prince of Orange

Anne Hyde = James II (1633–1701)

Elizabeth (1635–80)

Henry Duke of Gloucester (1640–60)

Henrietta (1644–70)

William III (1650–1702) = Mary II (1662–94)

Anne (1664–1714)

Instead, he thought that the Dutch preparations were for war against the French king, Louis XIV. James was unprepared when William's fleet landed in Torbay, Devon, on 5 November, 1688.

At the news of the Dutch invasion, James panicked. He refused to send his army to confront the invaders because he thought they were too unreliable. Indeed, many Protestant officers deserted and went to join the Dutch force. When he heard that his second daughter, Anne, had also deserted him for the Protestant cause, James made plans to flee. After one unsuccessful attempt, he escaped to France to join his wife and baby.

William marched to London without a shot being fired. This was the 'Glorious Revolution' – a change of monarch without bloodshed.

When James II ordered freedom of worship for Catholics and other dissenters, the Archbishop of Canterbury and six other bishops sent a petition to the king asking him to withdraw the order. James's reaction was to send them to the Tower of London. The bishops were tried and found not guilty.

James II was England's last Catholic monarch. Attempts by his male heirs to restore Catholic rule failed from lack of popular support.

The title of this picture is 'Popery's downfall and the Protestant's uprising'. It celebrates the victory of the Protestant King William over James II.

Towns and Trade

On 2 September, 1666, the Great Fire of London began in a London baker's shop and quickly raged out of control. A large part of the city was destroyed and about 100,000 people were left homeless.

King Charles II was determined that fire should not so easily sweep through the city again. He ordered that all new buildings must be made from brick and stone.

No other town in 17th-century Britain could equal London in size and importance. Not only was it the seat of government but it was also a major port and commercial centre. One of the next largest towns in terms of population was Norwich (20,000 in the 1660s). In the West Country, Bristol was an expanding port.

During the second half of the 17th century, Britain became a powerful trading nation. Trade routes reached far beyond Europe to North America, the Caribbean and Asia, and goods such as tobacco and sugar flooded into Britain. The boom in trade made merchants rich. But there was a human cost. English ships sailed to West Africa where they exchanged goods for African captives. These captives were then transported across the Atlantic Ocean in appalling conditions and sold as slaves in the colonies. The ships then sailed back to England with cargoes of sugar and tobacco. This terrible trade became known as the 'Triangular Trade'.

Merchants of the Dutch East India Company trade with locals on the Cape of Good Hope. The Dutch East India Company was set up in 1602 to protect Dutch trade in the Indian Ocean. The English East India Company was created by Royal Charter in 1600. Both companies imported spices and textiles such as silks, as well as calico, chintz and muslin that were all made from cotton.

A busy scene in a coffee house. Much business was done in the coffee houses that opened in the second half of the 17th century. Samuel Pepys wrote in his diary in 1660: 'To the coffee-house where was a great confluence of gentlemen; ... admirable discourse until 9 at night...' There were over 2,000 coffee houses in London by 1700.

New Discoveries

The 17th century saw great advances in all branches of science in England. Men such as William Harvey, Robert Hooke and Isaac Newton made discoveries that have laid the foundations for modern science.

These advances were part of an intellectual movement across Europe which saw new ideas and discoveries being exchanged across frontiers. For example, William Harvey (1578–1657) studied at the university medical school at Padua in Italy. With an expert grounding in anatomy, Harvey dissected every kind of living thing. From his observations he demonstrated how the blood circulates around the body, pumped by the heart. His findings made him famous throughout Europe.

Isaac Newton (1642–1727) was also influenced by European thinkers, such as the Italian scientist Galileo Galilei (1564–1642), and drew on the work of other English scientists, such as the chemist Robert Boyle (1627–91) who built the first air pump. Newton applied his brilliant mind to many different problems. His discoveries about light, his laws of force, motion and gravity, and his formulation of calculus in mathematics provide the basis for our modern-day understanding of the world. Newton's new ideas were frequently challenged – one of his main rivals being Robert Hooke (1635–1703). Hooke was also interested in optics and gravity, and his ideas brought him into frequent conflict with Newton. However, Newton's genius was recognized in his own lifetime, and he was the first scientist to be knighted for his work.

In 1703, Newton was made president of the Royal Society. This society was set up in 1660 by a group of English scientists including Robert Boyle and Christopher Wren to discuss scientific subjects. In 1662, Charles II granted a royal charter to the society, calling it the 'Royal Society of London for the Promotion of Natural Knowledge'.

The first Eddystone lighthouse was designed by Henry Winstanley. It was one of the first lighthouses to be exposed to the open sea. Constructed from timber, it was anchored by 12 iron cables and stood 136 metres tall. The lighthouse stood from 1699 to 1703 when it was swept away by a ferocious storm. Its designer, Winstanley, was in the lighthouse at the time and drowned in the storm.

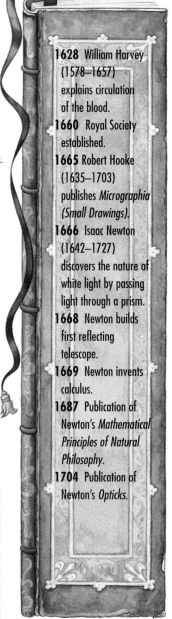

1628 William Harvey (1578–1657) explains circulation of the blood.
1660 Royal Society established.
1665 Robert Hooke (1635–1703) publishes *Micrographia (Small Drawings)*.
1666 Isaac Newton (1642–1727) discovers the nature of white light by passing light through a prism.
1668 Newton builds first reflecting telescope.
1669 Newton invents calculus.
1687 Publication of Newton's *Mathematical Principles of Natural Philosophy*.
1704 Publication of Newton's *Opticks*.

ARCHITECTURE

In the 1660s, Christopher Wren visited Paris to see its architectural glories. On his return, he began designing a dome for the old St Paul's Cathedral. After the Great Fire of London, Wren's plans for a new, grand cathedral were accepted in 1675 and the building was completed in 1711.

Robert Hooke used a microscope to study the structures of natural objects such as snowflakes. The first powerful lens microscope was built by the Dutch scientist Antonie van Leeuwenhoek in 1674.

William and Mary

Although Mary had the first claim to the English throne, William refused to accept an inferior role to his wife – he said that he would not be tied to the 'apron strings'. So parliament decided to make William and Mary joint king and queen of England and they received the Scottish crown in May 1689.

This china plate *commemorates the accession of William and Mary to the throne as joint rulers.*

At the coronation of William and Mary, a Declaration of Rights was presented. This stated that the monarch could not be a Catholic, or be married to a Catholic. It also limited the powers of the monarchy. In future, no king or queen could suspend a law without the consent of parliament. The Bill of Rights passed through parliament in October 1689.

William had taken the English throne without a fight, but holding on to it was more of a problem. With the backing of the French king, Louis XIV, James invaded Ireland and defeated Protestant forces there. William himself led an army to Ireland and crushed James's forces at the Battle of the Boyne (1690).

1688 'Glorious Revolution'.

1689 William and Mary accept Declaration of Rights and become joint monarchs (February). James II lands in Ireland with French troops. William and Mary accept Scottish crown (May).

1690 William defeats French troops at Battle of the Boyne (1 July). James flees to France.

1691 Battle of Aughrim (July). Treaty of Limerick designed to protect Irish Catholics but is soon proved worthless.

1692 1 January: date by which Highland chiefs to swear allegiance to William and Mary. Massacre in Glencoe, Scotland (13 February).

1694 Death of Queen Mary.

1697 Treaty of Ryswick: William is recognized by French king as rightful ruler of Britain.

1701 Act of Settlement ensures a protestant succession.

1702 Death of William. He is succeeded to the throne by Mary's sister, Anne.

The Battle of the Boyne *was fought on 1 July, 1690. The two sides were drawn up on either side of the river Boyne. William's cavalry managed to cross the river and began to surround James's troops. James fled and his troops withdrew. The battle is still celebrated today in Northern Ireland as a landmark Protestant victory.*

In Scotland, William also faced dissent and rebellion. Fighting in the early 1690s brought no definite conclusion.

William was persuaded to offer peace terms to the Highland clans if they would swear allegiance to him. When the leader of the MacDonalds of Glencoe missed the deadline for the oath of allegiance, William decided to make an example of him. He ordered the massacre of the MacDonald clan in Glencoe – an act of violence which lives on to this day in Scottish memory.

Mary had no children, so her sister Anne succeeded to the throne on William's death in 1702.

Irish Catholics flee from their homeland. *After Protestant victories at the Battle of the Boyne and Aughrim (1690), the English parliament confiscated the estates of many Catholic landowners. This was despite the Treaty of Limerick which aimed to protect Irish Catholics, but which proved worthless.*

TAX ON WINDOWS

During the reign of William and Mary, a new tax was introduced on windows. Houses were allowed only six untaxed windows. Many people bricked up windows in their houses in order to avoid paying this unusual tax.

The Eighteenth Century

p114 Ballet was performed in public for the first time.

p116 Tower mills were used to grind wheat and corn into flour to make bread.

p118 Slaves were taken from Africa to the Caribbean usually under very harsh conditions.

p123 British soldiers wore red coats into battle.

p125 Steam became the main source of power during the 18th century, going on later to drive locomotives.

The 18th century opened with William of Orange on the British throne (Mary died in 1694) and the Act of Settlement (1701), which ensured a Protestant succession. Despite plots and rebellions, William was succeeded peacefully by his sister-in-law Queen Anne and, on her death in 1714, the crown passed to the first of the Hanoverians, George I.

Life for most ordinary people in 18th-century Britain was relatively prosperous and peaceful. Nevertheless, wars and rebellions in distant places still made an impact. The Seven Years War (1756–63) was fought not only in mainland Europe but also in India, North America, the Caribbean and Africa as Britain battled to keep and increase its overseas colonies. In 1776, colonists in the 13 American states declared their independence from Britain. After another seven years of bitter fighting, Britain was forced to recognize the independence of the United States of America. In 1789, and partly inspired by the Americans' revolutionary example, the people of France overthrew their own monarchy at the start of the French Revolution.

In the wake of this revolution, the century ended with Britain once again at war with France.

Meanwhile, two different sorts of revolution were happening in Britain. Both were, in fact, gradual changes that gathered pace throughout the century. The first, often known as the Agricultural Revolution, involved different ways of organizing and owning land, and the application of scientific principles to growing crops and breeding animals. The second, known as the Industrial Revolution, started in the 1760s although pioneers such as Abraham Darby, Thomas Newcomen and John Kay were at work earlier in the century. Industrialization involved new methods of powering machinery and of manufacturing goods.

p128 Captain Cook commanded three voyages of discovery around the globe.

p120 The Battle of Culloden was an overwhelming victory for the English army over the Scots, under the command of Charles Edward, or 'Bonnie Prince Charlie'.

The Hanoverians

1660 Birth of George Ludwig, son of Elector of Hanover and Sophia (granddaughter of James I of England).

1682 George Ludwig marries Sophia Dorothea of Celle. Birth of son George Augustus (1683).

1698 George succeeds father as Elector of Hanover.

1701 English parliament passes Act of Settlement ensuring Protestant succession to throne.

1714 Death of Queen Anne (1 August). The Elector of Hanover is proclaimed George I.

1727 Death of George I. He is succeeded by George II.

1760 Death of George II. George III becomes king.

1776 Declaration of American Independence.

1788 Illness of king provokes 'Regency Crisis'.

1810 King ill once again, Prince of Wales is made Prince Regent.

1820 Death of George III. He is succeeded by George IV.

In 1714, two British ministers sent word to the exiled son of James II, James Edward (the 'Old Pretender'). If he would renounce his Roman Catholic faith and become an Anglican, they would support his claim as heir to the British throne. But James Edward refused. And so, when Queen Anne died on 1 August, 1714, the crown passed to a German prince, George, Elector of Hanover.

George I excluded from office the ministers who had tried to place James Edward on the throne instead of him. These ministers belonged to the political party known as the Tories. In their place he promoted ministers of the opposing party – the Whigs. One of these ministers, Robert Walpole, became an extremely powerful figure in government. He was the first prime minister of the British parliament.

George I was succeeded by his son. George II took a close interest in matters at home and abroad. He was also the last British monarch to appear in person on the battlefield.

George I was the first of the Hanoverians to rule in Great Britain. He could not speak English, so he talked with his ministers in French. He was backed by the Whig political party.

HANOVERIAN FASHIONS

Court fashions in Hanoverian England became increasingly elaborate. Women wore frilled skirts that were stretched out from the waist and around the hips with hoops. Queen Mary started a fashion for wearing patterned chintzes and calicoes. As the century progressed curled and powdered headdresses became taller and more elaborate. Delicate silk and satin shoes were worn indoors. Outdoors in muddy weather, women still wore clogs.

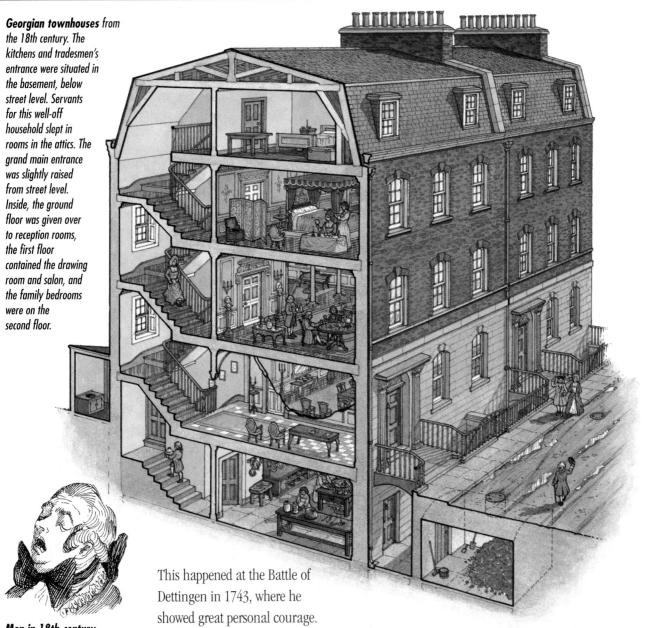

Georgian townhouses from the 18th century. The kitchens and tradesmen's entrance were situated in the basement, below street level. Servants for this well-off household slept in rooms in the attics. The grand main entrance was slightly raised from street level. Inside, the ground floor was given over to reception rooms, the first floor contained the drawing room and salon, and the family bedrooms were on the second floor.

Men in 18th-century Britain wore powdered, curled and perfumed wigs tied at the back with a bow.

This happened at the Battle of Dettingen in 1743, where he showed great personal courage.

George II's son, Frederick Louis, died, so his heir was his grandson, also called George. The reign of George III was a turbulent one. War in the American colonies started with the American Declaration of Independence in 1776. Revolution was in the air in Europe too, boiling over in France in 1789. George III battled with illness and insanity throughout his life. In 1811, his son became Prince Regent, standing in for his father until George III's death in 1820.

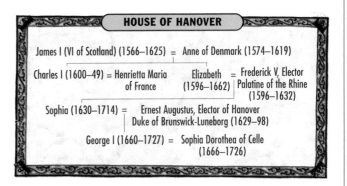

HOUSE OF HANOVER

James I (VI of Scotland) (1566–1625) = Anne of Denmark (1574–1619)

Charles I (1600–49) = Henrietta Maria of France
Elizabeth (1596–1662) = Frederick V, Elector Palatine of the Rhine (1596–1632)

Sophia (1630–1714) = Ernest Augustus, Elector of Hanover Duke of Brunswick-Luneborg (1629–98)

George I (1660–1727) = Sophia Dorothea of Celle (1666–1726)

The Enlightenment

Just as the scientific advances of the 17th century were part of a Europe-wide movement, so the Enlightenment grew out of ideas that were discussed across the Continent. The ideas of the Enlightenment led people to question the traditional teachings of the Church and to celebrate the power of human reason.

1632 Birth of John Locke.

1668 Locke becomes a member of the Royal Society.

1675–9 Locke lives in France.

1689 Publication of *Essay Concerning Human Understanding* by Locke.

1690 Publication of *Two Treatises of Government* by Locke.

1693 Publication of *Some Thoughts Concerning Education* by Locke.

1694 Birth of Voltaire.

1704 Death of John Locke.

1726–8 Voltaire exiled in England.

1728 Publication of Ephraim Chambers' *Cyclopaedia*.

1734 Publication of Voltaire's *Lettres Philosophiques*.

1737 Birth of Thomas Paine.

1751–72 Publication of the French *Encyclopédie* edited by Denis Diderot.

1776 Declaration of American Independence.

1789 Publication of *An Introduction to the Principles of Morals and Legislation* by Jeremy Bentham. Revolution in France.

1791 Publication of the *Rights of Man* by Thomas Paine defending the French Revolution.

Enlightenment thinkers believed that knowledge about the universe and the world around them could be gained only by experience. This idea grew partly out of the work of the 17th-century scientists, particularly Sir Isaac Newton. Newton's experiments and his rigorous application of logic led to theories, such as his law of gravity, that helped people understand the universe.

A major figure of the Enlightenment, John Locke, wrote many books and essays setting out his beliefs about the power of reason.

In the 18th century ballet was performed in public for the first time. The clothes that dancers wore became less restrictive and much easier to dance in.

An evening of music, readings and conversation in a 17th-century middle-class house. The 'middle sort' ranged from farmers to professionals such as clergymen and lawyers. They were better educated and had more money to spend than ever before, leading to a growth in publications such as magazines and novels.

In his *Essay Concerning Human Understanding* Locke said that at birth the human mind was empty (a 'clean slate') and that it was experience that created every individual character.

As a result, Locke insisted on the importance of a good and broad education for every child.

He also wrote about government in the influential *Two Treatises of Government*. He insisted that the rulers of any country were entrusted with the 'public good', and if they failed to fulfil that trust then the people could overthrow them. Together with the work of other writers such as Jeremy Bentham and the French author Voltaire these ideas eventually led to revolution in America and France, and reform in Britain.

Britain in the 18th century was regarded with great admiration by many European thinkers and writers. They wrote about the civilized character of English society and the way in which there was tolerance and moderation in all things. Voltaire wrote: 'The English nation is the only one on earth which has succeeded in controlling the power of kings... and in which the people share in the government without confusion.' Although this was rather an optimistic view, Britain did come closer to the ideals of the Enlightenment than other European countries at that time.

The **Encyclopédie** *was published in parts between 1751 and 1772 in France. It was inspired by the success of an English publication called* Cyclopaedia *published in 1728. The* Encyclopédie *was edited by the philosopher Denis Diderot, and it embraced the tolerance and open-mindedness of Enlightenment ideas.*

The Agricultural Revolution

The Agricultural Revolution was not a sudden, revolutionary change as its name might suggest. It was a slow change that took place throughout the 18th century and continued into the 19th century.

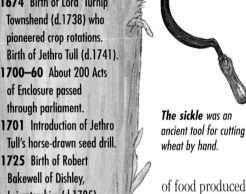

The sickle was an ancient tool for cutting wheat by hand.

1674 Birth of Lord 'Turnip' Townshend (d.1738) who pioneered crop rotations. Birth of Jethro Tull (d.1741).

1700–60 About 200 Acts of Enclosure passed through parliament.

1701 Introduction of Jethro Tull's horse-drawn seed drill.

1725 Birth of Robert Bakewell of Dishley, Leicestershire (d.1795).

1731 Publication of *The New Horse Houghing Husbandry* by Jethro Tull.

1741 Birth of Arthur Young (d.1820), writer and supporter of agricultural improvements.

1753 Birth of George Culley of Northumberland (d.1813) who worked on selective breeding of sheep.

1754 Birth of Thomas Coke of Holkham Hall, Norfolk (d. 1842).

1760–80 Over 1,000 Acts of Enclosure passed through parliament.

In the 18th century, agriculture had to provide enough food to feed the entire population of Britain. Grains such as wheat, barley, oats and rye provided the staple diet together with foods such as potatoes, peas, beans and cheese. Most ordinary families ate very little meat. The only foods that were usually imported at this time were exotic and expensive imports such as spices, chocolate, sugar, coffee and tea. The amount of food produced in Britain rose steadily throughout the 18th century. This happened because of two main changes: an increase in land enclosures and improvements in agricultural techniques.

From medieval times, much of the land across Britain was common land. Often, this was divided into strips, each cultivated by one farmer. Meanwhile, animals were kept on common land. But in some areas land was enclosed by hedges or ditches to make fields. The process of enclosing land had been going on for centuries, but its pace increased in the 18th and early 19th centuries. Sometimes, wealthy landowners bought up land cultivated by poorer farmers.

This type of windmill was known as a tower mill. The vane (on the left) turned the top part of the mill, called the head, so that the sails were always facing into the wind. The sails turned to provide power for grinding wheat and other grains.

New methods of crop rotation were developed in the 18th century. Previously, land was left to lie fallow (unplanted) for one year out of three in order to regain its fertility. But the introduction of fodder crops meant that the land could be planted continuously. The 'Norfolk rotation' was usually wheat, turnips, barley and clover. The turnips provided food for livestock; the clover fertilized the soil.

A farmer takes wheat to the mill to be ground into flour. Wheat was the most important of the grain crops because it was used to make bread – the staple food for most families in 18th-century Britain.

In other cases, the land was enclosed by an Act of Parliament. The result was more large farms on which the land was leased (rented) to tenant farmers. It was mainly on these larger farms that experiments with new methods of agriculture were carried out.

Jethro Tull was one of the first of the pioneers who applied his mind to the improvement of agricultural techniques. He invented a horse-drawn seed drill which sowed the seeds in rows. Another improvement, introduced from the Netherlands, was the cultivation of 'fodder' crops such as clover or turnips. Fodder crops improved the fertility of the soil and provided food for livestock. The manure from livestock was also used to fertilize the soil.

It was not only arable farming (growing crops) that was subject to improvement. Men such as Robert Bakewell (1725–95) experimented with breeding animals to give the best meat, milk and wool (called selective breeding). In Norfolk, another pioneering landowner Thomas Coke (1754–1842) lived at Holkham Hall. Coke bred sheep, pigs and cattle and held huge sheep-shearing meetings at Holkham; these meetings were the forerunners of today's agricultural show.

The horse-drawn seed drill was introduced in 1701. Traditionally, seed was scattered by hand which meant that quite a lot of seed went to waste. However, the seed drill planted seeds in neat rows, called furrows.

Farmers employed labourers such as cowhands, ploughmen, milkmaids and shepherds to work on their farms. Labourers often lived in the farm house with the farmer and his family. Many were employed on one farm for 12 months at a time.

A Trading Nation

Household goods were made by machine for the first time during the 18th century.

1717 Birth of John Metcalfe (d.1810) who improved road building and constructed over 300 kilometres of road, mainly in the Pennines.

1736 Smugglers Act imposed harsh penalties on smugglers.

1751–60 Over 180 Turnpike Acts passed through Parliament.

1756 Birth of John McAdam (d.1836) who invented mixture of tar and small stones known as 'tarmac' used to surface roads.

1757 Birth of Thomas Telford (d.1834), the engineer who oversaw building of London to Holyhead road and the Menai Bridge.

1761–72 Over 200 Turnpike Acts passed through parliament.

1773 Stock Exchange founded.

1807 Slave trade abolished in Britain.

1833 Slavery abolished in British Empire.

Daniel Defoe, writing in the 1720s, described Britain as the 'most flourishing and opulent country in the world'. And so it must have seemed as communications within Britain improved, and trade into and out of Britain continued to expand throughout the 18th century.

Trade within Britain at the opening of the 18th century still depended largely on markets and fairs. In London, there were large specialized markets at Billingsgate (fish), Smithfield (meat) and Covent Garden (vegetables). Supplies for these markets came from all over the country. There were smaller markets in regional centres where people came to buy and sell goods. Transporting goods from one place to another was both difficult and expensive. Each parish was responsible for looking after the roads in its area. In the early 18th century, local businessmen began to set up turnpike trusts to improve stretches of road and links to the main cities and travelling around the country became easier. However, most heavy goods were sent by river and on the canals that were constructed during the late 18th and early 19th centuries.

By the beginning of the 18th century the 'triangular trade', which involved transporting slaves from Africa to the Caribbean and taking goods back to Britain, was thriving.

The wealth that the 'triangular trade' brought to ports such as Liverpool and Bristol had a terrible human cost. As part of the trade, native Africans were taken from their homeland to work on plantations in the West Indies. Their treatment at the hands of the European traders was often both cruel and inhumane.

Ships were frequently wrecked along the rocky shores of southwest Britain and often provided welcome supplies of luxury goods such as brandy or tea for local communities. Smuggling was also common in coastal areas. Goods such as tea, tobacco, brandy and lace were all subject to customs duties (taxes), so smuggling these items into the country was a widespread and lucrative business.

As demand for imports such as tobacco and sugar rose, ports along the west coast of Britain flourished. Bristol, Liverpool and Glasgow all expanded rapidly. In 1700 Liverpool had a population of about 5,000 people. One hundred years later, it was a major transatlantic port with a population of over 80,000.

Many goods that were imported, such as tobacco, tea, coffee and sugar, were re-exported to other destinations in Europe. In addition, exports of manufactured goods to Britain's colonies, for example in North America, became an increasingly valuable market. However, throughout the 18th century Britain's most important export was textiles. The manufacture of woollen textiles was centred in the West Country, East Anglia and Yorkshire. But, after the 1780s, cotton manufacture began to replace wool in importance. Cotton was to play a major role in the Industrial Revolution in Britain.

These decorated vases come from China. Trade with Asia brought many exotic goods to Britain including Chinese porcelain and tea, spices such as pepper and cinnamon, and cheap cotton from India.

Jacobite Rebellion

1707 Act of Union unites England and Scotland to form Great Britain.

1708 'Old Pretender' James Edward (son of James II) attempts unsuccessfully to invade Scotland.

1715 John Erskine, Earl of Mar, raises support for Jacobite cause. James arrives in Scotland (December).

1716 Jacobite rebellion dies out. James and Earl of Mar flee to France.

1720 Birth of Charles Edward (the 'Young Pretender').

1745 Young Pretender lands in Scotland (July). British army defeated at Battle of Prestonpans (September). Jacobite army marches south as far as Derby.

1746 British army defeats Jacobites at Battle of Culloden (16 April). Escape of Young Pretender to France.

1766 Death of Old Pretender.

1788 Death of Young Pretender.

Although the Glorious Revolution took place without bloodshed, many people in Britain still looked on James II as the rightful king. Supporters of James were known as 'Jacobites' from the Latin word for James, 'Jacobus'.

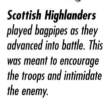

Scottish Highlanders played bagpipes as they advanced into battle. This was meant to encourage the troops and intimidate the enemy.

James II died in France in 1701, but the fight for the Jacobite cause continued for many years. After the massacre of Glencoe, Jacobite support strengthened in Scotland. The Act of Union (1707) which joined Scotland and England was also bitterly opposed by many in Scotland. The scene was set for Jacobite supporters to try to put James II's son, James Edward (known as the 'Old Pretender'), on the throne.

The Old Pretender had the backing of the French king, Louis XIV, but attempts to invade Britain in 1708, 1715 and 1719 all failed. The task of reclaiming the British throne was left to his son, Charles Edward, also known as 'Bonnie Prince Charlie' and the 'Young Pretender'. Charles Edward was born and brought up in Rome yet when he landed for the first time on Scottish soil in 1745 he declared: 'I am come home'.

The Young Pretender raised an army of Highlanders and after defeating the government army at the Battle of Prestonpans, he marched southwards as far as Derby.

James Stuart was known as the 'Old Pretender' to distinguish him from his son, the 'Young Pretender'. The word 'Pretender' comes from the French word 'prétendant', meaning claimant. Both father and son were claimants to the British throne.

The Battle of Culloden Field, the last major land battle fought on British soil, lasted only 40 minutes. The 5,000 Highlanders in the army of the Young Pretender were overwhelmed by the much larger government army. More than 1,000 Highlanders died. Later in his life, Charles Edward would say, 'I should have died with my men at Culloden'.

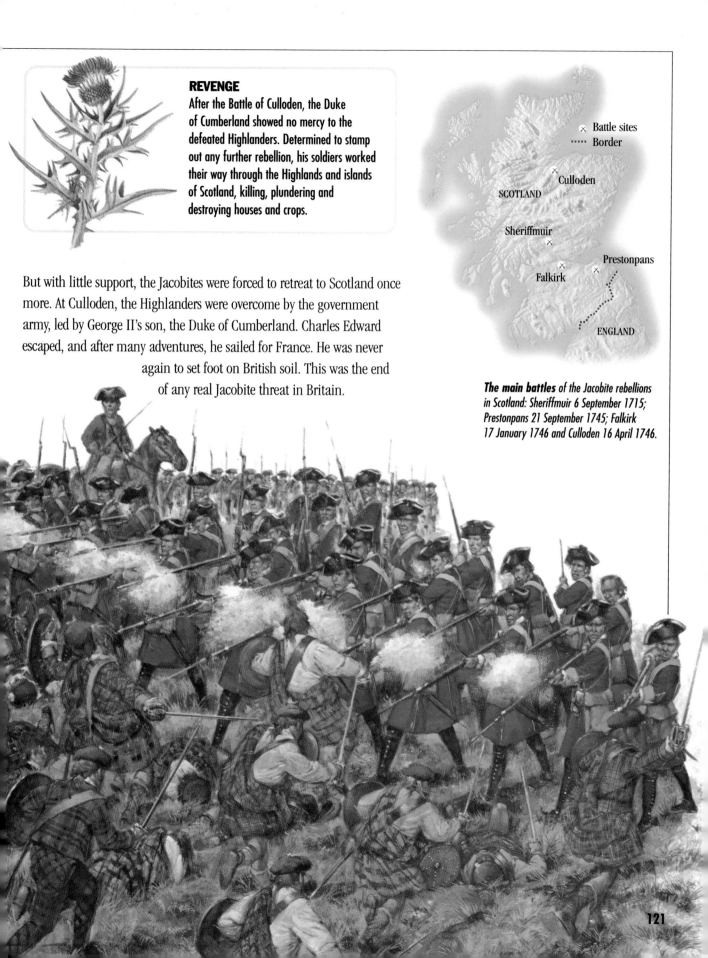

REVENGE

After the Battle of Culloden, the Duke of Cumberland showed no mercy to the defeated Highlanders. Determined to stamp out any further rebellion, his soldiers worked their way through the Highlands and islands of Scotland, killing, plundering and destroying houses and crops.

× Battle sites
····· Border

Culloden

SCOTLAND

Sheriffmuir
×

Prestonpans
×

Falkirk
×

ENGLAND

But with little support, the Jacobites were forced to retreat to Scotland once more. At Culloden, the Highlanders were overcome by the government army, led by George II's son, the Duke of Cumberland. Charles Edward escaped, and after many adventures, he sailed for France. He was never again to set foot on British soil. This was the end of any real Jacobite threat in Britain.

The main battles of the Jacobite rebellions in Scotland: Sheriffmuir 6 September 1715; Prestonpans 21 September 1745; Falkirk 17 January 1746 and Culloden 16 April 1746.

121

The Loss of America

Britain's victory over France during the Seven Years War (1756–63) meant that British colonists in America no longer feared a French invasion from the north. Many colonists thought that there was little need for the British army to remain in North America – especially as the colonists had to pay towards their upkeep. But the British had different ideas.

On 18 April 1775, riders carried a message to warn Boston of a British attack.

Ministers in the British government were determined to protect the valuable trade to and from North America. In order to meet some of the expense of keeping a military force in North America the government decided to impose new taxes on the colonists. As they had no representatives at Westminster, there was no one to argue the colonists' cause. During the 1760s and 1770s, the government in Britain imposed a whole series of taxes on the American colonists.

1765 American Stamp Act (tax on legal transactions) passed.

1767 Townshend's Act passed imposing taxes on various goods imported into America.

1770 Act passed to remove taxes on paper, glass and paint, but not on tea.

1773 Boston Tea Party (16 December).

1775 First battles of American War of Independence at Concord and Lexington (19 April). George Washington appointed commander of rebel armies (15 June).

1776 American Declaration of Independence (4 July).

1777 Surrender of British at Saratoga (17 October).

1778 Treaty signed between France and American rebels. France declares war on Britain (17 June).

1779 Spain declares war on Britain (21 June).

1780 Britain declares war on Netherlands (20 December).

1781 Cornwallis surrenders at Yorktown (19 October).

1783 Treaty of Versailles signed by Britain, France, Spain and the United States. Britain recognizes United States (3 September).

1784 Treaty signed with the Netherlands.

The army of the American colonists was not made up of professional soldiers, like the British troops, but of untrained working men such as farmers. They were ill-equipped to fight in the European manner, but had more success with guerrilla tactics such as ambushing and sniping to surprise and outwit the British troops.

Thomas Jefferson (1743–1826) was the main author of the Declaration of Independence which set out the reasons for the break of the 13 American colonies with Britain.

Finally, in 1775, the colonists' resentment boiled over into armed resistance.

In April 1775, British troops were sent from Boston to destroy military supplies held by the colonists at Concord, Massachusetts. However, the colonist rebels were warned and the first battles of the American War of Independence were fought at Concord and nearby Lexington. The American colonists declared themselves independent from Britain on 4 July, 1776, but the fighting continued until 1783.

Under their general, George Washington, the Americans used their local knowledge to harass the British troops. In 1778, help came for the Americans when France declared war on Britain. The French sent armies and fleets to America, but they also attacked British colonies in India and the West Indies. Similarly, Spain and the Netherlands joined the fighting in 1779 and 1780. Finally, Lord Cornwallis, who commanded the British army in America, was forced to surrender when French and Spanish fleets cut off his supply lines between Britain and the colonies. In 1783, Britain formally recognized the independence of the United States.

On 16 December, 1773, American colonists disguised as Native Americans boarded ships belonging to the British East India Company in Boston harbour. In protest at the tax imposed on tea by the British government they threw more than 300 chests of tea overboard. This event became known as the Boston Tea Party.

British soldiers were often called 'Redcoats' because of the red coats of their uniforms. About 42,000 British soldiers fought in the American War of Independence.

TAXES ON GOODS
The British government attempted to force the American colonists to pay taxes on many different commodities including lead, glass, paint, cotton, coffee, tea and paper. The new taxes were met with fierce opposition from the Americans. The eventual outcome was war and the declaration of American independence.

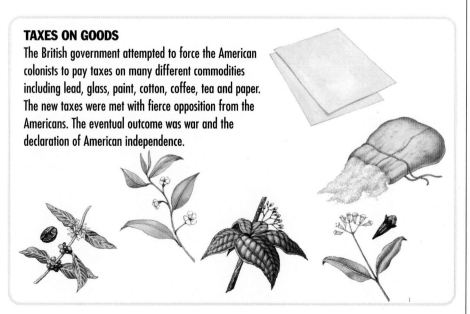

The Industrial Revolution

The Spinning Jenny was a multi-spool weaving machine that dramatically increased productivity.

1698 Thomas Savery develops steam pump.

1709 Abraham Darby develops coke-fired blast furnace.

1712 Thomas Newcomen develops steam-powered pumping engine for use in mines.

1733 John Kay develops flying shuttle.

1764 James Hargreaves develops 'Spinning Jenny'.

1769 Richard Arkwright patents water-frame (water-powered spinning machine). James Watt patents improved steam engine.

1776 Adam Smith writes *Wealth of Nations.*

1779 First iron bridge built across River Severn.

1782 Watt develops rotary steam engine.

1784 Henry Cort develops puddling iron.

1785 Edmund Cartwright invents power loom.

1815 Invention of Davy safety lamp for use in mines by Sir Humphry Davy.

1825 Stockton to Darlington railway opens.

Like the Agricultural Revolution, the phrase Industrial Revolution is used to describe a gradual rather than a sudden change. The Industrial Revolution is usually said to have started around the 1760s. By 1830, Britain was the most industrially advanced country in the world.

Britain was the first country to experience an Industrial Revolution, although industrial advances soon followed in Europe, America and elsewhere. There were many reasons for Britain's industrialization. Improved roads and the construction of canals and railways meant that transporting goods was relatively cheap and easy. There were rich natural resources such as coal and iron. Britain also had overseas colonies to provide cheap raw materials, such as cotton from India. These same colonies provided a ready market for manufactured goods.

The effects of the Agricultural Revolution meant that there were ample supplies of food for the rapidly growing population of Britain.

This increasing population provided the workforce for massive industrial development.

As new mines, mills and factories opened, many people left the rural areas and moved into towns and cities. London and the industrial towns of northwest England and South Wales all grew rapidly – Bradford, for example, had a population of 13,000 in 1800 which increased to over 100,000 by 1850.

The power that drove the Industrial Revolution was steam. In 1769, Scottish engineer James Watt patented a much improved steam engine. Other inventors who had a major impact in the development of the Industrial Revolution included Abraham Darby (coke-smelting), John Kay (flying shuttle), James Hargreaves (Spinning Jenny) and Richard Arkwright (water-powered spinning machine).

STEAM POWER

Steam power was in use as early as 1698 when Thomas Savery developed a steam-driven engine to pump water out of mines. The engine was improved by Thomas Newcomen and later by James Watt. Steam gradually took over as the main power source to drive machinery in mines, factories and mills. By 1825, steam power had taken to the rails, starting a transport revolution.

The Industrial Revolution completely changed the landscape in parts of Britain. Factories, smoking chimneys and powerful machinery appeared in places where there were once only green fields. Many people were awestruck by the industrial landscapes of northwest England or South Wales, but not everyone approved.

Canals and Railways

1757 Sankey Brook Navigation completed from St Helens to Mersey.

1761 Bridgewater Canal from Worsley to Manchester opened.

1777 Trent and Mersey canal completed.

1779 Stroudwater canal opened.

1789 Thames and Severn Canal completed.

1790 Forth and Clyde canal completed.

1804 Richard Trevithick's steam locomotive.

1825 Opening of Stockton to Darlington railway.

1829 Success of George Stephenson's *Rocket* at Rainhill steam trials.

1830 Opening of Liverpool and Manchester railway.

1843 Launch of Brunel's steamship *Great Britain*.

1858 Launch of iron ship *Great Eastern*.

The first half of the 19th century was the age of great engineers such as Isambard Kingdom Brunel, George Stephenson, Thomas Telford and James Brindley.

Isambard Kingdom Brunel's steamship Great Western *was the world's largest vessel in 1837. Brunel used his fame to persuade his railway employers to invest in ship building.*

In 1761, an 11-kilometre canal was opened between Worsley and Manchester. It was planned and paid for by the wealthy Duke of Bridgewater.

The Duke owned coalmines in Worsley, but carrying the coal the 11 kilometres from Worsley to Manchester by road was very expensive. After the opening of the Bridgewater Canal, he was able to transport his coal for a much lower price. The success of this canal aroused a lot of interest. Soon, landowners and business people around the country were forming companies to raise money to build canals linking towns and cities with industrial centres.

The canals brought many different benefits. They provided cheap transportation for goods such as coal, and linked up parts of the country that had previously been without access to navigable waterways, such as the 'Potteries' area around Stoke on Trent. The building of canals also called upon considerable engineering skills to construct tunnels, locks and aqueducts. Engineers such as James Brindley and Thomas Telford worked on many famous canal-building projects.

Another engineer, George Stephenson, designed the first railway. It went from Stockton to Darlington and was opened in 1825. Like the canals, its purpose was to carry coal. The first passenger-carrying railway opened in 1830. It ran from Liverpool to Manchester. This was the beginning of the age of railway construction. Between 1830 and 1850, about 10,000 kilometres of track were built. The engines that ran along the railway tracks were powered by steam. The first engineer to design a successful steam locomotive was Richard Trevithick in 1804.

Another use of steam was to power ships. The 1830s, 1840s and 1850s saw the launch of three great steam-powered ships all designed by Isambard Kingdom Brunel. The *Great Eastern*, launched in 1858 was iron-hulled and twice as large as any other ship of the time.

This map shows the main centres of industrial activity after 1760 for cotton, wool and iron. It also shows the route of the Grand Union Canal which linked the northwest, the Midlands and the southeast.

Travel by railway in the middle of the 19th century. Railways provided a cheap, efficient and fast way to move both people and goods around the country, and Britain was soon exporting its railway technology to countries around the world.

IRON BRIDGE
The first bridge to be made out of iron was erected in 1779 across the river Severn at Coalbrookdale. The bridge was constructed at the ironworks of the Darby family. It was Abraham Darby (1687–1717) who, in 1709, had discovered how to smelt iron ore using coke (made from coal) rather than charcoal (made from wood) as a fuel — an important breakthrough.

Captain Cook

In 1768, the Royal Society decided to send a scientific expedition to the Pacific Ocean. The scientists were to include astronomers, botanists and artists. The little-known James Cook was appointed commander of the voyage.

The **Endeavour** *was a sturdy ship about 30 metres in length. It was designed to carry coal along the east coast of Britain, but Cook had the cargo hold converted to carry stores and water for the expedition. The Endeavour carried 94 people on the long voyage to the Pacific Ocean.*

Cook had been at sea since the age of 18, and having worked on merchant ships he then joined the navy and saw action in the Seven Years War. He spent the years after the war making charts of the coast of Canada for the navy. His talents as a navigator, surveyor and astronomer, and his powers of command, made him an ideal choice to lead the Royal Society's scientific expedition.

One of Cook's orders was to look for a great Southern Continent. At the time, Europeans had little idea about the geography of the southern hemisphere. People thought that there was a large landmass to balance the huge landmass of Europe and Asia in the northern hemisphere. On his first round-the-world voyage (1768–71), Cook sailed around New Zealand and up the east coast of Australia.

Captain Cook was *an excellent commander who took good care of his sailors. He insisted that the crew's quarters should be clean and well ventilated. He prevented scurvy (a disease caused by malnourishment on board) by including cress and a kind of orange marmalade in the sailors' diet.*

PLANTS
One of the scientists on Cook's first voyage was the young botanist, Joseph Banks. He was the first European to see the plants and wildlife of New Zealand and Australia. After his return to Britain, Banks became famous for his reports on the plants and animals of the southern hemisphere.

Captain Cook met Pacific islanders and the Maoris of New Zealand during his epic voyages. To help him talk with the Maoris, he had with him an interpreter from Tahiti. Cook made the first accurate charts of New Zealand's coastline.

On his second voyage (1772–5), he explored the southern Pacific Ocean, crossing the Antarctic Circle and sailing farther south than anyone had ever ventured before. He almost discovered Antarctica but turned back north to resupply his ship. Cook wrote in his journal that there was at last a 'final end put to the searching after a Southern Continent'.

The aim of Cook's third and final voyage (1776–9) was to find a northwest passage around Canada and Alaska. But disaster struck in Hawaii. After a bad-tempered exchange with the local people of the islands, Cook was killed. His body was buried at sea on 21 February, 1779.

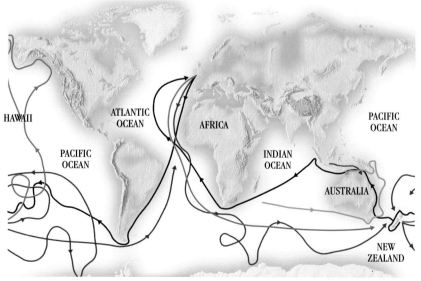

The routes of Captain Cook's three voyages are shown here. Black is the Endeavour 1768–71; red is Resolution and Adventure 1772–75; blue is Resolution and Discovery 1776–80.

— **Cook's first voyage (1768–71)**
— **Cook's second voyage (1772–75)**
— **Cook's third voyage (1776–79)**
— **Tasman (1642–44)**

The Nineteenth Century

p136 Queen Victoria became Britain's longest reigning monarch.

p152 American inventor Thomas Edison developed the first electric light bulb in the 1870s.

p151 Many important medical discoveries were made in the 19th century.

p158 Vast quantities of diamonds were discovered in southern Africa between 1869 and 1871.

p144 Failure of the potato crop led to famine in Ireland in the 1840s.

By the beginning of the 19th century, the process of industrialization was already well under way in Britain. By 1858, as Britain's factories turned out textiles, pottery, ironware and many other goods, Benjamin Disraeli was able to describe Britain as the 'workshop of the world'. About one-quarter of all world trade passed through British ports, and over 90 per cent of exports from Britain were goods manufactured in British factories.

This increase in trade and industrial production brought huge wealth to people such as factory owners and landowners. For the thousands of people who flocked to the new industrial centres, it brought dramatic changes in ways of living and working. Many people, particularly women and children, suffered from working long hours in harsh and often dangerous conditions. Throughout the 19th century, governments passed a series of Factory Acts to control the way that employers treated their workers. Workers also banded together to form 'combinations' (trade unions) to negotiate improvements in pay and working conditions with their bosses. These trade unions became more and more powerful organizations throughout the 19th century.

Unrest and reform were ever-present issues in the 19th century.

These ranged from the Luddite riots and Peterloo Massacre in the early years, to the fight for Home Rule that gathered pace in Ireland towards the end of the century. Despite the Reform Act of 1832, which gave the right to vote to many more men than ever before, demands for electoral reform continued in the 1840s, as campaigners called the Chartists presented huge petitions to parliament. They were all rejected.

The 19th century was an age of railway building in Britain. By 1880, there were about 25,000 kilometres of track open in the country. Long-distance travel was safe and affordable for many ordinary people. Millions began to enjoy day trips to seaside resorts. And in 1851 there was a new attraction – the Great Exhibition in London.

p153 The invention of the internal combustion engine in the 1860s led to the development of the first cars by the end of the 19th century.

p147 Florence Nightingale is credited with developing modern nursing methods.

p160 Many diamond mines in southern Africa in the 1870s used slave labour to dig for the precious stones.

War with France

In July 1789, a mob in Paris stormed the Bastille prison. This event marked the beginning of the French Revolution. Inspired by the example of the Americans, the revolutionaries declared that France was no longer to be ruled by a monarch but by the National Assembly.

*A **popular British cartoon** of the time depicts the Duke of Wellington in the boots that were named after him.*

In Britain many people welcomed the Revolution and its slogan 'liberté, égalité, fraternité' ('liberty, equality, brotherhood'). Others feared that violence would break out in Britain's towns and cities. The British prime minister, William Pitt, waited to see which side would emerge victorious in the Revolution. However, Pitt was forced to take action when France declared war on Britain in 1793.

The British government agreed to help its European allies to fight France on the continent by contributing towards the cost. Meanwhile, the British army and navy concentrated on fighting the French at sea, and defending the British colonies.

1783 William Pitt the Younger becomes prime minister at the age of 24.

1789 Revolution in France starts with storming of the Bastille Prison (14 July).

1793 France declares war on Britain and Holland (1 February).

1796 Napoleon becomes commander of French army.

1798 Napoleon invades Egypt. Nelson destroys French fleet at the Battle of the Nile (1 August).

1802 Treaty of Amiens.

1803 War breaks out once more (May).

1804 Napoleon crowns himself Emperor of France.

1805 Nelson defeats French–Spanish fleet at the Battle of Trafalgar (21 October).

1812 French army forced to retreat from Moscow.

1814 Treaty of Chaumont. Napoleon goes into exile on the island of Elba (May).

1815 Napoleon returns to France. Wellington defeats the French at the Battle of Waterloo (18 June).

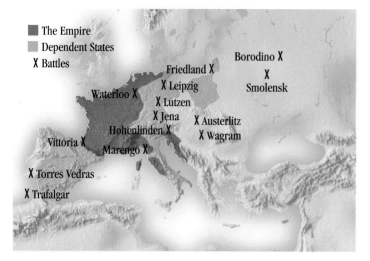

The Empire
Dependent States
X Battles

Borodino X
Friedland X
X Leipzig
Waterloo X
X Lutzen
Smolensk
X Jena
Hohenlinden X
X Austerlitz
Vittoria X
X Wagram
Marengo X
X Torres Vedras
X Trafalgar

This map shows the French Empire under Napoleon and the dependent states that were virtually part of it. The main battles of the Napoleonic Wars are also shown.

Horatio Nelson was born in Norfolk in 1758. He died at the Battle of Trafalgar, hit by a bullet from a French sniper. Although Trafalgar was an important victory for the British, the whole nation went into mourning for their great naval hero.

Pitt was forced to raise new taxes to pay for the war, and in 1795 there were widespread riots in protest. To make matters even worse, a brilliant new military commander had taken command in France and was winning victories over Britain's allies. His name was Napoleon Bonaparte.

In 1798, Napoleon invaded Egypt in an attempt to cut off Britain from its colonies in India. He was driven back when the British fleet, under the command of Admiral Nelson, defeated the French at the Battle of the Nile. Nelson scored another momentous victory in 1805 when he defeated a combined French and Spanish fleet at Trafalgar. Napoleon could not invade Britain, but he did try to take over Spain and Portugal, where British troops fought against the French during the Peninsular War. In 1812, he invaded Russia but was driven back by the savage winter conditions. The French emperor then went into exile, but escaped in 1815 to fight one last battle – Waterloo, against the Duke of Wellington's army which was made up of Germans, Dutch, Belgians, British and Prussians.

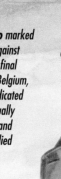

The Battle of Waterloo marked the end of Britain's war against France. Napoleon met his final defeat near Waterloo, in Belgium, on 18 June, 1815. He abdicated soon after and was eventually exiled to St Helena, an island in the Atlantic, where he died in 1821.

Napoleon Bonaparte was born in Corsica in 1769. He became a general in the French army in 1796 and quickly showed his military brilliance. In 1804 he became Emperor of France.

Regency Britain

When George IV succeeded to the throne on 29 January, 1820, he had already been ruler of Great Britain and Ireland for nine years. He had taken over from his ill father as Prince Regent in 1811, giving the Regency period its name.

During the early 19th century, romantic poets, novelists and artists became household names in Britain.

1785 Prince of Wales has relationship with Maria Fitzherbert.

1795 Prince of Wales marries Caroline of Brunswick.

1810 George III becomes ill.

1811 Prince of Wales is made Prince Regent. Beginning of Luddite disturbances.

1814 Abdication of Napoleon.

1815 Defeat of Napoleon at Waterloo.

1819 'Peterloo Massacre' in Manchester.

1820 George III dies. Prince Regent becomes George IV.

1821 Riots in London at funeral of Queen Caroline.

1830 Death of George IV. Succeeded by his brother as William IV.

By the time he became Regent, the Prince already had a reputation as a man rather 'too fond of women and wine'. In 1785 he had become informally and secretly married to Maria Fitzherbert, who was a Roman Catholic. This marriage was never acknowledged and, in 1795, he officially married Caroline of Brunswick. Only a year later, the two separated. Caroline's behaviour was outrageous, but her harsh treatment at the hands of the Prince Regent earned her public sympathy. He refused to allow her to attend his coronation in 1821, and after her death a few weeks later there were riots at her funeral.

The Royal Pavilion in Brighton was one of the projects of the Prince Regent. He first went to Brighton in 1783 and it was there that he met Maria Fitzherbert in 1784. As a result of the Prince's patronage, Brighton quickly became a fashionable resort. The Prince used his favourite architect, John Nash, to create the Royal Pavilion in Indian style with Chinese decorations.

Three Regency ladies. These high-waisted gowns became fashionable in the late 18th century. They were a reaction to the fussy, frilled fashions of the past.

George Gordon, Lord Byron (1788–1824) *was famous in his own lifetime as poet and author of* Childe Harolde's Pilgrimage. *He also sat in the House of Lords and spoke out in 1812 against the measures taken to stop the Luddite attacks. He compared the conditions of the British workers unfavourably to the poorest parts of Turkey and Greece, where he had recently travelled.*

Unrest and riot characterized much of the Regency period. After 20 years of Napoleonic War, people across Britain were sick of the hardships it brought. Many workers received pitifully low wages and others were losing their jobs. High food prices and poor harvests created widespread fear of starvation. In 1811, there were attacks on machinery and mills by people who claimed allegiance to a man called Ned Ludd. He probably did not exist, but the protestors became known as Luddites.

The attacks ended in 1812, only after the arrest and execution of 17 Luddites. Further evidence of the bitterness felt towards the government came when Prime Minister Spencer Perceval was shot in the House of Commons. His assassin was a businessman who had gone bankrupt as a result of the war. By many, he was hailed as a hero.

Victorian Britain

In the early hours of 20 June, 1837, a carriage raced as fast as possible from Windsor Castle to Kensington Palace in London. Inside were two men bearing important news – King William IV was dead. At Kensington they greeted their new queen, the 18-year-old Victoria. The Victorian age had begun.

1837 Death of William IV. Succeeded by Queen Victoria.

1840 Marriage of Queen Victoria to Prince Albert of Saxe-Coburg-Gotha.

1851 Great Exhibition in Crystal Palace.

1854–56 Crimean War.

1861 Prince Albert dies (14 December).

1877 Queen Victoria is proclaimed Empress of India.

1879 Zulu War.

1881 First Boer War.

1899–1902 Second Boer War.

1901 Death of Queen Victoria (22 January).

At first, the young queen was a lonely figure relying heavily on the advice of her prime minister, the leader of the Whig party, Lord Melbourne. Victoria's friendship with Lord Melbourne and her enthusiasm for the Whigs caused several scandals in the early years of her reign. However, after her marriage to the German Prince Albert in 1840, she was more careful to avoid favouring one party over another, working closely with her ministers, whatever their political beliefs.

In fact, as Victoria gave birth to nine children, she was obliged to hand over many of the responsibilities of monarchy to her husband. As a result, he became an increasingly powerful figure in the early years of her reign. When Albert died in 1861, Queen Victoria was distraught. She went into mourning and withdrew almost entirely from public life. As the years spent in mourning passed, public sympathy gave way to discontent with the absent monarch. Only the persuasiveness of the Tory prime minister, Benjamin Disraeli, brought Victoria back to her public duties.

A Victorian lady of fashion. Women's fashion during the Victorian era was dominated by the bustle gown, with its exaggerated, full skirts and tiny waist.

Queen Victoria was the first British monarch to be photographed. She also travelled widely around her kingdom thanks to the new railway network. She and Albert especially loved Scotland, where they stayed at Balmoral Castle, and the Isle of Wight, where they stayed at Osborne House.

Victoria's golden and diamond jubilees in 1887 and 1897 (celebrating 50 and 60 years on the throne) were huge successes. When she died in 1901, she was buried alongside the love of her life, Albert, in a mausoleum near Windsor Castle. Of Victoria and Albert's nine children, the first in line to the throne was Edward, Prince of Wales, who became Edward VII on the death of his mother in 1901. Many of Victoria's children went on to marry members of other European royal families. At her death, Victoria had 37 great-grandchildren.

THE SALVATION ARMY

The Salvation Army was formed by Catherine and William Booth in 1878. It was made up of members from their Whitechapel Christian Mission. The Salvation Army offered help to the poor, homeless and sick during the Victorian period. Today, it is a worldwide organization that helps those in poverty.

The Victorian era saw a change in business methods and the advent of advertising. This advert for Cadbury's cocoa dates from the second half of the 19th century.

Dancing at the Royal Cremorne Gardens in Chelsea, London. There were all sorts of amusements in these pleasure gardens including fireworks, dancing, puppet shows and hot-air balloons.

Trade and Industry

1840 Introduction of Penny Post by Rowland Hill improved the postal service.

1842–4 Prime Minister Sir Robert Peel introduces reduction or abolition of duty on many goods.

1844 Bank Charter Act.

1846 Repeal of Corn Laws. Free trade in corn established.

1848 Revolutions across Europe.

1850 Over 10,000 kilometres of railway track open.

1851 Great Exhibition held in Crystal Palace, Hyde Park, London.

1860 Final abolition of duties on many goods.

1880 Over 25,000 kilometres of railway track open.

In 1858, Benjamin Disraeli called Britain the 'workshop of the world'. Both trade and industry were booming. About one-quarter of all world trade passed through British ports, and most of this was carried in British ships. By the middle of the 19th century, over 90 per cent of the exports from Britain were goods manufactured in British factories.

Industrial innovations of the Victorian era saw the invention of many mechanical marvels, including the motor car. The first practical model was built by German engineers Karl Benz and Gottlieb Daimler in 1885.

The most important of the exports were textiles. By 1830, they made up 75 per cent of all Britain's exports, and half of this amount was cotton goods. Raw cotton was imported from North America and turned into cloth in the factories and mills in northern Britain. It was then exported either as cloth, or manufactured into cheap goods. Many of these cotton goods were sold in India.

Rioting breaks out in Germany in 1848. While Europe was in a state of turmoil, British industry went from strength to strength. Britain soon became a leading industrial nation.

The amount of railway track in Britain increased rapidly in the 19th century. The railways revolutionized travel, providing cheap and efficient transport across the country. Soon, British engineering and technology was being used in many overseas countries for railway building projects. From the 1840s, iron became a major British export – much of it destined for the construction of railways in other nations around the globe.

The introduction of free trade in the middle of the 19th century also helped to boost British commerce abroad. For many years, British products had been protected by charging duties (taxes) on goods imported from overseas. These duties were gradually removed by successive governments, making the importing of raw materials, such as cotton, a lot cheaper.

The event that best showed off the power of British trade and industry was the Great Exhibition of 1851. It displayed the finest British technology and engineering, proving Britain's leadership in industry at the time.

Mailbags being delivered through a pneumatic tube. In 1840, Rowland Hill started a new scheme in which the cost of postage over any distance was a penny, and it was paid by the sender. This was the Penny Post, and it was a huge success.

HORSE-DRAWN CARRIAGES

The arrival of the railways in the 19th century brought an end to long-distance journeys by carriage. The railways were far more efficient and more reliable than the old stagecoaches. However, carriages continued to be used for shorter journeys, and town streets were choked with horse-drawn traffic.

Bank notes being printed. The British banking system started in the late 17th century. At first, each bank issued its own notes. However, the Bank Charter Act of 1844 aimed to control the number of banknotes issued, and gradually limited the issue of notes to the Bank of England.

Labourers at work on a new railway track. Thousands of kilometres of track were laid in Britain in the 19th century. Gangs of construction workers often came from Scotland or Ireland and were known as 'navvies' (short for 'navigation', another word for canal). The building of the railways provided unskilled work for many thousands of labourers.

Life in Victorian Britain

One of the effects of the Industrial Revolution was that large numbers of people moved to work in the factories and mills of the industrial areas. These workers had to become accustomed to new ways of working – including long hours and the discipline of factory life.

Ladies' summer fashions of 1844. These full skirts would have been supported by several starched petticoats. In the 1850s crinolines appeared. They were frameworks of steel and whalebone that were lighter and more comfortable than thick, heavy petticoats.

Life in the country was not easy either. A 12-hour day was normal, and it could be longer during busy times of year, such as harvest. However, during the winter, shorter daylight hours meant that the working day was also shorter.

1799 Combination Act prevents 'combinations' of workers.

1807 Britain ends slave trade.

1811 Beginning of Luddite disturbances.

1813 Elizabeth Fry begins reform of the prison system.

1819 'Peterloo Massacre' in Manchester.

1824 Repeal of the Combination Act.

1825 New Combination Act confines combinations to peaceful negotiation over wages and hours.

1834 Trade unions join together to form Grand National Consolidated Trades' Union (GNCTU). 'Tolpuddle Martyrs' sentenced to transportation for swearing illegal oaths in connection with Friendly Society of Agricultural Labourers. Public outcry and demonstrations lead to pardon of the six men.

1844 'Ragged Schools' set up for the poorest children.

1848 Public Health Act to set up boards of health.

1850 Factory Act establishes standard working day.

1868 First Trades Union Congress in Manchester.

1893 Keir Hardie sets up Independent Labour Party.

Two wealthy ladies visit the home of a poor family. *Many well-off people in Victorian times were deeply concerned with the plight of the poor. Many charities were set up, as well as voluntary hospitals and the 'Ragged Schools' – free schools for poor children.*

A street flower seller. *Many poor people were forced to take whatever work they could in order to survive.*

In the factories, the 12-hour working day operated throughout the year and workers had to be very disciplined. For example, if they turned up late for work the factory gates were shut, they were turned away and they lost any pay they would have earned that day.

In some places, workers combined into groups to demand better conditions. These groups were known as 'combinations' (and later as 'unions'). Although they faced many legal challenges, the unions grew in power and importance throughout the 19th century.

For many working-class women, jobs in factories or mills offered an opportunity to earn their own money for the first time, although they were usually paid less than men for the same work. The largest group of women workers was domestic servants.

A bustling scene on London Bridge. The streets of Victorian London were usually filthy and choked with traffic. For short journeys in town, people travelled by foot, on horseback, or by carriage — for example in a two-wheeled hansom cab (front left).

CHILDHOOD

Most children in middle-class homes in the 19th century were brought up largely by nurses and governesses. Parents were often remote figures, to be treated with respect. Great emphasis was laid on good manners, and children would often address their father as 'Sir'. Boys were usually sent away to school but, until the later years of the century, most girls were educated at home by a governess.

Unrest and Reform

Since Elizabethan times, there had been a system in England of helping those who were sick or who could not find work, as well as poor widows and orphans. Known as the 'Poor Law', the money for this system came from the householders in each parish.

1819 Factory Act limits working day for children in cotton mills to 12 hours.

1832 Reform Act gives vote to men living in property worth £10 per year.

1833 Factory Act limits work for children in textile factories.

1834 New Poor Law Act.

1839 First Chartist petition presented to parliament.

1842 Second Chartist petition rejected by parliament.

1847 Factory Act limits women and children to 58-hour working week.

1848 Feargus O'Connor presents third Chartist petition. It is rejected by parliament.

1850 Factory Act establishes standard working day.

1867 Second Reform Act gives vote to about one in three working men.

1885 Third Reform Act passed by parliament.

Mounted police move in to quell a riot in Trafalgar Square on 13 November, 1887. The disturbance started after a meeting of unemployed people. Such clashes were common throughout the 19th century, as workers demanded reforms and rights.

In 1832, a government commission was set up to look into the workings of the Poor Law. Many people were unhappy with the cost of the system and the way it was run. The New Poor Law, passed in 1834, targeted people who were able bodied yet unemployed. Out-of-work labourers were no longer to get relief (money). Instead they were to go to the workhouse, where they would be separated from their families and fed the poorest food. The New Poor Law saved money, but it caused misery to thousands of people.

For those in work, life was sometimes little better. Conditions in many mines, mills and factories were atrocious, with women and children working long hours with dangerous equipment. Various Factory Acts limited working hours and the age of children being put to work, but the acts were largely ineffective until inspectors were employed to check that the new laws were being obeyed.

Many governments throughout the 19th century attempted to improve life for poorer people by passing various acts. Many of these acts, however, proved worthless without the proper organizations to check on their application.

A scene from one of Charles Dickens's novels, **Oliver Twist.** Oliver is famous as the workhouse boy who dared to ask for more food because he was hungry. In Oliver Twist, Dickens highlighted the conditions and the treatment of poor children in workhouses.

In the late 1830s, unrest over working conditions and the New Poor Law broke out in the north of England. Out of this unrest grew the movement called Chartism. Supporters of Chartism were called Chartists, and they believed that the only way towards fairer laws was if more working men had the vote. Until 1832, only wealthy landowners were allowed to vote. In 1839 a group of Chartists presented the People's Charter to parliament. It called for the vote for men of 21 years and over, but it – and further petitions – were rejected. After 1848, Chartism died out, but parliamentary reform continued.

Women at work in the workroom of a Victorian workhouse. The inhabitants of a workhouse were made to wear uniforms and were not allowed to receive visitors or to leave the building.

SERVANT EMPLOYMENT

In the 19th century, domestic service was a large source of employment for both men and women. Even modestly well-off households employed a maid or two, and in larger households there were teams of maids and men servants. The servants' living quarters were usually in the basement and at the top of a large house (right). Their employers lived and slept in greater luxury in the main rooms (left).

Great Hunger

1838 Poor Law introduced in Ireland.

1841 Population of Ireland is 8,175,000.

1845 Potato blight first reported in southern England (August). Blight appears in Ireland (September). Beginning of famine in Ireland. Peel orders shipment of corn from United States to feed starving people in Ireland.

1846 Repeal of the Corn Laws. Sir Robert Peel resigns and Lord John Russell becomes prime minister (June). Potato crop fails again and famine worsens. More than 100,000 people emigrate from Ireland.

1847 Potato crop succeeds but it is very small and insufficient to feed the population. About 215,000 people emigrate from Ireland.

1848 Blight reappears and potato crop fails.

1849 Only partial failure of potato crop brings an end to the famine.

1851 Population of Ireland has fallen to 6,552,000. Over 250,000 people emigrate this year.

The potato plant was first brought to Europe from North America in the 16th century. The fungus that killed the Irish potato crop also came from America, arriving in 1845. The fungus destroyed both the leaves and the roots of the potato plant, leaving a rotting mess behind.

Between 1845 and 1849 a famine struck Ireland, killing an estimated one million people from starvation or disease. Many thousands more emigrated across the Atlantic to the United States to escape the great hunger.

In 1841, just over eight million people lived in Ireland. About half depended on potatoes as their main food source. In 1845, a fungus affected the potato crop in southern England. It soon moved to Ireland, and in an unusually cold, wet year the fungus quickly swept across the country. Many people found that their potatoes had rotted in the ground. Others picked seemingly healthy potatoes only to find that they rotted later on.

The situation was made worse by the Corn Law, which protected British landowners by taxing imported corn. This kept the price of British corn too high for the Irish to afford to buy. Prime Minister Sir Robert Peel ordered £100,000 worth of corn to be imported from the USA. It was sold cheaply in Ireland, helping to prevent starvation. In 1846, Peel persuaded MPs to vote for the repeal (cancellation) of the Corn Laws. Many Conservative MPs were landowners and they saw the repeal of the Corn Laws as a threat to their profits. The vote split the Tory party and led to Peel's resignation. He was replaced by a Whig, Lord John Russell. When the harvest failed in 1846, the famine worsened.

A starving woman and her children search for edible potatoes in Ireland. Starvation was not the only cause of death during the great famine. Diseases such as typhus and dysentery spread, killing thousands of people.

Famine-struck Ireland in 1845. One writer said of the scenes he saw: 'In many places the wretched people were seated on the fences of their decaying gardens, wringing their hands, and bewailing bitterly the destruction that had left them foodless.'

The new government did little to help the people of Ireland. Prime Minister Russell expected Irish landowners to take responsibility for their starving tenants. The government limited its help to building extra workhouses and opening soup kitchens. However, each year brought with it further crop failures and the famine continued. It was not until 1849 that conditions for the millions of Irish people left slowly began to improve.

Irish emigrants wait at the dockside to board ships to the United States of America. Between 1846 and 1849 thousands of people emigrated, desperate to escape from the famine in Ireland. Conditions on board ship were often appalling. One in nine emigrants from the Cork region died before they reached their destination.

145

The Crimean War

The Crimean War takes its name from the region where the war was fought – the Crimean Peninsula, on the Black Sea in present-day Ukraine. The war was fought between Russia and the allied armies of Britain, France and the Ottoman empire (Turkey), with the army of Sardinia–Piedmont joining this alliance in 1855.

1853 Ottoman empire (Turkey) declares war on Russia. Turkish fleet destroyed by Russians at Sinope. French–British fleet goes to Black Sea to protect Turkish coast.

1854 France and Britain declare war on Russia. Siege of Sebastopol begins. Major battles at Alma River, Balaklava and Inkerman. Florence Nightingale and a team of nurses arrive in Scutari.

1855 French capture Malakhov and Russians evacuate Sebastopol.

1856 Russians accept peace. Treaty of Paris (March).

1857 Royal Commission on the Health of the Army set up. Foundation of Army Medical School.

The war started because of religious conflicts between Russia and the Ottoman empire. Britain also had concerns about Russia's wish to expand its territories and any threat this might present to British colonies and trade. In 1853 Russia invaded Turkish-held provinces on the river Danube, and Great Britain and France declared war. Most British ministers wanted a peaceful settlement to the conflict, but public opinion forced Britain and France to declare war on Russia.

The Russian armies withdrew from the Danube provinces in the summer of 1854, but the British and French decided to send a force to attack their stronghold at Sebastopol on the Crimea. The aim was to launch a swift attack to frighten the Russians and increase security for the Ottoman empire. What actually happened was a year-long siege in which many thousands of soldiers died.

The Crimea is a large peninsula which juts out into the Black Sea.

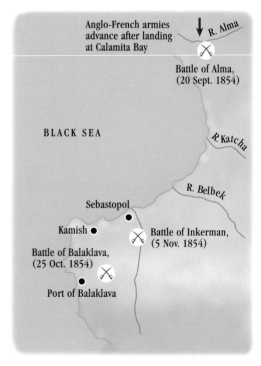

This map shows the main battles of the Crimean War, including the Battle of Balaklava in which the famous charge of the Light Brigade took place.

The Victoria Cross is a medal presented to members of the British armed forces for acts of extreme bravery. It was set up by Queen Victoria during the Crimean War, and the first crosses were awarded to soldiers who fought in this war. The medals are made from the metal of captured Russian cannons.

Florence Nightingale was called the 'lady with the lamp' because of her late-night ward rounds during which she comforted the sick troops. When she arrived in Scutari, Florence Nightingale found filthy hospitals full of dying men lying on bare boards. She ordered 200 scrubbing brushes, and then she cleaned the wards. Next, she organized the delivery of mattresses and sheets, and opened a kitchen to prepare food for her patients.

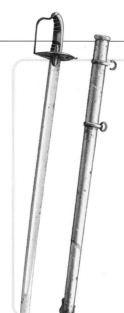

CRIMEAN WEAPONS
While cavalry fought with traditional swords and weapons in the Crimea, many new weapons and innovations were used by both sides. These included steam ships and the first military use of railways to move supplies to the battlefield and the telegraph to aid communications.

The end came when French troops captured the Russian position at Malakhov. The Russians blew up their forts and ships at Sebastopol and withdrew. A peace treaty was signed in March 1856.

Many of the British troops who died in the Crimea were killed not by Russian attacks but by disease. The sick were taken to makeshift hospitals at Scutari in Turkey, where they were left to die of typhus or of their wounds. Their suffering was described in *The Times* newspaper by its correspondent Sir William Russell. His reports caused a public outcry, and prompted the minister for war to ask Florence Nightingale to go to Scutari with a team of nurses. She had soon earned her well-known nickname: 'the lady with the lamp'.

The charge of the Light Brigade happened at the Battle of Balaklava on 25 October, 1854. A set of confused orders sent the Light Brigade towards a well-armed Russian position and as a result about 250 out of the 673 men died. The event was made famous in a poem by the English poet, Alfred, Lord Tennyson.

Ireland and Home Rule

1800 Act of Union establishes the United Kingdom of Great Britain and Ireland.

1828 Daniel O'Connell elected as an MP, although as a Catholic he could not take up the post.

1829 Catholic Emancipation Act gives Catholics political equality.

1843 Meeting at Clontarf to promote repeal of the Union put down by troops.

1845–9 Great famine.

1848 Leaders of the Young Ireland movement arrested and transported after an unsuccessful uprising.

1858 Founding of Fenian Brotherhood to fight for Irish independence.

1870 Home Rule League founded in Dublin by Isaac Butt.

1880 Charles Stewart Parnell becomes leader of the Home Rule League.

1884 Franchise Act gives vote to many supporters of Home Rule.

1886 First Home Rule Bill defeated in House of Commons.

1893 Defeat of Second Home Rule Bill.

Eamon de Valera (1882–1975) continued the Irish struggle for independence after the turn of the century. De Valera went on to become president of Ireland in 1959.

In 1800, the Act of Union joined Great Britain and Ireland to form the United Kingdom. Ireland was now represented by 100 MPs at Westminster in London. However, Irish Catholics, who made up 90 per cent of the Irish population, could not vote or become MPs.

Trying petty cases in an Irish courtroom in 1853. Justice was weighted heavily in favour of the English landlord in 19th-century Ireland. The fate of Irishmen brought to court was often already decided before the trial began.

An Irish tenant farmer and family are evicted by their landlord. Tenants were thrown out if they could not pay their rent. Some landlords tried to 'clear' their estates by offering tenants incentives of money to emigrate.

The fight for political equality for Catholics was led by Daniel O'Connell. Although he could not legally become an MP, he stood for election in County Clare in 1828 and won a huge number of votes. In 1829, Catholics gained the right to become MPs. O'Connell wanted the Act of Union to be repealed (cancelled), and Ireland to be independent from Britain and to have its own parliament again. O'Connell died in 1847, but the campaign for repeal continued with the Young Ireland movement and the Fenian Brotherhood.

In 1870, Isaac Butt founded an organization that used the slogan 'Home Rule'. Under the leadership of Charles Stewart Parnell, the Home Rule League played a major part in the fight for independence. In 1884, the Franchise Act gave the vote to many more Catholics, and in 1885 over 80 Irish 'Home Rulers' were elected. Prime Minister William Gladstone was convinced of the need for Home Rule. However, between 1886 and 1893 two Home Rule bills were defeated in parliament.

In March 1867, there was a Fenian uprising. It was unsuccessful, lasting only one night. Many of the Fenian leaders had already been rounded up and imprisoned by the government.

Health and Education

The first half of the 19th century saw a massive movement of people from the countryside to industrial centres such as Manchester and Leeds. Huge numbers of houses were built to accommodate these workers, but towns quickly became overcrowded and unhealthy places.

The most basic problem was one of sanitation. The new houses were built back to back, or around a courtyard. They were overcrowded, and there was often just one toilet and one clean-water pipe for several houses. There were no sewerage systems, so sewage drained directly into rivers or was dumped in heaps.

1828 Thomas Arnold becomes headmaster of Rugby School and begins the reform of public schools.

1833 Factory Act includes education for children working in textile factories, and provides government fund for education.

1844 'Ragged Schools' set up for poorest children.

1848 Public Health Act to set up boards of health.

1850 Factory Act establishes standard working day.

1870 Education Act sets up School Boards and aims to 'cover the country with good schools'.

1875 Public Health Act sets up authorities to oversee areas such as housing, health and sanitation.

1880 Education Act makes school compulsory for children aged 5–10.

1891 Assisted Education Act funds each child, so schools did not have to charge fees.

KING CHOLERA
Cholera is a disease spread through dirty water, although the way it spread was not understood in the 19th century. There were outbreaks of cholera in 1831, 1848, 1853 and 1866, killing thousands of people each time.

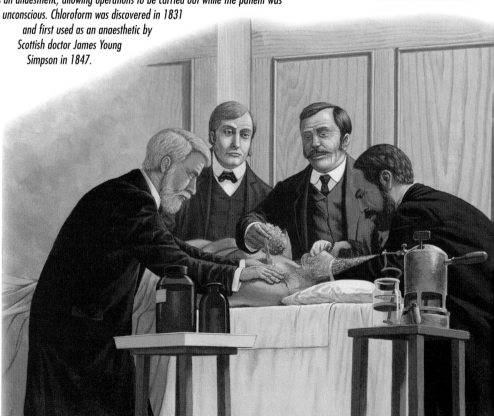

Operating on a patient with the use of chloroform. This drug acted as an anaesthetic, allowing operations to be carried out while the patient was unconscious. Chloroform was discovered in 1831 and first used as an anaesthetic by Scottish doctor James Young Simpson in 1847.

It is not surprising that water for drinking was often dirty, spreading many fatal diseases such as cholera.

In the 1840s, people began to accept the links between the filthy conditions in towns and the spread of disease. Plans were drawn up for water and sewerage systems, and conditions in towns slowly began to improve. However, in the 1860s a writer could still complain that the town of Kidderminster in the West Midlands 'stank from end to end'!

For most children of working-class families in the early 19th century, there were few opportunities for education. Church organizations ran some Sunday schools, and there were 'Dame' schools (so called because they were run by women) for young children. In 1844, 'Ragged Schools' were set up to provide basic education for orphans and very poor children. As more men were given the right to vote, people began to realize the importance of educating future voters.

This ornamental washstand is typical of the style of the late 19th century. Fitted bathrooms were found only in the houses of the well-to-do at this time.

MEDICINE

Health and cleanliness became an important issue during the Victorian era. Various medicines and sanitary products were introduced and a number of medical discoveries made. One of the most important medical breakthroughs of the age was the use of Joseph Lister's carbolic antiseptic spray during operations.

A Victorian schoolroom. In many schools pupil-teachers helped with the teaching. The pupil-teachers were boys and girls of 13 and over. After five years of apprenticeship they could themselves become teachers.

Inventions and Discoveries

The 19th century saw major developments that made travel, communications and trade much easier for many people. The railways allowed people to travel cheaply and rapidly around the country, opening up new possibilities for both rich and poor. The postal service expanded after the introduction of the 'Penny Post'.

The first practical electric telegraph was demonstrated by two British inventors, William Fothergill Cooke and Charles Wheatstone, in 1837. It used electric signals running along a wire to make a needle point to specific letters and numbers at the receiving end. It provided, for the first time, a method of fast, long-distance communication. Soon telegraph wires were being laid alongside railway tracks, and strung between poles to link towns and cities.

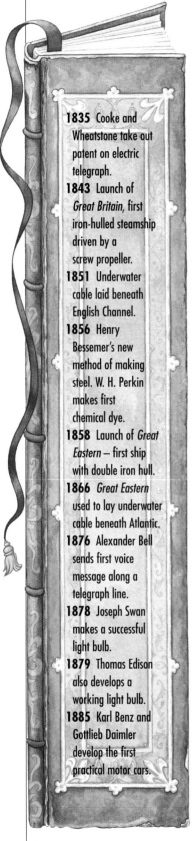

1835 Cooke and Wheatstone take out patent on electric telegraph.

1843 Launch of *Great Britain*, first iron-hulled steamship driven by a screw propeller.

1851 Underwater cable laid beneath English Channel.

1856 Henry Bessemer's new method of making steel. W. H. Perkin makes first chemical dye.

1858 Launch of *Great Eastern* – first ship with double iron hull.

1866 *Great Eastern* used to lay underwater cable beneath Atlantic.

1876 Alexander Bell sends first voice message along a telegraph line.

1878 Joseph Swan makes a successful light bulb.

1879 Thomas Edison also develops a working light bulb.

1885 Karl Benz and Gottlieb Daimler develop the first practical motor cars.

An early light bulb, made by the American inventor Thomas Alva Edison. Both Edison and the British scientist Joseph Wilson Swan worked independently on a design for a practical light bulb in the late 1870s.

An early phonograph, or gramophone. The earliest practical phonograph was developed by the American inventor Thomas Alva Edison, in 1877. In the 1880s, a German-born American called Emil Berliner improved on Edison's design by using a flat disc to store the recorded sound, instead of a wax tube used by Edison. A needle-like stylus picked up the information stored in the grooves on the disc and converted it back into sound.

Isambard Kingdom Brunel
was one of the most famous engineers of the period. With his first ship, the Great Western, he proved that it was possible to cross the Atlantic Ocean using only steam power.

In 1876, there was another communications breakthrough when the Scottish-born inventor Alexander Bell sent a voice message along a telegraph line. This was the first telephone message ever sent.

The 19th century was also a time of advances in scientific knowledge about the natural world. It was a naturalist called Charles Darwin who, in 1859, published one of the most controversial books of the century. *The Origin of Species* was the result of many years of research, including a round-the-world voyage on *HMS Beagle*, a Royal Navy survey ship. Darwin's theories of evolution and natural selection challenged the teachings of the Church – that God created all living things. It caused a huge outcry at the time and was opposed by many prominent members of the clergy. But the discovery of dinosaur fossils and other evidence of early life on Earth soon convinced many people.

A microscope *was one of the essential pieces of equipment for scientists in the 19th century. Charles Darwin's microscope still sits on his desk in his study at his house in Kent. Darwin's controversial theories were backed up by the discovery of dinosaur fossils and other evidence of early life on Earth, and were soon accepted by many people.*

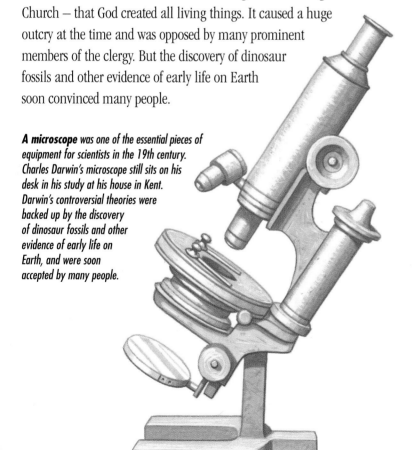

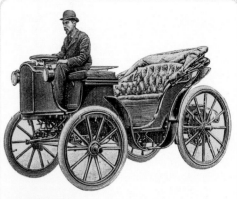

AUTOMOBILES

While British engineers were busy improving steam power, a new breakthrough was made in France in the 1860s with the invention of the internal combustion engine. Around 1885, two German engineers, Karl Benz and Gottlieb Daimler, used this new type of engine to power the earliest motor cars. Cars began to appear on British roads during the 1890s, and the first cars were manufactured in Britain in 1895.

The British Raj

1833 East India Company becomes administrative agent in India on behalf of the British government.

1845–56 Lord Dalhousie pursues policy of introducing Western ideas about religion and education into India.

1857 Indian Mutiny begins at Meerut on 10 May.

1858 Peace proclaimed. British government assumes control of India.

1876 Queen Victoria is created Empress of India.

1885 Indian National Congress founded.

1892 First Indian members sit on legislative council.

A British soldier in tropical uniform. The British army in India was made up of a mixture of British and Indian troops.

Rudyard Kipling was born in India in 1865. He was sent to school in England from the age of six, but returned to India in 1882 to work as a journalist. He became famous for his poems and short stories about life in India. He also wrote many children's stories including The Jungle Book *and the* Just So Stories.

On 10 May, 1857, sepoys (soldiers) in the service of the East India Company in Meerut shot their British officers. This was the start of the uprising known to Indians as the First War of Independence, and to the British as the Indian Mutiny.

By the middle of the 19th century, British rule was well established in India. The East India Company, set up in the 17th century to trade with countries in the East, was responsible for administration across British-ruled India.

Although the poor treatment of the sepoys and religious intolerance were the root causes of the mutiny, the spark that caused the uprising was the introduction of a new kind of rifle.

The cartridges for this rifle had to have the ends bitten off before the bullet inside could be used. A rumour began that the grease used in these cartridges was made of a mixture of cow's and pig's fat. This was unacceptable to both the Hindu and Muslim sepoys, as Hindus consider the cow to be a sacred animal and Muslims consider pigs to be unclean. When the sepoys in Meerut refused to use the new cartridges, they were thrown into prison. Their comrades then mutinied against the British officers.

The main battles of the mutiny were fought in Delhi, Cawnpore and Lucknow. The massacre of 200 women and children at Cawnpore outraged the British. However, they took equally violent revenge on the sepoys, killing hundreds of Indian soldiers. Peace was finally declared on 8 July 1858. The Indian Mutiny shocked the British, and changes were made to prevent any similar uprisings in the future. The administration was taken away from the East India Company and a new government department was set up to run India. Before the mutiny, British policy was to introduce Western ideas about religion and education, which threatened both Hindu and Muslim ways of life. After 1858, a new policy aimed at preventing British interference with religious matters in India was introduced.

CARRIAGE AND BEARERS
The British officials of the British East India Company were often very wealthy and could afford to be carried around in an enclosed litter, called a palanquin. After the Indian Mutiny, most British officials in India lived in well-guarded military towns, or camps, built outside local towns.

Chintz was made in India for export to Europe. It is printed and glazed calico (a type of Indian cotton), and became popular for clothes in India and in Britain, where it was also used for furniture coverings. Different patterns were used on the cloth for the home market and the cloth for export, following the fashions of the time. The word 'chintz' comes from a Hindu word meaning 'spotted'.

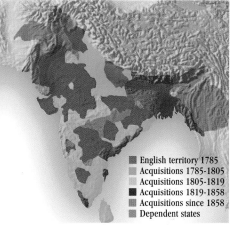

Indian cavalry of the British army fight a battle in Burma. There were three wars between Britain and Burma, in 1824–26, 1852 and 1885. Britain invaded Burma in order to protect the safety of India, but also because of greed for Burma's valuable natural resources of teak, oil and rubies.

■ English territory 1785
■ Acquisitions 1785-1805
■ Acquisitions 1805-1819
■ Acquisitions 1819-1858
■ Acquisitions since 1858
■ Dependent states

This map shows how the British expanded their rule over India. The British took over some states by force, while others were occupied when their rulers died and there was no obvious heir. The dependent states were governed by Indian princes who ruled with protection from British forces. Until 1947, India also included the countries of Pakistan and Bangladesh (which was East Pakistan until 1971).

Opium Wars

A pipe used to smoke opium. *Britain did not want to stop the use of opium. Instead they wanted to control its trade in Southeast Asia.*

Although China exported large amounts of tea and silk to countries in Europe, the Chinese government restricted imports. Foreign traders were allowed to do business in only one Chinese port, Guangzhou.

1839 Chinese officials seize opium from British merchants. Start of First Opium War (lasted until 1842).

1841 Guangzhou captured by British forces (24 May).

1842 Shanghai captured (19 June). Treaty of Nanjing (29 August). Hong Kong leased to Britain and five Chinese ports opened for foreign trade.

1856 Chinese seize British ship *Arrow* (October). Start of Second Opium War (lasted until 1860).

1858 Treaty of Tientsin.

1859 Construction of Suez Canal begins (25 April).

1860 British and French forces occupy Beijing. Treaty of Beijing (24 October).

1869 Opening of Suez Canal (17 November).

1875 British government buys shares in Suez Canal.

1882 British take control in Egypt.

1883 Sudanese defeat Egyptian army led by British commander.

1885 General Gordon is killed by Sudanese forces.

1888 International convention agrees that Suez Canal open to all nations.

The British steamship Nemesis attacked Chinese junks (sailing vessels) in 1841 during the First Opium War. Opium addiction became a problem in China in the 18th and 19th centuries. By 1890, it was estimated that about 80 per cent of all Chinese men used the drug.

British merchants tried to get round these restrictions by illegally importing opium from India into China. Although the dangers of opium were well known, the British government backed the merchants in their illegal trade. In 1839, Chinese officials seized all the opium stored in the British warehouses in Guangzhou. The First Opium War started in 1839 and ended with the British forcing a settlement on the Chinese in 1842. Under this treaty, Hong Kong became a British colony.

In 1856, the Second Opium War began. The British government wanted to extend its trading rights in China, and forced the Chinese to settle with the Treaty of Tientsin. When the Chinese tried to block this treaty, British and French troops occupied Beijing, the Chinese capital. In 1860, the Chinese signed the Treaty of Beijing in which they agreed to accept the terms of the Treaty of Tientsin.

Egypt and Sudan

The opening of the Suez Canal was important for trading nations in Europe. Instead of sailing around the southern tip of Africa, ships travelling between Europe and Asia could now take a short cut from the Mediterranean Sea to the Red Sea.

Benjamin Disraeli was prime minister in 1868 and again from 1874 to 1880. In 1875, he bought a large number of shares in the Suez Canal Company from the Khedive (viceroy) of Egypt, Isma'il Pasha. This purchase gave the British government a financial interest in the management of the canal.

The British government took no part in the canal's funding or construction. Nevertheless, the canal was vital for British trade. When political disturbances in Egypt threatened the canal, Britain quickly stepped in and took control of Egypt. In 1888, an international convention agreed that the canal should open for use by ships of all countries.

British rule in Egypt coincided with rebellion in neighbouring Sudan. Under their leader, the Mahdi, Sudanese rebels defeated an Egyptian army in 1883. Prime Minister Gladstone sent General Charles Gordon to oversee the withdrawal of Egyptian troops from Sudan. Gordon then tried to overthrow the Mahdi. By March 1884, he was besieged in Khartoum, and in 1885 Gordon was killed. Sudan came under British and Egyptian control in 1898.

The Sphinx and pyramids at Giza, just outside the Egyptian capital of Cairo. During the 19th century, European influence in Egypt increased as France and Britain competed to control the region. Egypt's importance was increased by the completion of the Suez Canal in 1869 which cut thousands of kilometres off the trade route between Europe and Asia.

The Scramble for Africa

A spiked helmet worn by British soldiers. European powers were desperate to control regions of Africa and the raw materials there. Thousands of troops were sent to the continent to defend these 'interests'.

Between 1880 and 1900, European nations took over most of the African continent. The activities of these 20 years have become known as the 'Scramble for Africa', as Europeans rushed to stake their claims and establish new colonies.

By the 1860s, France, Germany and the United States had all become successful industrial nations, threatening Britain's position as the leading power in both industry and trade. Across Europe, factories were producing cheap manufactured goods and European nations looked to Africa as a massive potential market in which to sell them. Europeans also believed that Africa was a source of valuable raw materials, such as rubber from the tropical forests. The discovery of diamonds and gold in southern Africa only added to these expectations.

In the late 1870s and early 1880s, several European nations laid claim to regions in Africa. The French and Belgians controlled much of the west, the Germans and British were interested in the east and south. To prevent conflict over their African ambitions, the European powers held a conference at Berlin, Germany, from 1884-5.

The Europeans decided how to divide up Africa without regard for African peoples and their cultures.

Henry Stanley and David Livingstone meet in 1871 at Ujiji on the shores of Lake Tanganyika. Stanley was a journalist who went to Africa to look for explorer Livingstone. When he found him, the story made headlines in newspapers all around the world.

1880 Leopold II, king of Belgium, claims a large area of the Congo as his own personal territory.

1882 British take control in Egypt.

1884–5 Berlin Conference. European countries negotiate over control of West Africa.

1885 Leopold II proclaims his personal territory the 'Congo Free State'.

1888 The British conquer the Matabele people and take their land (later Rhodesia, now Zimbabwe).

1889 British South Africa Company founded.

1890 Cecil Rhodes becomes prime minister of Cape Colony.

1891 British Protectorate in Nyasaland (present-day Malawi).

1894 Uganda becomes a British protectorate.

1895 Kenya becomes a British protectorate, called British East Africa.

1899 Start of Boer War.

DIAMONDS

Between 1869 and 1871, vast deposits of diamonds were discovered in the region of modern-day Kimberley in southern Africa. People flocked there from all over Africa, Europe, America and Australia. One immigrant was Cecil Rhodes, a Briton who made a fortune in the diamond fields. His company, De Beers, took over all of the mining operations at Kimberley.

After the Conference, the 'Scramble' began. The African people fought to defend their lands, but the invention of the Maxim-gun (a type of machine gun) gave European armies a major advantage over their African opponents. Many thousands of Africans died in the wars against European powers.

By the beginning of the 20th century, almost all of Africa was ruled by seven European nations – Britain, France, Germany, Spain, Portugal, Belgium and Italy.

The British advance against the Zulus in southern Africa in 1879. *The Zulu army, under its leader Cetewayo, defeated the British army at Isandhlwana, killing 1,700 British soldiers. However, the Zulus were then defeated at Rorke's Drift.*

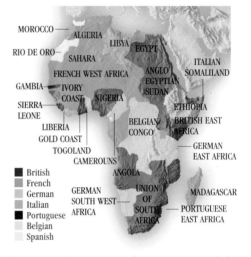

The map of Africa in 1914, *after European nations had established colonies in almost every region. The only two remaining independent countries were Ethiopia and Liberia.*

The exploration of Africa by Europeans in the 19th century *marked a turning point in African history as European nations scrambled to claim their 'share' of the continent.*

159

War in South Africa

1836–44 'Great Trek' northwards of the Boers.

1854 Boers form Orange Free State.

1857 Boer Republic established in Transvaal.

1869 onwards Discovery of diamonds near Kimberley.

1877 Britain annexes Transvaal.

1880 Boers proclaim their independence.

1881 British defeated at Battle of Majuba (27 February). Convention of Pretoria (5 April) restores the independence of Transvaal.

1886 Gold discovered in Witwatersrand.

1897 Paul Kruger signs military alliance with Orange Free State.

1899 War is declared between Britain and the Boer alliance (October). The Boers besiege the towns of Ladysmith, Mafeking and Kimberley.

1900 Reinforcements arrive from Britain and end sieges of Kimberley and Ladysmith (February). End of siege in Mafeking (May). Boer capital captured (June).

1902 Treaty of Vereeniging.

Cape Colony, the largest European settlement in Africa, came under British rule in 1806. Most of the colonists were descendants of Dutch farmers, known as Boers. Many Boers quickly came to dislike the new administration and in the 1830s, thousands of them started a long trek northwards, known as the 'Great Trek'. They founded two Boer states: the Orange Free State and a Boer Republic in the Transvaal region.

This map shows two Boer States: the Orange Free State and a state in the Transvaal.

A Zulu shield. Prior to European expansion in the 19th century, the Zulus controlled a large empire covering much of southern Africa under the leadership of Shaka.

A diamond mine in southern Africa. The mines were owned by European companies, and many used slave labour.

Zulu troops attack British soldiers. When the Boers trekked northwards in the 1830s, they moved into traditional Zulu homelands. The Boers attempted to set up a republic in Natal, but they were defeated by the Zulus. In the 1870s, Zulus, under the leadership of Cetewayo, organized an army to defend against British incursions. After initial victories, the Zulus were finally defeated at Ulundi and Zululand was annexed in 1887.

In the 1870s the British government tried to persuade the Boers to unite its states with the British colonies (Cape Colony and Natal). The British not only wanted to increase their power in southern Africa, they also wanted a share of the diamond deposits that were coming to light along the Vaal River, particularly around Kimberley. When British troops were sent to force the Boers to accept these proposals, the Boers fought back. The British were defeated at the Battle of Majuba in 1881.

In 1886, major gold deposits were discovered in the Transvaal. Britain feared the growing power and wealth of the Boer states and war broke out again in 1899. The Boer armies attacked the British settlements at Ladysmith, Mafeking and Kimberley. It was not until reinforcements arrived in early 1900 that these sieges ended. The British went on to capture Pretoria, the capital of Transvaal. By mid-1900, there were about 250,000 British troops in southern Africa compared to only 30,000 Boer soldiers. Yet the Boers continued to fight a guerrilla war, attacking the British in raids. The British retaliated by burning Boer farms, and women and children were put in concentration camps. The conditions were appalling, and over 40,000 people died from disease. The Boers finally surrendered to the British and signed the Treaty of Vereeniging in 1902.

Thousands of Boer farmers trekked northwards from Cape Colony in southern Africa in the late 1830s and early 1840s, in what became known as the 'Great Trek'. The Boers left in rebellion against British rule.

The Modern Age

As the 20th century dawned, Queen Victoria was in her 63rd year on the throne. Despite competition from other imperial powers, Britain remained at the centre of the largest empire the world has ever known – covering over one-fifth of the planet's land surface. Motor cars were still an unusual sight on the streets of Britain. Most British men could vote, but the right to vote was denied to women. As the century progressed, many things were to change.

p168 A British Sopwith Camel fighter aircraft from World War I.

p194 Countries in Europe join together to form the European Union (EU).

p190 Compact discs and DVDs can store huge amounts of information, such as music and movies.

p189 Margaret Thatcher was prime minister from 1979 to 1990.

p198 Technological advances such as the laptop computer have revolutionized the ways we live and work.

The first shock was the death of Victoria in January 1901. She was succeeded by her elderly son, Edward. The 'Edwardian era' is often regarded as an idyllic time – the 'calm before the storm' of World War I. In fact, the prewar years were a time of political uncertainty and social unrest, and they seem peaceful only in comparison with the terrible carnage that followed.

The 20th century will be remembered for its two terrible world wars. During the four years of World War I, from 1914 to 1918, over 900,000 soldiers of the British empire died. After the horrors of this slaughter, people hoped that World War I would be the 'war to end all wars', but the rise of Fascism in Germany and other parts of Europe eventually sparked off World War II in 1939. For six years Britain and its allies fought against Germany and the Axis powers, including Italy and Japan. This war spread around the globe.

In the second half of the century, Britain gave up most of its empire, and was no longer a world power of the first rank. It joined the European Union, as ties with the evolving Commonwealth weakened. British society became multicultural, with the immigration of people from the Caribbean, Asia and Africa.

Scotland and Wales gained their own parliamentary assemblies, while in Northern Ireland a peace agreement towards the close of the century brought hope of an end to the long years of troubles there. As the 21st century began, Britain was greatly altered, yet still a rich and creative nation with much to offer the world.

p197 The remains of a London bus destroyed by an explosion during the terrorist attacks of 7 July, 2005. Three suicide bombers attacked the underground system and a fourth blew himself up on this bus. In total, 56 people were killed in the attacks.

p180 The Battle of Britain was fought between the Royal Air Force (RAF) and the German airforce, the Luftwaffe.

Edwardian Britain

Only three weeks after celebrating New Year in 1901, people were mourning the death of Queen Victoria, who died on 22 January. She was succeeded by her son, Edward.

1901 Death of Queen Victoria. Succeeded by Edward VII (22 January). Start of Edwardian era.

1903 Edward VII visits Paris and encourages more friendly relations with France.

1904 *Entente Cordiale* between Britain and France (April).

1906 Labour Party formed.

1909 Lloyd George's 'People's Budget' rejected by House of Lords. Trade Boards fix wages in low-paid industries.

1910 Death of King Edward VII. Succeeded by George V. Strike by miners in South Wales lasts 10 months.

1911 Parliament Act passes through House of Lords, abolishing Lords' power of veto (August).

1912 Strike by miners in support of national minimum wage.

1914 Start of World War I.

The fun-loving King Edward VII was hugely popular. His favourite activities were racing, sailing and shooting and he had a wide social circle both in Britain and on the continent. His willingness to speak French was put to good use when he visited Paris in 1903 and prepared the ground for the *Entente Cordiale* ('Friendly Relationship') which was signed between Britain and France in 1904.

Edward was king not only of the United Kingdom, but also of the world's biggest empire. Despite the wealth and power that the empire continued to bring, there were some concerns about Britain's world position. Several countries that had industrialized later than Britain were now threatening British trade – the USA and Germany, in particular. Worse, Germany was building a navy to rival Britain's. In response, the government ordered the construction of several new and up-to-date warships, called dreadnoughts.

For rich people, life in the first decade of the 20th century was good. The wealthy enjoyed their money openly, with fine food, large houses staffed with servants, and a social life based around their favourite outdoor pursuits. However, the gap between rich and poor was huge.

King Edward VII and Queen Alexandra at the king's coronation in 1902. *Alexandra was the eldest daughter of the king of Denmark. She and Edward had married in 1863.*

Edwardian schools were often run by clergymen, *sometimes helped by their wives who acted as matrons. Academic subjects such as reading, writing and mathematics were taught, along with a stern respect for the Church and British empire.*

An Edwardian corset.
The fashion of the day called for narrow waists that were held in place by stiff whale bones in the corset and by tying the corset together tightly at the back.

Alexandra Palace, built in 1875, was named after the Princess of Wales. *Its concert hall, containing one of the largest organs in the world, could seat 14,000 people. It burned down just days after opening and had to be completely rebuilt.*

A tiny minority of people enjoyed this affluent lifestyle – one estimate is that 13 per cent of the population owned 92 per cent of the wealth at that time. For the poor of the country, the story was rather different.

In 1901, the manufacturer Seebohm Rowntree published a report called *Poverty: A Study of Town Life*. It was the result of his own investigations into poor households in York and it showed that even in a small cathedral city, many people lived in desperate conditions. Rowntree found that 28 per cent of adults could not afford enough food to keep themselves healthy, and that 40 per cent of children suffered illness and stunted growth from lack of food. A similar survey on a much larger scale was carried out by Charles Booth in London. He collected information over a period of 17 years, publishing his report in 1903.

Social and Political Change

1906 Education Act to provide free school meals for poor.

1907 Education Act to provide medical inspections in schools.

1908 Coal Mines Act fixes working day to eight hours. Old Age Pensions Act introduces pensions for first time.

1909 Labour Exchanges Act to help people find work. Lloyd George's 'People's Budget' is rejected by the House of Lords.

1910 Death of King Edward VII. Succeeded by George V. First trade union strikes.

1911 National Insurance Act to provide insurance against sickness and unemployment. Parliament Act limits powers of the House of Lords.

1912 Sinking of the *Titanic*.

1914 Plans for a 'Triple Alliance'. Outbreak of World War I.

David Lloyd George (1863–1945) was born in Pembrokeshire, Wales. He became Liberal MP for Caernarvon in 1890, a seat he kept for 55 years.

The work of Seebohm Rowntree in York and Charles Booth in London focused public attention on poverty in Britain. As a result of these and other reports, the period from 1906 until the outbreak of war in 1914 saw the introduction of laws that formed the basis of the welfare state.

In 1906, the Liberal Party won 84 seats more than any other party in the general election and introduced a programme of welfare. The two ministers most active in these reforms were David Lloyd George and Winston Churchill. Their ideas were not new – Germany already had a system of old-age pensions and national insurance against unemployment and sickness.

They started in 1906 with an act that gave free school meals for poor children. This was followed by other measures including medical inspections in schools and pensions for the poorest people.

In 1908, the Coal Mines Act limited the working day of a miner to eight hours. Nevertheless, miners in South Wales went on strike for ten months in 1910. When the government sent in troops to help the police, there were riots. The miners went on strike again in 1912.

The Boy Scout Movement was founded in 1908 by Robert Baden-Powell, a cavalry officer who wrote a book entitled Scouting for Boys.

*The Titanic **sinks in the early hours of 15 April, 1912,** after hitting an iceberg about 640 kilometres south of Newfoundland. There were not enough lifeboats to accommodate all the passengers and crew and about 1,500 people drowned.*

In 1909, Lloyd George read out the details of his 'People's Budget' in the House of Commons. He wanted to tax the rich more heavily, in order to pay for the fight against 'poverty and squalidness'. Conservative MPs complained, but they did not have enough power in the House of Commons to defeat the budget. However, the budget was thrown out by the House of Lords. The Liberals called and won a general election, forcing the Lords to back down. The Liberals were now determined to go further. With the support of the new king, George V, they forced the Lords to pass the Parliament Act which limited the powers of the Lords.

Throughout the 1900s, membership of trade unions grew steadily. Workers' demands for better conditions and pay resulted in a series of strikes between 1910 and 1912. In 1914, three of the main unions agreed to work together to form a powerful 'Triple Alliance'. However, their plans were interrupted by the outbreak of war.

MOVIEMAKING

Cinema started when Auguste and Louis Lumière showed their films to an audience in Paris in 1895. The first purpose-built cinema opened in Britain in 1907. Early films had no soundtrack. The Italian actor Rudolph Valentino, shown below, was one of the biggest stars of these films, known as 'silent movies'.

World War I

In June 1914, Archduke Franz Ferdinand and his wife Sophie visited the Austrian-Hungarian province of Bosnia. On 28 June, they were assassinated in the streets of the capital, Sarajevo. Their deaths sparked the outbreak of World War I.

28 June, 1914
Assassination of Archduke Franz Ferdinand of Austria at Sarajevo.

July 1914 Austria-Hungary declares war on Serbia.

August 1914 Germany invades Belgium. Austria-Hungary invades Russia. Britain declares war on Germany and Austria-Hungary.

September 1914 First Battle of the Marne.

November 1914 Britain declares war on the Ottoman empire. First Battle of Ypres.

April 1915 Allied troops (mainly Australian, New Zealander and Indian) land at Gallipoli.

May 1915 Second Battle of Ypres. Germans use poison gas for the first time. German submarine sinks British liner *Lusitania*. Over 1,000 people drown including 128 Americans: USA protests but does not enter war. Italy enters war on side of the Allies.

The Archduke was assassinated by a Serbian terrorist who was protesting about Austrian-Hungarian rule in Bosnia. This caused Austria-Hungary to declare war on Serbia on 28 July. Germany supported Austria-Hungary's action, but Russia promised to defend Serbia, and France backed Russia. Germany declared war on Russia and France and the German army marched through Belgium and into France. The German aim was to defeat France quickly with a rapid dash to encircle Paris, before turning around and attacking Russia to the east. However, the German invasion of the neutral country of Belgium brought Great Britain into the war on 4 August.

The pressures that led to war had been building up for years, with increasing rivalry between the various countries of Europe. They competed for industrial power, control of trade, and also for control of the many colonies around the globe. Germany had built up a strong, well-trained army and a navy containing some of the most powerful war machines of the day – battleships. Other European nations felt threatened and rapidly expanded their own military forces.

World War I was the first war in which aeroplanes were widely used. They were first used to spy on enemy trenches and later in air combat and bombing raids. Different types of aircraft were designed for different roles, from large bombers to fast and agile fighters. This Sopwith Camel flew with the Royal Flying Corps and was a fighter, designed to shoot down other aircraft.

In an attempt to increase their security, several countries made agreements to support each other. Germany, Austria-Hungary and Italy formed the Triple Alliance, promising to go to war in the case of an attack. France, Russia and Great Britain had a similar agreement, called the Triple Entente. After the outbreak of war, Germany and Austria-Hungary were known as the Central Powers. The nations who fought against the Central Powers were known as the Allies.

In 1914, the Germans were confident of victory on the Western Front in France. They wanted to defeat France quickly, but the Allies blocked their advance. By November 1914, neither side could gain any advantage on the Western Front. The deadlock lasted for over three years.

KITCHENER'S ARMIES

This poster was intended to encourage men to sign up as volunteers at the beginning of World War I. It features war minister Lord Kitchener with the caption "You are the man I want". Kitchener expected a long war, and he organized the enlisting of thousands of untrained volunteers, into what were known as 'Kitchener's armies'.

A British dreadnought battleship.
HMS Dreadnought *was a new type of battleship, built for the British navy in 1906. By 1914, the British navy had 22 dreadnoughts.*

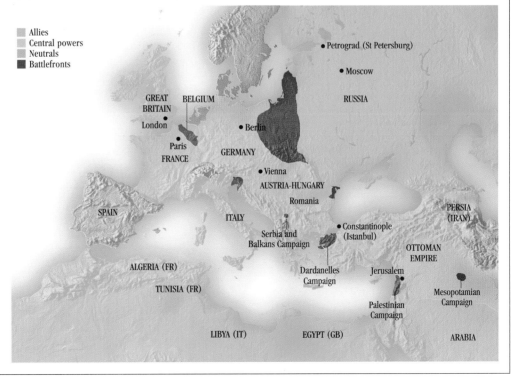

This map shows neutral countries, and the groupings of Allies and Central Powers. It also shows the main battlefronts, including the Western Front. The war on the Eastern Front between Russia and the Central powers was more mobile than on the Western Front and covered a far greater area. There were also several attempts to open other fronts against the Central Powers. These included the Dardanelles Campaign as well as the campaigns in the Middle East.

Allies
Central powers
Neutrals
Battlefronts

Petrograd (St Petersburg)

Moscow

GREAT BRITAIN
BELGIUM
RUSSIA
London
Berlin
Paris
GERMANY
FRANCE
Vienna
AUSTRIA-HUNGARY
Romania
PERSIA (IRAN)
SPAIN
ITALY
Constantinople (Istanbul)
Serbia and Balkans Campaign
OTTOMAN EMPIRE
ALGERIA (FR)
Dardanelles Campaign
Jerusalem
TUNISIA (FR)
Mesopotamian Campaign
Palestinian Campaign
LIBYA (IT)
EGYPT (GB)
ARABIA

Life in the Trenches

January 1916 Evacuation from Gallipoli. Over 250,000 Allied troops wounded or killed.

January 1916 Conscription introduced in Britain.

5 June, 1916 Lord Kitchener, British secretary of state for war, is drowned when the ship he is on, *HMS Hampshire*, hits a German mine.

July–November 1916 Battle of the Somme. Over 400,000 British soldiers die.

December 1916 David Lloyd George becomes prime minster.

April 1917 USA declares war on Germany. Revolution in Russia. Battle of Vimy Ridge.

December 1917 Over 300,000 British and Canadian soldiers die. Russia signs an armistice with Germany.

A British soldier's helmet. *Soldiers on both sides had to endure terrible conditions in the trenches, especially during the winter when the cold and rain turned the ground into mud.*

By the end of 1914, the Western Front stretched over 700 kilometres from the English Channel to Switzerland. Thousands of Allied and German troops had dug themselves into parallel lines of trenches.

Trench warfare was a result of the power of modern weapons, which made it too dangerous to fight a battle on open ground. For over three years, Allied and German soldiers attacked each other from their own trenches, often gaining only a few metres of ground at a time. The numbers of dead were horrific. For example, on the first day of the Battle of the Somme in 1916, 57,000 British soldiers were either killed or wounded.

The Western Front was only one of the battle zones of World War I. The Russians attacked the Central Powers along the Eastern Front, which ran the length of the Russian border with Germany and Austria-Hungary. In 1914, the Ottoman empire (Turkey) joined the Central Powers. Italy joined the war in 1915 on the side of the Allies.

TE Lawrence (1888–1935) *became known as 'Lawrence of Arabia'. In 1916, he was involved in the Arab revolt against the Turks. He wrote an account of the revolt in his book* The Seven Pillars of Wisdom.

A cross-section drawing of a trench. *Trenches were lined with sandbags and protected by rolls of barbed wire which lay in the area between the two sets of trenches, known as 'no man's land'.*

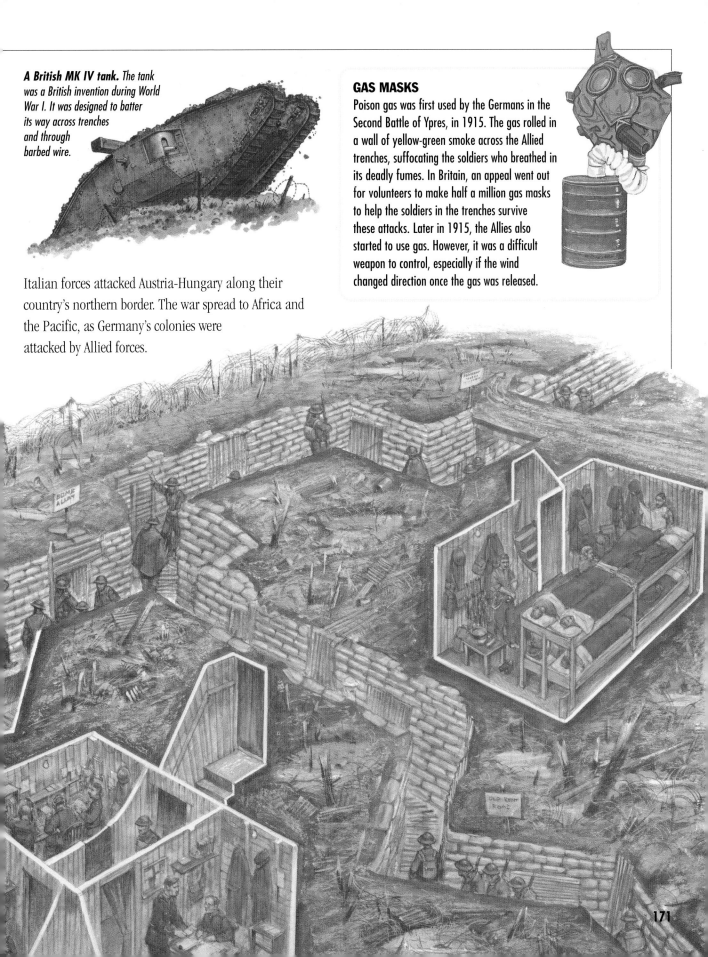

A British MK IV tank. *The tank was a British invention during World War I. It was designed to batter its way across trenches and through barbed wire.*

GAS MASKS

Poison gas was first used by the Germans in the Second Battle of Ypres, in 1915. The gas rolled in a wall of yellow-green smoke across the Allied trenches, suffocating the soldiers who breathed in its deadly fumes. In Britain, an appeal went out for volunteers to make half a million gas masks to help the soldiers in the trenches survive these attacks. Later in 1915, the Allies also started to use gas. However, it was a difficult weapon to control, especially if the wind changed direction once the gas was released.

Italian forces attacked Austria-Hungary along their country's northern border. The war spread to Africa and the Pacific, as Germany's colonies were attacked by Allied forces.

The Armistice

At the start of World War I, the US had declared itself to be a neutral country. However, the sinking of the British ship the *Lusitania* in 1915 and other similar attacks against civilians drew American support for the Allies. The US declared war on Germany in 1917.

In 1918, the German forces launched a series of attacks to try to crush the Allies before the Americans arrived in force. In July and August, at the Second Battle of the Marne, the Allies and Germans fought over the same ground as in 1914, to the east of Paris. However, this time American soldiers helped the Allies to push the Germans back. By October it had become clear that Germany was on the point of collapse. The British naval blockade had led to severe food shortages and the German people were starving. There were riots and demands for peace. On 11 November, 1918, the Germans accepted the Allies' peace terms and the war ended.

The announcement of peace was greeted with euphoria in London, as large crowds gathered outside Buckingham Palace. But it was impossible to forget the terrible cost of the war – over 900,000 soldiers from the British empire had died, and the death toll for all the countries involved in World War I was over 8.5 million. People hoped that this was the 'war to end all wars'.

1918 US President Woodrow Wilson sets out war aims in 'The Fourteen Points'. Germany launches its final attacks against the Allies. The Allies begin final attack against the Germans (August). Bulgaria surrenders (29 September). Ottoman empire (Turkey) signs armistice (October). Austria-Hungary signs an armistice (3 November). Germany signs an armistice ending World War I (11 November).

1919 Paris Peace Conference. Peace settlement and agreement to set up a League of Nations (January). Treaty of Versailles signed by Germany (June).

1920 Treaty of Trianon signed by Hungary. Treaty of Sèvres signed by Ottoman empire (August).

A map of the 'New' Europe after the Treaty of Versailles. Austria-Hungary was broken up into smaller states, such as Yugoslavia, Czechoslovakia and Hungary.

In January 1919, members of the Allied countries met in Paris to agree a settlement. The US president, Woodrow Wilson, had already drawn up a plan, known as the 'Fourteen Points'. Although France and Britain refused to accept many of these points, they did agree to set up an organization called the League of Nations. The aim of this League was to prevent another similar worldwide conflict by settling international disputes by diplomacy and agreement. It was later replaced by the United Nations, after World War II in 1946.

In June 1919, the agreements made in Paris were accepted by Germany in the Treaty of Versailles. All the other Central Powers signed separate treaties. Under the Treaty of Versailles, Germany was forced to accept responsibility for starting the war and to pay reparations (compensation for war damages) to the Allied countries. Germany also lost territory to various European countries. The ending of World War I completely redrew the map of Europe, as boundaries changed and new countries emerged out of the old empires.

In January 1919, the Allied war leaders, President Woodrow Wilson (centre), Georges Clemenceau (left) and David Lloyd George (right) met in Paris to end the war formally.

By the end of World War I the trenches had claimed over 900,000 lives of British empire soldiers. Many vowed that this was a war to end all wars.

Anglo-Irish Relations

1905 Sinn Fein, meaning 'Ourselves Alone', founded by Arthur Griffiths with policy of non-cooperation with British.

1912 Third Irish Home Rule Bill introduced in parliament. Ulster Volunteers formed to fight against Home Rule.

1913 Home Rule bill rejected by House of Lords. Irish nationalists form Irish Nationalist Volunteers (later Irish Republican Army, or IRA).

1916 Easter Rising by Irish nationalists put down by British troops. Execution of leaders sparks off anti-British feeling.

1917 Eamon de Valera becomes leader of Sinn Fein.

1918 73 Sinn Fein MPs elected.

1919 Sinn Fein MPs set up a parliament 'Dáil' in Dublin. Clashes between British troops and the IRA.

1920 'Bloody Sunday': IRA gunmen kill 14 in Dublin.

1921 Signing of Anglo-Irish Treaty. Civil war breaks out.

1923 Republicans accept the treaty.

1932 Southern Ireland renamed Eire.

1949 Ireland Act recognizes Eire as an independent republic and confirms Northern Ireland as part of United Kingdom. Republic of Ireland leaves Commonwealth.

At the beginning of the 20th century, the issue of Irish independence from Britain was still unresolved. After two defeats in the 1880s and '90s, a third Home Rule bill was introduced in the British parliament in 1912, but its passage was interrupted by World War I.

This map shows Ireland after 1923. *Three of the nine counties of Ulster became part of the Irish Free State. The other six remained part of the United Kingdom.*

Not all Irish people supported Home Rule. It was backed by Irish Catholics who believed that Ireland should have its own parliament in Dublin. Irish Protestants, who were in the majority in the province of Ulster, were opposed to Home Rule. In 1912 and 1913, both sides formed armed organizations: those against Home Rule set up the Ulster Volunteers and the nationalists formed the Irish Nationalist Volunteers, later the Irish Republican Army (IRA).

The start of war in 1914 prevented a crisis over the Home Rule issue, but in 1916, nationalist protestors seized buildings in Dublin and proclaimed Ireland a republic. The British government sent in troops and bombarded the rebels with artillery until they surrendered. Most Irish people disapproved of the rebels' actions. But when the British arrested and imprisoned suspects without trial, and then executed 15 of the republican leaders, public opinion quickly changed. The rebels of the 'Easter Rising' were seen as heroes. In 1918, the republican movement, Sinn Fein, won 73 seats in the general election. However, Sinn Fein's MPs refused to take their seats at Westminster.

BLACK AND TANS

The British soldiers sent to Ireland to help the Royal Irish Constabulary in 1920–21 were known as the 'black and tans' because of the colour of their uniform. They were hated by the Irish because of their ruthless attacks in revenge for IRA actions.

The Easter Rising in 1916 was led by Patrick Pearse and involved about 1,600 nationalists. They believed that Ireland would only become a republic by force. Pearse took over the Post Office as his headquarters, and barricades were set up in the Dublin streets with British soldiers on one side and republicans on the other.

Instead, they declared Ireland a republic and set up a parliament, called the Dáil Eirann, which was based in Dublin.

This started three years of fighting between the Royal Irish Constabulary, backed by British troops, and the IRA. In July 1921, British Prime Minister Lloyd George proposed a compromise in which the 26 counties of southern Ireland would become a dominion within the British empire, known as the Irish Free State. The Dáil approved the Anglo-Irish Treaty in 1921. This led to more civil war, between the Republicans who wanted independence, and the 'Free Staters'. A ceasefire was called in 1923 when the Republicans, led by Eamon de Valera, accepted the treaty. By 1949, Eire (Southern Ireland) had become an independent republic. The six counties of Northern Ireland remained within the United Kingdom.

Michael Collins (1890–1922) took part in the Easter Rising in 1916. He was one of the 73 Sinn Fein MPs elected in 1918, and he was leader of the IRA during the troubles of 1920–21. He signed the Anglo-Irish Treaty believing it was the best deal for Ireland. The following year he was assassinated.

The Custom House in Dublin. In 1921, it was burned down by the IRA to destroy the public tax records stored there.

Strike and Depression

A tram from the 1920s.
The general strike of 1926 brought the country's transport network to a standstill.

On 3 May, 1926, the Trades Union Congress (TUC) called a general strike in support of the miners. Over two-and-a-half million men and women, including transport workers, gas and electricity workers, and printers joined the one million miners who were already locked out of work. The strike lasted for nine days.

The immediate cause of the strike was the mine owners' demands that workers should accept lower pay and longer working hours. There were problems in the British mining industry. Foreign mines produced coal more efficiently and cheaply than British suppliers. Demand for coal was declining because of a new fuel – oil. To make matters worse, the government returned Britain to the gold standard. This was a way of fixing the value of the pound to a set amount of gold. However, the effect was to make British exports more expensive – and therefore even less competitive abroad. To try to avert a strike, the government commissioned a report on the mining industry.

During the Depression, soup kitchens were set up in many towns and cities to feed the hungry. Britain was not the only country hit by the Depression. Millions of people in the USA lost their jobs and were forced to rely on government hand-outs and charity for survival.

Despite the government's attempts, the country was still brought to a standstill by the general strike. Troops were ordered to do the strikers' work. After nine days, the TUC called off the strike leaving the miners to fight on alone. Eventually, the miners were forced to accept their employers' demands.

Even though the strikers were back at work, the problems of British industry remained. Britain was still paying off massive debts from World War I. In 1929, there was a financial crisis in the US, and many banks, businesses and individuals were ruined. Americans no longer had enough money to buy goods from abroad and, as demand fell, more people lost their jobs. In 1931–32, the number of unemployed people in Britain reached almost three million.

The regions hardest hit by the Depression of the 1930s were the industrial areas in the north of England, South Wales, Scotland and Northern Ireland. In some towns, over half the workforce was out of work. Despite 'dole' money paid to the unemployed, people suffered severe hardships. The 1920s and '30s saw many protest marches to London to draw attention to the plight of the hungry unemployed.

The mines were dangerous places – thousands of miners were killed each year. Many more suffered from severe health problems as a result of their work. Even before the general strike in 1926, there was a long history of miners' strikes about pay and working conditions.

The Jarrow Crusade on the road to London. *In 1936, 200 unemployed men set off from Jarrow in the northeast of England to take a petition to parliament. More than two-thirds of the workforce was out of work in Jarrow, and the men wanted new industry to open in the town. The petition was presented to parliament by the marchers' MP, Ellen Wilkinson.*

Strikers on a protest march during the general strike. *The government said that the strike was an attempt by the unions, led by the TUC, to take over the running of the country. The government printed its views in a newspaper called the British Gazette.*

Votes for Women

1903 Emmeline Pankhurst and her daughters Christabel and Sylvia found Women's Social and Political Union (WSPU).

1905 Christabel Pankhurst and Annie Kenney become the first suffragettes to be sent to prison.

1908 About 500,000 women attend suffrage demonstration in London.

1909 Over 100 suffragettes arrested while trying to meet the prime minister.

1911 Suffragette riots in West End of London.

1913 Emily Davison throws herself under the king's horse at the Derby. She dies from her injuries.

1918 Vote given to women over 30, if they are rate payers or wives of rate payers.

1928 Vote given to all women over 21.

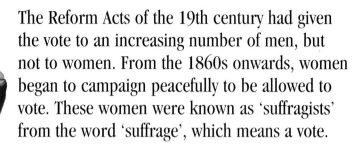

Emmeline Pankhurst is arrested during a suffragette demonstration. The slogan of the WSPU was 'Deeds not Words', and the suffragettes' tactics included actions such as disrupting public meetings and damaging property.

The Reform Acts of the 19th century had given the vote to an increasing number of men, but not to women. From the 1860s onwards, women began to campaign peacefully to be allowed to vote. These women were known as 'suffragists' from the word 'suffrage', which means a vote.

In 1903, Emmeline Pankhurst and her daughters Christabel and Sylvia decided that peaceful means were not sufficient. They set up the Women's Social and Political Union (WSPU), aiming to use direct militant action to get publicity. Their campaign started in 1905 when Christabel and another member of the WSPU, Annie Kenney, shouted suffrage slogans at a meeting where the foreign secretary was speaking. They were arrested and imprisoned. The militant campaigners of the WSPU became known as 'suffragettes'.

The suffragettes continued their campaign until the outbreak of war in 1914. They were often arrested and badly treated by the police. In prison, some suffragettes went on hunger strike and were forcibly fed. If they became too ill to stay in prison they were released, but were re-arrested once they had recovered. During World War I, the suffragettes stopped their violent actions and engaged in war work. Women took men's places in industry and trade. In 1918, they also got the vote.

Many women campaigned peacefully for the vote and disapproved of the violent methods of the WSPU. Women were eventually given the vote in two stages, in 1918 and 1928.

Abdication

The abdication of Edward VIII threw the British monarchy into a deep crisis.

'I have found it impossible to carry on the heavy burden of responsibility and to discharge the duties of king as I would wish to do without the help and support of the woman I love.'

George VI and his wife, Elizabeth. George reigned from 1936, through the dark days of World War II (1939–45) until his death in 1952. He was succeeded by his eldest daughter, Elizabeth II.

With these words, King Edward VIII became the only British monarch ever to abdicate (resign) from the throne voluntarily. In the early 1930s, he had met and fallen in love with an American called Wallis Simpson. Mrs Simpson had been married twice and divorced once. When her divorce to her second husband came through, the king was determined to marry her. However, the king was the head of the Church of England, which opposed divorce. George V died in January 1936 and was succeeded by the Prince of Wales as Edward VIII.

The prime minister of the day, Stanley Baldwin, advised the new king that he could not marry Mrs Simpson and remain on the throne. On 10 December, 1936, Edward made his choice and abdicated in order to marry Mrs Simpson.

His place was taken by his brother, who became King George VI. Edward became Duke of Windsor and he married Mrs Simpson in 1937. The Duke and Duchess of Windsor spent the rest of their lives in exile abroad, living mainly in France.

'High society' encompassed a fashionable and glamorous circle of people. Women particularly had a new freedom, and displayed this in their appearance. Hair was worn bobbed (short) and instead of accentuating curves, clothing was designed to disguise them, creating a boyish appearance. People of society enjoyed a whirl of cocktail parties and foreign holidays and, as Prince of Wales, Edward moved in this world.

World War II

Many people had hoped that World War I had been the 'war to end all wars'. But the peace settlements drawn up by the victorious nations in 1919 were the start of a whole new set of problems that led, eventually, to the outbreak of an even more vicious and destructive worldwide war.

1933 Hitler becomes Chancellor of Germany.

1936 Germany occupies the Rhineland, defying terms of Treaty of Versailles.

1938 Germany occupies Austria.

1939 Germany occupies much of Czechoslovakia. Germany invades Poland. Britain and France declare war on Germany.

9 April, 1940 Germany invades Denmark and Norway.

May 1940 Germany invades Belgium and the Netherlands. Italy declares war on France. British troops evacuate France.

22 June 1940 France signs armistice with Germany.

July–September 1940 Battle of Britain.

September–October 1940 'Blitz' in London. German air raids on Coventry.

Many children were evacuated from major towns and cities and taken to live in the country to avoid the bombing.

The 1920s and '30s saw the growth in many European countries of a movement called fascism. In Germany, support quickly grew for the fascist Nazi Party, which promised strong leadership and to restore national pride. In 1933, the Nazi Party, under its leader Adolf Hitler, was declared to be the only political party in Germany and took control of government.

Hitler began to build up the German armed forces and to reclaim the territories lost by Germany after World War I. This was in defiance of the Treaty of Versailles, but the League of Nations was too weak to stop Hitler's aggression. When Hitler tried to occupy part of Czechoslovakia, the Czechs turned to their allies for help. In 1938, Hitler promised the British prime minister, Neville Chamberlain, in the Munich Agreement that this was the last of his demands. Chamberlain wanted to avoid war at all costs, so he and the French prime minister forced Czechoslovakia to accept Hitler's wishes.

The Battle of Britain was fought between the Royal Air Force (RAF) and the German airforce, the Luftwaffe. The British used a radar system that warned of approaching German planes.

Neville Chamberlain, the British prime minister, waves a copy of the Munich Agreement. Chamberlain believed he had negotiated 'peace for our time'.

However, in March 1939, Germany took the whole of Czechoslovakia and threatened Poland. Britain guaranteed to help Poland if its independence was threatened. Hitler invaded Poland on 1 September, 1939; France and Britain declared war two days later.

The Germans swept through Poland, Denmark, Norway, Belgium, the Netherlands and France. The Allied forces of Britain and France were trapped by this invasion and had to evacuate their troops from the French port of Dunkerque across the English Channel. Next, Hitler planned his invasion of Britain. First of all he needed to gain control of the skies and to defeat the British airforce. The Battle of Britain began in July 1940.

Hitler at a Nazi rally *in Nuremberg in 1938.*
The rise of fascism affected other countries as well as Germany, including Italy and Spain.

SWASTIKA
The swastika is an ancient symbol which is used by Hindus and Buddhists as a mark of good fortune. However, the swastika was reversed and adopted by the Nazis as their symbol. It quickly came to stand for all the horrors of the Nazi regime.

The Home Front

Winston Churchill, the British prime minister, became a focal point for rallying propaganda.

1941 Lend-Lease Act signed by US President Roosevelt.

May 1941 German invasion of USSR begins.

June 1941 Germany invades Greece and Yugoslavia.

December 1941 Royal Navy sinks German battleship the *Bismarck*. Britain and United States agree Atlantic Charter pledging world freedom. Japanese attack US fleet in Pearl Harbor. Allies declare war on Japan. Germany and Italy declare war on USA.

1942 'United Nations' declare they will not make separate peace with Axis.

30 May, 1942 Allied bombing of Cologne.

August 1942 Battle for Stalingrad begins.

1943 Roosevelt and Churchill agree to accept only unconditional surrender of Axis. German troops surrender in Stalingrad. Allies invade Sicily. Italy surrenders to Allies.

The Battle of Britain came to an end in September 1940, when the Germans turned their attention to bombing civilian targets in London and other major cities. This was the beginning of the 'Blitz'. The Germans hoped to weaken the morale of the British public and force a surrender.

Starting on 7 September, 1940, London was bombed every night for 58 nights. The wail of the air-raid sirens would send people running for cover in air-raid shelters, or in the deep tunnels of the underground railway. Every day, hundreds of Londoners died in the raids and thousands more were injured. The Blitz also destroyed cities such as Portsmouth, Coventry and Liverpool. However, British fighters continued to shoot down the German bombers and, by the end of 1940, it was clear that the Germans could not control the skies. The invasion of Britain was postponed indefinitely.

Later in the war, Allied bombers made massive bombing attacks on German cities. The first raid was on Cologne in May 1942 when 900 Allied bombers battered the city. By the end of the war many German cities were reduced to rubble and many thousands of civilians had been killed by Allied bombing.

Unlike World War I, which was mainly fought by soldiers, World War II involved the whole civilian population. Many children were evacuated from cities and away from the Blitz, to live in safer country areas. Some were even sent abroad.

Women workers in a munitions (arms) factory. During the war, women took the place of men who had been called up to the armed forces. Women worked in all sort of jobs – for example, on the railways, in shipyards and in aircraft factories.

The Land Army was the name given to the thousands of women who went to work in the country, harvesting crops on farms to ensure that a supply of food was available to the civilian population.

Food rationing was introduced on 8 January, 1940. People were also encouraged to grow their own fruit and vegetables. Clothes were rationed from 1941. Throughout the war, Britain depended for its survival on supplies brought across the Atlantic Ocean from North America. German submarines (U-boats) were a constant threat. The Allies organized convoys of cargo ships that were escorted and protected by naval ships. Radar and sonar were also used to detect submarines. By the middle of 1943, many U-boats had been detected and destroyed.

The American B-17 bomber *was also known as the 'Flying Fortress' because it was so heavily armoured. The Americans joined the Allies in the war against Germany in 1941, and American bombers took part in many raids over Germany from 1942.*

The scene after an air raid. *Both British and German civilians suffered terribly during bombing raids. Towards the end of the war, Allied bombing raids destroyed many German cities. In 1945, over 80,000 civilians were killed in one night in Dresden.*

Kill him – with War Savings

War bonds *were sold by the government as a way of borrowing money from people to pay for the war, which was very expensive. The USA also gave aid to countries fighting the Nazis. By the end of the war, Britain was left with huge debts.*

War in Africa

The British Bren gun could fire at a rate of 500 bullets a minute.

On 10 June, 1940, Italy joined its Axis ally Germany and declared war on Britain and France. Italy's fascist leader, Benito Mussolini, immediately ordered an invasion of North Africa where he expected to overrun the small Allied forces very quickly.

1940–41 Italian and British forces fight in North Africa.

1941 Germans send tank units to North Africa.

December 1941 Japanese attack US fleet in Pearl Harbor. Allies declare war on Japan.

April 1942 Singapore falls to Japanese. US bombers attack Tokyo in Doolittle Raid.

May 1942 Allies stop threat to Australia at Battle of the Coral Sea.

June 1942 Allies defeat Japanese fleet at Battle of Midway.

October–November 1942 Battle of El Alamein in North Africa.

1943 Axis forces in North Africa surrender to Allies. Allied forces begin slowly to drive Japanese forces from Pacific.

The main priority for the Allies in North Africa was to retain control over Egypt and the Suez Canal, in order to keep open supply routes to Asia and the oilfields of the Middle East. From the summer of 1940, the fighting swept across North Africa, but by February 1941 the Allies had the upper hand. Hitler sent reinforcements to help the Italians.

The reinforcements were tank units trained for desert warfare, and were under the leadership of General Rommel. Rommel was a clever commander, nicknamed 'Desert Fox'. The Battle of El Alamein in October 1942 marked a turning point for the Allies who, commanded by General Montgomery, broke through the Axis defences and forced the Axis troops to retreat. Soon after this victory, Allied troops landed in Algeria and Morocco and moved towards Tunisia. The Axis surrendered in North Africa in May 1943. North Africa provided a base from which the Allies could take control of southern Europe. They invaded Sicily in July 1943 and Italy signed an armistice with the Allies in September.

A British soldier (or 'Tommy') fighting in the North African desert campaign of 1940–42.

Under the leadership of Montgomery, the British 8th Army's tanks and infantry force, known as the 'Desert Rats', fought a tough war against the German 'Africa Korps'.

War in the Pacific

Torpedoes *could be fired from submarines or dropped from low-flying torpedo bombers.*

Japan joined the two Axis powers, Germany and Italy, in 1940. The Japanese wanted an empire in Southeast Asia, but to do so they had to destroy the American Pacific fleet. On 7 December, 1941, Japanese aircraft attacked Pearl Harbor, Hawaii, where the US fleet was at anchor.

The attack was unexpected and it inflicted great damage on the American fleet. It also brought the USA into the war – the USA and the Allies declared war on Japan the following day. The Japanese quickly took control of much of Southeast Asia. In Malaysia, they forced British troops to retreat to the island of Singapore. On 15 February, 1942, Singapore surrendered to the Japanese and 85,000 soldiers were taken prisoner – Britain's worst-ever military defeat.

The Japanese also advanced towards Australia and the Hawaiian Islands. In June 1942, the Americans halted the Japanese advance at the Battle of Midway. This was the first major Allied victory against the Japanese. Between 1942 and 1945, the Allies continued the slow process of driving the Japanese out of their newly captured territories.

An Allied warship *is attacked by a Japanese warplane. A second ship (in background) joins in the fierce anti-aircraft barrage.*

The war in the Pacific *began with the Japanese bombing of Pearl Harbor. Japan quickly occupied all the areas coloured orange on the map, which also shows important battles.*

USSR
KOREA
JAPAN
PACIFIC OCEAN
CHINA
✗ Okinawa
✗ Iwo Jima
BURMA
✗ Philippine Sea   ✗ Eniwetok
Leyte Gulf ✗   ✗ Guam   ✗ Saipan   ✗ Kwaljalein
✗ Pelehu   Tarawa ✗
THAILAND
✗ Bougainville
NEW GUINEA
FRENCH INDO-CHINA
AUSTRALIA

End of the War

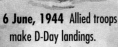

The atomic bomb dropped on Hiroshima on 6 August, 1945 claimed the lives of more than 70,000 people.

6 June, 1944 Allied troops make D-Day landings.

20 July, 1944 Failure of plot to assassinate Hitler.

25 August, 1944 Allied troops and Free French liberate Paris. Battle of the Bulge in Belgium – last German attack against Allies.

1945 Soviet troops enter Warsaw, capital of Poland. Final assault on Germany by Allied troops. Yalta Conference – Roosevelt, Churchill and Stalin agree to divide Germany into four zones after war. Hitler commits suicide.

7 May, 1945 Germany surrenders to Allies. V-E Day.

August 1945 Americans drop atomic bomb on Hiroshima and Nagasaki, Japan.

2 September 1945 Japan surrenders. V-J Day.

October 1945 United Nations formed.

About 80 per cent of Hiroshima was destroyed by the explosion of the atomic bomb. The closest surviving building to the location of the bomb's detonation has been preserved as a memorial.

Ever since the evacuation of Allied troops from Dunkerque in 1940, Allied leaders had been waiting to return to France. By summer 1944, the time was right and thousands of troops were on standby in southern England.

The Germans knew that the Allies would attack somewhere along the north coast of France but they were not sure where. The most obvious place was near Calais, where the English Channel is narrowest. In fact, the Allies made their landing further west on the beaches of Normandy. D-Day was originally planned for 5 June, 1944, but bad weather postponed the landings for a day. On the morning of 6 June, Allied troops waded ashore.

Under the command of the American general, Dwight D. Eisenhower, the Allies advanced rapidly. By 25 August, they had reached Paris. Meanwhile, Soviet troops were advancing across eastern Europe and Allied forces had landed in southern France. Despite a last offensive by the Germans in Belgium, it was clear that victory was in sight in Europe.

In April 1945, as Soviet troops surrounded Berlin, Adolf Hitler committed suicide. The Germans finally surrendered on 7 May, and the Allies declared 8 May V-E (Victory in Europe) Day. However, in the midst of the rejoicing, the horrors of the Nazi concentration camps were revealed on 15 April 1945, when Allied troops reached Belsen concentration camp in Germany. During the war, the Nazis had imprisoned and killed millions of Jews. The starving camp survivors were terrible proof of Nazi brutality.

In the Far East, the war was not yet over. Japan seemed determined to fight on, despite defeat looking certain. The American president, Harry S. Truman, decided to use a secret weapon developed by American and British scientists during the war. This was the atomic bomb. President Truman wanted to end the war without losing the lives of thousands more Allied troops. On 6 August, 1945, an atomic bomb was dropped on the Japanese city of Hiroshima. Another was dropped on Nagasaki three days later. The Japanese surrendered on 2 September – V-J (Victory over Japan) Day. The war had cost millions of lives, and many more people died later from injuries and other illnesses.

Celebrations on V-E Day, 8 May, 1945.
People hung out flags, and huge crowds gathered in the streets of London and other towns and cities throughout the United Kingdom.

***During the D-Day** invasion on 6 June, 1944, over 156,000 American, British and Canadian troops landed on the beaches of Normandy. This was the largest sea-borne attack ever mounted. The Germans prepared for an invasion by putting mines and barbed wire along the beaches to slow down the advancing troops.*

WINSTON CHURCHILL
Before World War II, Winston Churchill argued strongly against Chamberlain's attempts to make peace with Hitler. He was prime minister throughout the war, and his own courage and faith in an Allied victory were an inspiration to the British people. Churchill's 'trademark' was the V-sign for victory.

Commonwealth of Nations

The British empire began to break up in 1947, when India and Pakistan became independent. The old Dominions of Australia and Canada were already self-governing. In the 1950s and 1960s, more colonies took the road to independence and the Commonwealth of Nations, a loose association of friendly countries, came into being.

1919 Massacre at Amritsar. First Government of India Act.

1920–22 Gandhi, leader of Indian National Congress leads policy of non-cooperation.

1930 Gandhi leads Salt March.

1935 Second Government of India Act passed.

1947 India and Pakistan become independent.

1948 Ceylon (Sri Lanka) and Burma (Myanmar) become independent.

1952 Start of Mau Mau rebellion in Kenya.

1957 Gold Coast becomes independent as Ghana.

1960 Cyprus, Nigeria and Somalia become independent.

1961 Tanganyika, Sierra Leone and Cameroon become independent.

1962 Uganda becomes independent.

1963 Malaysia and Kenya become independent.

The campaign for India's independence had started early in the 20th century, with the first Government of India Act (1919) and the campaigns of the Indian National Congress, led by Gandhi. By the end of World War II in 1945, the British government knew it could no longer ignore the calls for Indian independence.

Although a large majority of India's people were Hindus, there was a substantial number of Muslims, who did not want to live under Hindu rule. Under their leader, Mohammed Ali Jinnah, the Muslims demanded their own state of Pakistan. On 14 August, 1947, two regions in northeast and northwest India became the Muslim state of Pakistan. The following day, India became independent. Millions of people now found that they were in the 'wrong' country, and as Hindus and Muslims tried to move, violence broke out and hundreds of thousands of people were killed.

India was the most populous nation in the new Commonwealth, which soon had many new members as colonies in the Caribbean, Asia and Africa sought and won independence. Often, as in Ghana (1957), this was achieved peacefully, but in some countries there was violence.

The Indian flag was adopted when the nation became independent in 1947. At its centre is a wheel with 24 spokes, called the 'Ashoka Chakra'.

Jawaharlal Nehru (1889–1964) (left) and Mohammed Ali Jinnah (1867–1948) (right). Nehru took part in the struggle against British rule and became the first prime minister of India in 1947. Jinnah was leader of the Muslim League from 1935 and became governor-general of Pakistan in 1947.

In Kenya, the Mau Mau fought a campaign against the British from 1952, and Kenya did not become independent until 1963. There was also fighting in Malaya against Communist rebels before the emergence of the new nations of Malaysia (1963) and Singapore (1965).

Most Commonwealth nations are republics, but the Queen is recognized as head of the organization. Since 1966, meetings of Commonwealth leaders have taken place in different member countries.

Ghanaian chiefs wait for the first session of parliament to begin. Ghana, formerly known as the Gold Coast, became independent from Britain in 1957. It became a republic in 1960, under its leader Kwame Nkrumah.

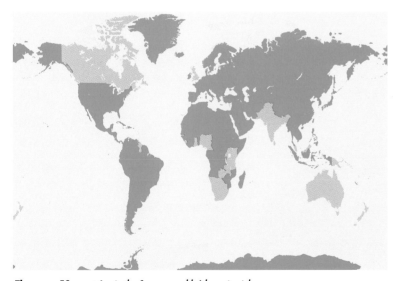

There are 53 countries in the Commonwealth (shown in pink on this map), with a total population of nearly 1.8 billion people, which is nearly one-third of the world's population. These countries include the world's second most populous nation, India, which is home to nearly 1.1 billion people, and the world's second largest country, Canada, which has a land area of more than 9 million square kilometres.

FALKLANDS WAR

Britain fought several small 'colonial wars': for example, in Kenya, Malaya, Cyprus and Aden. In 1982, the Falkland Islands in the South Atlantic were invaded by Argentina (which claims the islands). The British government led by Prime Minister Margaret Thatcher sent a naval task force to the South Atlantic to recapture the islands, which remain a British colony.

Social Change

Recycling *is seen as a way of reducing humans' impact on the environment.*

1956 John Osborne's play *Look Back in Anger* performed at Royal Court Theatre.

1957 Homicide Act abolishes death penalty except for specific offences. First atomic bomb exploded by Britain in Pacific Ocean.

1958 Formation of Campaign for Nuclear Disarmament (CND).

1959 Obscene Publications Act and failed attempt to prosecute publishers of D.H. Lawrence's *Lady Chatterley's Lover.*

1963 *Please Please Me* becomes Beatles' first number one hit. Robbins Report on higher education.

1965 Death penalty abolished.

1967 Abortion Act makes termination of pregnancies legal.

1969 Divorce Reform Act. Voting age reduced from 21 to 18 years.

1975 Equal Opportunities Act makes discrimination against women illegal.

1981 Riots in Brixton, London.

In July 1957, a few months after becoming prime minister, Harold Macmillan told an audience at a meeting: 'Let's be frank about it, most of our people have never had it so good. Go around the country... and you will see a state of prosperity such as we have never had in my lifetime...'.

After the difficulties of the post-war years, more families than ever before could afford goods such as cars, fridges, washing machines and television sets. This affluence extended to young people, too. After the war, there was a sudden increase in the birthrate and by the late 1950s and '60s the 'baby boomers' had reached their teens. For the first time a separate youth culture grew up in which teenagers challenged the adult world. Hooliganism was also seen increasingly on the streets, with gangs clashing with authority and each other.

The 1960s was a time of wide social change and a move towards a more 'permissive' society. There were more tolerant attitudes to matters such as abortion, family planning, homosexuality and censorship, and laws were passed to reflect these changes in attitudes. In 1965, the death penalty was abolished.

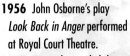

The compact disc (CD) *was introduced in 1982 and can be used to store data such as computer files, images and music.*

Education changed in the 1970s, with the ending of the 11-plus exam in most areas, and the switch to comprehensive schools, in which children of all abilities were taught together. By the year 2000, education (from nursery school to university) had become a priority for politicians of all parties.

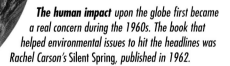

The human impact *upon the globe first became a real concern during the 1960s. The book that helped environmental issues to hit the headlines was Rachel Carson's* Silent Spring, *published in 1962.*

The women's liberation movement in Britain was inspired by writers such as Australian Germaine Greer who published her book The Female Eunuch *in 1970. The Equal Pay Act, which made it illegal to pay men and women different rates for the same work, came into effect in 1975.*

Other priorities included the National Health Service and Britain's ageing and overcrowded transport system.

During the 1980s and 1990s, large state-run industries such as gas, electricity, coal and railways were 'privatized'. In a fast-changing world, few people could expect to stay in the same job for all their working lives, as their grandparents might have done.

A hippy concert in the late 1960s. Pop music first came to Britain from the USA in the form of rock 'n' roll in the 1950s. After the Beatles had their first number one hit in 1963, Beatlemania hit Britain. The Beatles changed the face of pop music for ever.

FAMILIES ON HOLIDAY
By the 1990s, many people could take four or more weeks off a year. Theme parks, such as Alton Towers, became popular. As air fares became cheaper, more people chose to go abroad for their holidays.

Britain and the Cold War

1945 V-E Day and the end of World War II.

1946 Winston Churchill describes a 'special relationship' between Britain and the US.

1949 North Atlantic Treaty Organization (NATO) established military alliance between western nations.

1950–53 Korean War. Soldiers from the US, Britain and other western powers face Chinese and North Korean forces.

1953 Death of Josef Stalin. Succeeded by Nikita Kruschev.

1955 Warsaw Pact created to unite communist nations in eastern Europe.

1961 East Germany builds the Berlin Wall dividing former German capital.

1968 Nuclear Non-Proliferation Treaty signed.

1972 Strategic Arms Limitation Treaty I (SALT I) signed.

1979 Strategic Arms Limitation Treaty II (SALT II) signed.

1991 USSR officially dissolved. Cold War ends.

Britain's own nuclear missiles *have been carried by submarines.*

After the end of World War II, the two main Allied forces, the communist Soviet nations and the countries of the west, stood facing each other along a line that Winston Churchill famously described as the 'Iron Curtain'. Although they had once been allies, the two sides now faced an uneasy stand-off in a period that became known as the 'Cold War'.

The Cold War started in 1947 following a deterioration in relationships between the Soviet Union and the West, and was to last until the final years of the century. This period saw an escalation in the numbers and sizes of the armed forces on both sides of the Iron Curtain, as each side tried to better the other in order to gain an advantage. The period saw a number of conflicts around the world where the Soviet Union and the US came close to all-out war, such as the Cuban missile crisis and the Korean War, but nowhere were tensions higher than in Europe.

Listening stations were established throughout the UK during the Cold War. Their task was to intercept Soviet radio transmissions and to decode their information.

The Campaign for Nuclear Disarmament (CND) was founded in February 1958.

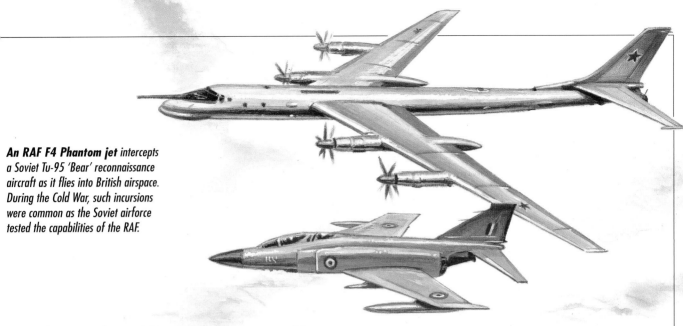

An RAF F4 Phantom jet intercepts a Soviet Tu-95 'Bear' reconnaissance aircraft as it flies into British airspace. During the Cold War, such incursions were common as the Soviet airforce tested the capabilities of the RAF.

As the region closest to the Soviet Union, Europe and Britain were seen as the potential frontline for any future war. Allied bases were established throughout western Europe, including Britain. Later, American nuclear missiles were stationed there, further escalating the tension.

Although the Cold War saw no direct hostilities between the Soviet Union and the West, the period did experience a number of other 'struggles', including economic embargoes, spying and propaganda.

During the 1980s, however, relationships between the two sides thawed, and a number of agreements were made, specifically about reducing the size of the armed forces and the numbers of nuclear missiles. At the start of the 1990s, the collapse of communism in the Soviet Union and other eastern European countries brought an end to the Cold War.

The Berlin Wall became a symbol of the tensions between the Communist countries and the West. It divided the city of Berlin, splitting the Soviet-controlled eastern half from the western half which, after World War II, had been controlled by the western allies of France, America and Britain. The wall was demolished in 1989, but some parts remain as a memorial to the people who died trying to cross it.

Britain and Europe

After the end of World War II, many people in Europe believed that the best way to recover from the ravages of the war and to prevent future conflict was increased and stronger cooperation between European nations.

The flag of the European Union features a circle of 12 gold stars on a blue background.

1951 Treaty of Paris establishes European Coal and Steel Community (ECSC).

1957 Treaty of Rome establishes European Economic Community (EEC).

1958 EEC comes into operation with six member states.

1960 Britain sets up European Free Trade Association (EFTA) as rival to EEC.

1961 Britain opens negotiations to join EEC.

1963 Britain's application to join EEC rejected by French leader General de Gaulle.

1967 France rejects Britain's second application to join EEC.

1973 Britain, Denmark and Ireland become members of EEC (1 January).

1975 Referendum in Britain. Majority vote for staying in EEC.

1993 Establishment of European Union (EU).

1995 Austria, Finland and Sweden join EU.

2004 EU expands to 25 members.

In 1951, several European countries set up the European Coal and Steel Community (ECSC). The nations in this organization agreed to trade coal and steel without charging each other customs duties. In 1957, this idea was extended by the creation of the European Economic Community (EEC). The six countries that signed up to the EEC agreed to trade all goods in a single market. To begin with, Britain did not join either the ECSC or the EEC.

In the 1950s, many British politicians still believed that Britain had a wider role to play in the world. There were strong ties with the remaining countries in the British empire and the other Commonwealth nations. Britain also felt a close link with the USA, often referred to as the 'special relationship'.

By 1961, the situation had changed enough for Britain to open negotiations to join the EEC. It was becoming clear that the EEC was an economic success, but Britain's application to join was rejected by French leader General de Gaulle. He was suspicious of Britain's relationship with the USA, and of its trade links with Commonwealth countries.

Eurostar passenger trains run between London and Paris and Brussels, through the Channel Tunnel. The tunnel itself was completed in 1994 and provides a permanent link between the UK and continental Europe.

The same thing happened in 1967 when Britain applied for a second time. It was not until 1973, after de Gaulle had retired (in 1969) that Britain was finally admitted into the EEC. Even then, many people in Britain were unsure about becoming a member. In 1975, the Labour government held a referendum to find out whether Britain should remain a member of the EEC. Over 26 million people voted, and the result was two to one in favour of staying in.

In 1993, the EEC became the European Union (EU), and its membership has gone on expanding. It has its own money, the euro. Some people see a federal Europe as both inevitable and desirable, with a European president as well as the existing European parliament. Others believe that Britain should be free to make its own decisions, within an EU that remains an economic association of nation-states rather than a United States of Europe.

The euro came into existence as a currency on 1 January, 1999. By 2002, it had replaced the traditional currencies of most EU members, but not Britain's pound.

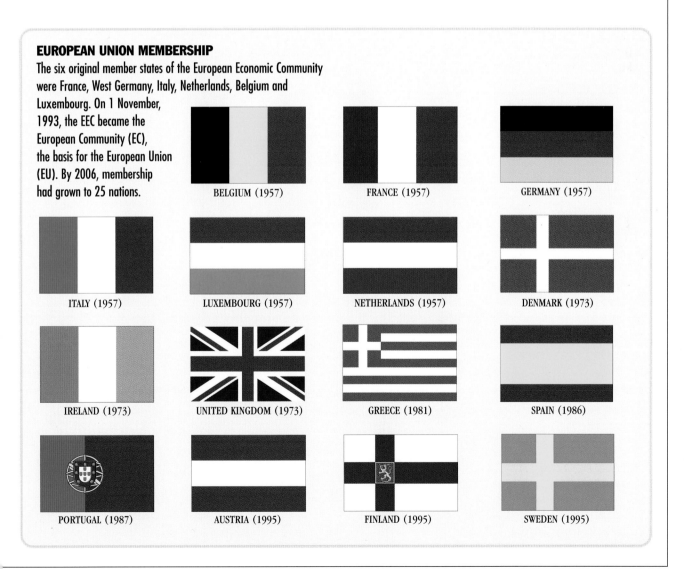

EUROPEAN UNION MEMBERSHIP

The six original member states of the European Economic Community were France, West Germany, Italy, Netherlands, Belgium and Luxembourg. On 1 November, 1993, the EEC became the European Community (EC), the basis for the European Union (EU). By 2006, membership had grown to 25 nations.

BELGIUM (1957)

FRANCE (1957)

GERMANY (1957)

ITALY (1957)

LUXEMBOURG (1957)

NETHERLANDS (1957)

DENMARK (1973)

IRELAND (1973)

UNITED KINGDOM (1973)

GREECE (1981)

SPAIN (1986)

PORTUGAL (1987)

AUSTRIA (1995)

FINLAND (1995)

SWEDEN (1995)

Terror and Unrest

Throughout the second half of the 20th century, trouble flared in Northern Ireland, as the struggle between Republican and Unionist militia and British forces continued. As the new millennium dawned, however, a new wave of terrorism began, taking the focus onto a more international stage.

August 1969 The Battle of Bogside. Catholics and Protestants clash near the Bogside area of Derry.

30 January, 1972 A march against internment is fired on by British soldiers who kill 14 – later known as 'Bloody Sunday'.

1985 The Anglo-Irish Agreement gives Dublin some control over Northern Ireland affairs.

31 August, 1994 Provisional IRA declares a ceasefire.

10 April 1998 Good Friday Agreement is signed.

15 August 1998 Bomb explodes in Omagh, killing 29 people. Splinter group the Real IRA admits responsibility.

11 September, 2001 Two jet airliners crash into the World Trade Center in New York, killing more than 2,500 people.

October 2001 US-led forces invade Afghanistan to topple the Taliban regime.

20 March, 2003 US-led forces invade Iraq.

7 July, 2005 Four bombs explode on the London underground and a bus, killing more than 50 people.

28 July, 2005 IRA relinquishes violence and instructs members to pursue political means.

November 2006 Iraq Special Tribunal convicts Saddam Hussein of crimes against humanity.

30 December, 2006 Saddam Hussein executed.

Since the formation of Northern Ireland in 1949, tensions between Catholics and Protestants had been rising. Many Catholics felt that they were not being treated equally by the Protestant majority. Civil rights protests increased throughout the 1960s, culminating in the rioting of the Battle of Bogside in August 1969, when Protestant marchers clashed with Catholics in Derry and Belfast. British troops were forced to intervene and barricades were erected around Catholic areas, separating them from Protestant ones. Attacks by the IRA on soldiers led to the British government imposing new legislation, such as the introduction of internment in August 1971 and the Prevention of Terrorism Act in 1974. The IRA responded by carrying out bomb attacks on targets on the British mainland.

In 1985, the governments of Britain and Ireland met to discuss the situation. The result of this meeting was the Anglo-Irish agreement, which allowed Dublin some control over affairs in Northern Ireland. Further discussions over the next decade between parties from both sides resulted in the Good Friday Agreement of 1998 which established the Northern Ireland Assembly. Despite some attacks by various terrorist splinter groups, the IRA gave up its military struggle and decommissioned its weapons in 2005.

The Parliament Buildings at Stormont, Belfast, are home to the Northern Ireland assembly established after the Good Friday agreement,1998.

However, a new wave of terrorism had already started with the attacks on New York on 11 September, 2001. Al-Qaeda claimed responsibility, and attention turned to their alleged bases in Afghanistan. An invasion of the country in 2001 was unsuccessful in capturing the al-Qaeda leader, Osama Bin Laden. The next country targeted in the 'War against Terror' was Iraq. But many people felt that Iraq had no links with al-Qaeda. Despite their protests, the invasion of Iraq went ahead, and the overthrow of the Iraqi dictator, Saddam Hussein, was completed in May 2003. Terrorist activities continued, however, with attacks on London on 7 July, 2005.

The Afghan capital city of Kabul. Following the terrorist attacks in New York on 11 September, 2001, the UK joined the US in the 'War on Terror'. The first country attacked was Afghanistan. The Taliban government of Afghanistan was believed to support the terrorist organization al-Qaeda, which many people blamed for the attacks on New York.

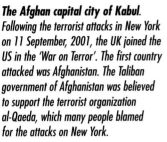

A massive march on the streets of London protesting against the US-led invasion of Iraq. After toppling the Taliban regime in Afghanistan, attention turned to Iraq and its leader Saddam Hussein. Many people felt that any action against Iraq was unjustified, but their protests were unsuccessful and the invasion of Iraq started in March 2003.

The remains of a London bus destroyed by an explosion during the terrorist attacks of 7 July, 2005. Three suicide bombers attacked the underground system and a fourth blew himself up on this bus. In total, 56 people were killed in the attacks.

Modern Living

The 20th and 21st centuries have seen a dramatic change in the way many people live their lives. In a little over 100 years, the population of the UK increased from 41.6 million in 1901 to 59.8 million in 2004. This has led to ever-larger cities and increased demands on infrastructure, such as the health service.

The development of the internet *has allowed more and more people to work from home, and to choose the hours that they work.*

22 June, 1948 The *Empire Windrush* arrives at Tilbury from the Caribbean. On board are migrants who have come to live and work in the UK.

1971 Population of the UK reaches 55.9 million.

1989 British computer engineer Tim Berners-Lee comes up with the idea for the World Wide Web.

1992 The Kyoto Summit of climate change attempts to limit the levels of polluting gases created by countries.

February 2003 London introduces a congestion charge in an attempt to reduce traffic levels.

2004 Population of the UK reaches 59.8 million. In the year up to 2004, the population has increased by some 281,200.

The increase in population size has been caused by a number of factors. Firstly, people are living longer due to improvements in diet, healthcare and lifestyle. In the years between 1971 and 2004, the percentage of people aged over 65 went up from 13 per cent to 16 per cent. During the same period the percentage of people under the age of 16 fell from 25 per cent to 19 per cent. As a result, the population of the UK is, on average, getting older. In 1971, the average age in the UK was 34.1 years, by 2004, this had increased to 38.6 years. This, however, brings its own set of problems. An ageing population means that more and more people are dependent upon pensions rather than salaries. This puts increased pressure on younger people who have to pay for these pensions through their tax contributions, as well as increased pressure on healthcare organizations that look after elderly people.

The second reason for the increasing population size has been immigration. Over the last 50 years, people have moved to the UK from a wide range of countries to live and work.

The population of Britain *is getting older. With improvements in healthcare and living conditions, people are living longer and, today, the over-65s make up one-sixth of the population.*

Greater demands for energy have increased the production of pollutants, which could be changing our climate.

Immigration has meant that Britain has a multi-racial society with people migrating to the UK from all over the world. However, this has increased racial tensions in certain parts of the country.

Alternative sources of energy are seen as one solution to the increasing levels of pollution. These include wind farms and tidal power stations. A more controversial plan involves the building of more nuclear reactors, a move which many people oppose.

These have included the countries of the Commonwealth, such as India and the West Indies, and, more recently, the latest countries to join the European Union. Today, about one in 12 people living in the UK was born overseas.

Technology has also played a major part in shaping our modern lives. Increased car ownership has given people greater freedom to travel to work or go on holiday. In 1961, there were fewer than 9 million vehicles on British roads. By 2004, this had soared to 32.3 million. This massive increase in car ownership has even changed the shape of our towns and cities with the arrival of enormous out-of-town shopping centres and supermarkets which some believe are driving high-street stores out of business. Traffic congestion has risen and some towns and cities have introduced congestion charging to try to reduce traffic levels, such as the scheme in London which was introduced in 2003.

Today, our homes are filled with modern appliances, many of which were too expensive or not available 50 years ago. These include washing machines, televisions, dishwashers and home computers. As a result, demand for power has increased dramatically and with it the release of polluting gases given off by the creation of this energy. In recent years, the UK government has tried to use alternative sources of energy which create less pollution, including solar power and wind farms. By 2003, these 'renewable sources' of energy accounted for 4 per cent of the UK's demand.

	500,000–5000 BC	5000 BC–AD 0	AD 0–300	300–600
POLITICS	c.230,000 BC Neanderthal peoples arrive, ousting original hominid settlers c.30,000 BC Advanced *homo sapiens* ousts Neanderthal species c.12,000 BC Human groups begin to return to Britain as Ice Age ends	c.2500 BC Beaker people migrate to Britain from Europe c.700 BC Celtic peoples begin to settle in Britain 55 BC Roman army led by Julius Caesar lands in southern England	43 Full-scale Roman invasion under Emperor Claudius 60 Revolt of the Iceni under Boudicca 296 Britain divided into four Roman provinces	367 Hadrian's Wall overrun by Picts and Scots 408 Saxon invasion begins; most Roman troops withdrawn 577 Decisive Saxon victory over Celts at Dyrham
EXPLORATION	c.500,000 BC First human settlers arrive in Britain c.10,000 BC Settlers reach northwest coast of England c.7000 BC First settlements in Scotland and Ireland	c.4000 BC Orkney, Shetland and other remote islands colonized	84 Roman troops under Agricola penetrate Scottish Highlands c.150 First detailed world map shows Britain and Ireland	c.555 St Brendan sails from West of Ireland and claims to have reached America
TECHNOLOGY	c.450,000 BC Use of fire and flint hand-axes developed c.7000 BC Hunters begin to use bows and arrows	c.4500 BC New Stone Age begins; farming techniques established in Britain c.2150 BC Bronze Age begins c.750 BC Iron Age begins	c.120 Road-building programme begins 122 Romans start construction of Hadrian's Wall 160 Iron smelting flourishes in Sussex	c.300 Pottery industry flourishes in central England c.325 Large iron foundry established in Silchester, Hampshire
ARTS		c.30 BC White Horse carved on chalk downs at Uffington, Oxfordshire	c.85 Lavish villas constructed, including Fishbourne in Sussex c.150 Romans redesign cities with grand civic buildings such as bath houses and fora	c.350 Silver treasure buried at Mildenhall, Suffolk c.590 Golden age of Anglo-Saxon jewellery making begins
RELIGION	c.24,000 BC Elaborate cave burial rituals at Paviland, South Wales	c.3700 BC Ritual burials in long barrows and chambered tombs common c.3000 BC Stone circles erected throughout British Isles c.70 BC Power of Druid priests grows	60 Romans destroy Druid stronghold on Anglesey c.200 Christianity reaches northern Britain	325 Christianity becomes the official religion of the Roman Empire 450 St Patrick begins the conversion of Ireland 597 St Augustine sent from Rome to convert the English
DAILY LIFE	c.23,000 BC Last Ice Age begins c.8500 BC Beginning of thaw; ice retreats again c.6500 BC Hunters burn patches of growing woodland to attract herds of game	c.4000 BC Farming settlements in most parts of Britain c.1500 BC Village communities develop, especially in southern England c.550 BC Hillforts built to protect scarce farmland	90–98 Roman colonies built at Lincoln and Gloucester 150 Bigger area of farmland brings bigger crops c.190 Six-hour working day introduced for all but slaves	c.370 Beginning of new villa-building boom, especially in southern England c.425 Economy collapses following end of Roman rule and Saxon attacks c.570 Anglo-Saxons now settled in small 'states' ruled by kings

	600–800	800–1000	1000–1100	1100–1200	
	736 Ethelbald declares himself first king of Britain 757–96 Offa unites and rules Mercia 789 First Viking raid on Britain	865 Danish Great Army lands in Kent 878 Alfred defeats the Danes at Edington 995 Irish victory over Norse invaders at Tara	1042 Edward the Confessor becomes king of England 1066 Norman conquest of England led by William 1087 William I succeeded by William II	1100 Death of William II; Henry I becomes king 1139–53 Civil War in England during reign of Stephen 1154 Henry of Anjou invades England and becomes King Henry II	POLITICS
	c.726 Inc, King of Wessex, is one of many to make dangerous pilgrimage to Rome	c.885 Ohthere arrives at Alfred's court after exploring Lapland	1030 New map of Europe, including Britain, produced in Kent	1170 Prince Madoc of Wales alleged to have established a colony in North America	EXPLORATION
	685 Completion of monastery at Jarrow, Tyne and Wear c.690 Development of new and better weapons, including double-edged swords of iron and steel 735 Bede states that the Earth is round	841 Vikings establish base at Dublin and dominate Irish Sea shipping	c.1000 Mint for gold coins founded at Bristol 1067 Programme of castle building in England and Wales begins 1097 Completion of White Tower (later part of the Tower of London)	1100 Westminster Hall completed 1110 'Exchequer' cloth devised to calculate royal accounts	TECHNOLOGY
	c.624 Ship burial of King Redwald with treasure at Sutton Hoo, East Anglia c.670 The monk Caedmon writes first Christian poems in Anglo-Saxon c.725 Anglo-Saxon poem *Beowulf* written	c.800 Completion of the illuminated *Book of Kells* in Ireland c.890 Alfred orders gold and crystal jewels for his bishops c.990 Collection of many Anglo-Saxon poems, including *The Wanderer* and *The Seafarer*	c.1050 Irish legends and sagas written down in Latin and Gaelic 1077 Bayeux Tapestry completed	c.1133 Durham Cathedral completed 1136 Geoffrey of Monmouth writes *History of the Kings of Britain* 1176 First Eisteddfod of poetry and music held in Dyfed	ARTS
	c.600 Death of St David, Welsh missionary 664 Synod of Whitby affirms Roman Christian calendar 731 Bede completes *History of the English Church*	806 Vikings ravage monastery on Iona for third time 875 Monks flee Lindisfarne to escape Vikings c.993 Alfric publishes *Lives of the Saints*	1059–65 Rebuilding of Westminster Abbey 1070 First Norman appointed as Archbishop of Canterbury 1083 Founding of new priory on Lindisfarne	c.1128 First Cistercian monastery founded in Surrey 1170 Murder of Thomas Becket 1190–92 Richard I on Crusade to Holy Land	RELIGION
	c.695 Southampton established as trading port c.710 Beginnings of feudal system, with kings rewarding bands of retainers c.750 London now Britain's largest town and major port	893 *Anglo-Saxon Chronicle* begun c.900 Norse establish settlements, and many Norse words enter the language 935 Tithes introduced	1013 England divided into shires 1067–69 Normans savagely put down rebellions in northern England 1086 Domesday survey carried out	1117 First leper hospital founded in London 1121 First royal Scottish burgh established at Berwick to encourage trade 1170 Population of London exceeds 30,000	DAILY LIFE

	1200–1300	1300–1350	1350–1400	1400–1450
POLITICS	1215 King John signs Magna Carta 1272 Death of Henry III; Edward I becomes king 1282–83 Edward conquers Wales	1314 Robert the Bruce defeats English at Bannockburn 1337 Beginning of Hundred Years' War with France 1346–47 English successes at Crécy and Calais	1381 The Peasants' Revolt in southeast England 1388 Major Scots victory over English at Otterburn 1399 Richard II deposed and replaced by Henry IV	1400–10 Revolt of Owain Glyndwr in Wales 1415 English defeat French at Agincourt 1449–50 French recapture Normandy
EXPLORATION	1280 New 'Mappa Mundi', or world map, drawn for Hereford Cathedral	1304–11 Nearly 40,000 sacks of wool exported to Europe each year. Network of trading routes established with Near East	1399 Richard de Clare's expedition to Ireland cut short by rebellion at home	1419–20 English conquest of Normandy
TECHNOLOGY	1222 Widespread introduction of windmills to East Anglia 1290 Completion of massive castle-building programme in Wales	c.1350 Introduction of plate armour	1352 First weight-driven striking clock installed at Windsor 1367 King David II orders new fortifications at Edinburgh castle	1410 Stone bridge built across the Clyde at Glasgow
ARTS	c.1200 New stained glass windows in rebuilt Canterbury Cathedral c.1201 First troubadours arrive at English courts 1245 Work begins on rebuilding Westminster Abbey 1250 Matthew Paris produces illuminated *Chronicles*	c.1325 A collection of poems and prayers, the *Book of Kildare*, completed in Ireland 1330 The illuminated *St Omer Psalter* completed in East Anglia	c.1370 English poem *Piers Plowman* written 1392 English poet Geoffrey Chaucer begins *The Canterbury Tales* c.1396 Religious painting, called the *Wilton Diptych*, commissioned by Richard II	1412 Cloisters of Gloucester Cathedral completed 1430 English poet John Lydgate writes *Pageant of Knowledge* 1446 Building begins of King's College Chapel, Cambridge
RELIGION	1221 Franciscan and Dominican friars arrive in England	1326 London mob murders the Bishop of Exeter 1338 Inspections by bishops reveal low moral standards in many monasteries	1373 Mystic Julian of Norwich cured after visions of God 1384 Death of heretic John Wycliffe, leader of the Lollards	1401 Death penalty introduced for heretics 1407 Archbishop of Canterbury leads campaign against Lollards
DAILY LIFE	1200 Links with France make greater variety of food available in England 1288 New 'piepowder' courts set up to try offenders at local fairs 1290 Jews expelled from England	1315–16 Widespread famine in England and Wales 1327 Rising wool exports bring prosperity to Scotland 1348 First outbreak of Black Death in Britain	c.1351 Peasants' wages rise as plague makes labour scarce 1360 Major outbreak of Black Death in Ireland 1363 Football banned on holidays in England, to encourage people to practise archery	1407 Bethlehem Hospital (Bedlam) in London becomes first institution for the insane 1424 King James imposes first tax in Scotland for 50 years 1443 Riots by tradesmen in Norwich

	1450–1500	1500–1550	1550–1575	1575–1600	
POLITICS	1453 English rule in France ends with defeat in Gascony 1455 Wars of the Roses begin in England 1485 Henry Tudor seizes power after defeating Richard III at Bosworth	1509 Henry VIII becomes king of England 1536 Union of England and Wales 1542 English victory over invading Scots at Solway Moss	1558 Death of Mary; Elizabeth I becomes queen	1587 Execution of Mary, Queen of Scots 1588 Defeat of the Spanish Armada	POLITICS
EXPLORATION	1481 Bristol merchants sponsor exploration of the Atlantic Ocean westwards 1497 John Cabot crosses Atlantic to Newfoundland	1508–09 Cabot sails into Hudson Bay 1527 Cabot explores South American rivers	1553–54 Willoughby and Chancellor search for Northwest Passage	1576 Frobisher explores Baffin Bay and Hudson Strait 1581 Drake completes circumnavigation of the world	EXPLORATION
TECHNOLOGY	c.1450 Invention of the astrolabe for studying the stars 1457 Giant siege gun, 'Mons Meg', manuactured in Edinburgh 1478 Caxton produces first printed book in England	1502 Coal mining begins in Bradford area 1507 Italian alchemist fails in attempt to fly from battlements of Stirling Castle, Scotland 1545 Henry VIII's flagship, the *Mary Rose*, sinks at Portsmouth	1564 Horse-drawn coach introduced from the Netherlands 1571 First Irish book, *A Gaelic Alphabet and Catechism*, printed in Ireland 1571 Theodolite for measuring angles invented by Digges	1582 London gets new water supply, pumped from Thames. 1589 William Lee invents a knitting machine. 1589 Sir John Harington installs a water closet in his home 1590 Microscope invented in Holland	TECHNOLOGY
ARTS	1469 Thomas Malory completed his *Morte d'Arthur*, an account of King Arthur c.1480 Scots poet Robert Henryson writes *The Testament of Cresseid* 1495 Morality play *Everyman* first performed in England	1516 Thomas More writes *Utopia* 1516 Wolsey builds Hampton Court Palace 1527 German painter Hans Holbein begins work in London	1552 Birth of Edmund Spenser, author of *Faerie Queene* 1564 Birth of William Shakespeare	1580 Nicholas Hilliard starts career as painter of miniatures c.1588–1613 Career of William Shakespeare 1590 Spenser writes *Faerie Queene* 1593 Christopher Marlowe, playwright, killed in brawl 1597 Completion of Hardwick Hall, Derbyshire	ARTS
RELIGION	1472 Scotland's first archbishop is appointed	1526 Bishops order the burning of Tyndale's English translation of the New Testament 1533 Henry declares himself head of the Church, beginning English Reformation 1549 *First Book of Common Prayer* compiled	1552 Cranmer completes *Second Book of Common Prayer* 1553 Mary restores Catholic rule, and Protestants Ridley and Latimer are burned at the stake 1565 Founding of Puritan movement in Cambridge	1575 Publication of collection of *Sacred Songs* by Thomas Tallis and William Byrd	RELIGION
DAILY LIFE	1479 Severe outbreak of plague in England c.1480 Extravagant fashions at English court c.1490 Wool trade brings great prosperity to East Anglia	1505 Royal College of Surgeons founded in Edinburgh 1518 Landowners enclose common lands for grazing sheep 1536 Beginning of dissolution of the monasteries	1557 Third successive year of bad harvests causes famine 1557 Protestant settlers 'planted' in Laois and Offaly, Ireland 1572 New Poor Law provides parish relief for the needy	1584 First potatoes planted in Ireland 1595 High-heeled shoes fashionable 1599 Globe theatre opens in London 1600 Food cost five times what it did in 1500	DAILY LIFE

	1600–1625	1625–1650	1650–1675	1675–1700
POLITICS	1603 James VI of Scotland becomes James I, first Stuart king of England and Ireland 1605 Gunpowder Plot to blow up Parliament fails and conspirators are executed 1621 Protestation of House of Commons stating right of MPs to free speech	1625 Death of James I. Charles succeeds as Charles I 1642 Civil War breaks out in England between supporters of King Charles and Parliamentarians 1649 Execution of King Charles I. England becomes a republic under Cromwell	1651 Defeat of Royalist troops at Worcester. Charles II escapes to France 1652 Act of Settlement — six Irish counties are cleared of Catholic landholders and settled by English Protestants 1660 Restoration of monarchy, Charles II takes throne	1685 Death of Charles II. Succeeded by his brother as James II 1688 'Glorious Revolution' 1689 Parliament declares abdication of James II. William and Mary take over throne jointly. James lands in Ireland and is defeated at Battle of the Boyne (1690)
EXPLORATION	1607 Colony of Virginia founded 1609 'Plantation of Ulster' Protestant settlers move on to land taken from Irish Catholics	1629 Massachusetts Bay Company obtains charter from Charles I 1630 About 1,000 Puritans settle in Massachusetts under Governor John Winthrop	1661 Bombay becomes British trading post, ceded by Portugal 1663 Royal African Company set up to trade in slaves, ivory and gold	1686 East India Company base established at Calcutta, India 1691 Plymouth Colony is annexed to Massachusetts Bay
TECHNOLOGY	1613 British trading station opens in Surat, India	1645 Meetings of the 'Invisible College' — group of scientists who met in London and Oxford	1666 Isaac Newton discovers nature of white light by passing light through prism 1668 Newton builds first reflecting telescope 1669 Newton invents calculus	1675 Royal Observatory opens in Greenwich 1687 Publication of Newton's *Mathematical Principles of Natural Philosophy* 1698 Thomas Savery develops steam pump 1699–1703 Eddystone lighthouse designed by Henry Winstanley
ARTS	1616 Death of Shakespeare	1634 John Milton writes *Comus* 1642–60 Theatres shut down in England	1653 Izaak Walton writes *The Compleat Angler* 1659 Samuel Pepys begins his diaries 1660 Royal Society is founded 1667 Milton writes *Paradise Lost*	1680 Henry Purcell is organist at Westminster Abbey 1689 Publication of *Essay Concerning Human Understanding* by John Locke 1689 First production of Purcell's *Dido and Aeneas*
RELIGION	1611 Publication of the Authorized Version of the Bible, known as the King James Bible	1637 Riot in Edinburgh after Charles tries to force Scots to use a new Anglican prayerbook 1639–40 Bishops' Wars fought between Charles and the Scots	1645 Presbyterianism is made official religion in England 1648 George Fox founds the Society of Friends (Quakers)	1675 Rebuilding of St Paul's Cathedral begins 1678 John Bunyan writes *The Pilgrim's Progress*
DAILY LIFE	1618 James I issues Book of Sports which permits a variety of sports. It provokes objections from Puritans 1621 Publication of the *Corante*, the first English newspaper	1634 Opening of Covent Garden Market, London	1650 Tea first drunk in England 1652 First coffee house opens in London 1665 Great Plague causes thousands of deaths 1666 Great Fire of London (3–6 September)	1692 Lloyd's Coffee House, London, becomes insurance office 1694 Bank of England set up 1695 Window tax enforced in England

	1700–1725	1725–1750	1750–1775	1775–1800	
POLITICS	1701 English Parliament passes Act of Settlement 1702 Death of William. Anne succeeds to the throne 1707 Act of Union 1714 Death of Queen Anne. The Elector of Hanover is proclaimed George I 1715 Jacobite rebellion fails	1721 Robert Walpole becomes Britain's first prime minister 1727 Death of George I. He is succeeded by Prince of Wales as George II 1745–46 Jacobite rebellion led by Bonnie Prince Charlie. British army defeats Jacobites at Battle of Culloden	1756–63 Seven Years' War 1760 Death of George II. He is succeeded by his grandson (son of Frederick Louis) as George III 1773 Boston Tea Party (16 December) 1775–83 American War of Independence	1776 American Declaration of Independence 1783 Treaty of Versailles. Britain recognises United States 1788 Illness of king provokes 'Regency Crisis' 1789 Start of French Revolution 1793 France declares war on Britain	
EXPLORATION	1708 Rescue of Alexander Selkirk, the model for Robinson Crusoe, from an island off the coast of Chile	1740 George Anson begins round-the-world voyage	1768–71 First voyage of Captain Cook on *Endeavour*. Scientific voyage to Pacific Ocean 1772–75 Second voyage on ships *Resolution* and *Adventure* to cirumnavigate and investigate the Antarctic	1776 Third voyage on ships *Resolution* and *Discovery* to look for northwest passage around Canada and Alaska 1779 Cook is killed in Hawaii 1780 *Resolution* and *Discovery* return to Britain	
TECHNOLOGY	1701 Introduction of Jethro Tull's horse-drawn seed drill 1705 Thomas Newcomen develops steam-powered pumping engine for use in mines 1709 Abraham Darby develops coke-fired blast furnace	1731 Publication of *The New Horse Houghing Husbandry* by Jethro Tull 1733 John Kay develops flying shuttle	1757 Sankey Brook Navigation completed 1761 Bridgewater Canal from Worsley to Manchester opened. 1764 'Spinning Jenny' developed 1769 Richard Arkwright patents water-frame; James Watt patents improved steam engine	1779 First iron bridge built across river Severn 1782 James Watt develops rotary steam engine 1784 Edmund Cartwright invents power loom 1796 Edward Jenner proves vaccination theory	
ARTS	1715 G. F. Handel writes *Water Music* 1719 Daniel Defoe writes *Robinson Crusoe*	1726 Jonathan Swift writes *Gulliver's Travels* 1728 *The Beggar's Opera* written by Pepusch and John Gay 1737 Start of censorship of plays in England 1747 Samuel Johnson starts work on his dictionary	1759 Opening of British Museum 1768 Royal Academy of Arts is founded	1776 Adam Smith writes *Wealth of Nations* 1789 William Blake writes *Songs of Innocence*	
RELIGION	1710 Building of St Paul's Cathedral completed	1739 John Wesley begins his life as an open-air preacher 1744 First Methodist conference held at Foundry Chapel, London	1756 John Wesley publishes *Twelve Reasons against a Separation from the Church*	1795 Separation of Methodist and Anglican churches	
DAILY LIFE	1720 Collapse of South Sea company leaves thousands of people financially ruined	1725 Guy's Hospital founded 1732 Completion of first Covent Garden Theatre 1744 First official cricket match in Britain	1751–72 Over 380 turnpike Acts passed through Parliament 1752 Britain adopts Gregorian calendar and 'loses' 11 days 1773 Stock Exchange founded	1779 Derby horse race at Epsom runs for the first time 1782–1820 First period of Highland Clearances 1799 Combination Act prevents 'combinations' of workers	

	1800–1825	1825–1850	1850–1875	1875–1900
POLITICS	1800 Act of Union establishes the United Kingdom of Great Britain and Ireland 1805 Nelson victorious at the Battle of Trafalgar (21 October) 1815 Wellington defeats the French at the Battle of Waterloo (18 June) 1820 George III dies. George IV succeeds	1830 George IV dies. William IV succeeds 1834 Slavery abolished in British Empire 1837 Death of William IV, succeeded by Victoria 1846 Repeal of Corn Laws. Free trade in corn established	1861 Prince Albert dies (14 December) 1867 Second Reform Act gives vote to about one in three working men	1877 Queen Victoria is proclaimed Empress of India 1879–1902 Boer Wars in South Africa 1885 Third Reform Act 1885 First Home Rule Bill defeated in House of Commons
EXPLORATION	1812 William Moorcroft explores Tibet	1831 James Clark Ross reaches North Magnetic Pole 1833 East India Company becomes administrative agent in India for British government	1852–56 David Livingstone explores the Zambezi river 1858 John Speke and Richard Burton reach Lake Tanganyika 1871 Henry Stanley sets out to look for Livingstone	1876–77 Henry Morton Stanley explores Lake Tanganyika
TECHNOLOGY	1804 Richard Trevithick's steam locomotive 1815 Invention of Davy safety lamp for use in mines by Sir Humphry Davy 1825 Opening of Stockton to Darlington railway	1829 Success of George Stephenson's *Rocket* at Rainhill steam trials 1830 Opening of Liverpool and Manchester railway 1835 Cooke and Wheatstone take out patent on electric telegraph 1843 Launch of *Great Britain*, first propeller-driven iron-hull steamship	1850 Over 10,000 km of railway track open 1851 Underwater cable laid across English Channel 1856 Henry Bessemer's new method of making steel 1858 Launch of *Great Eastern*, first ship with double iron hull	1880 Over 25,000 km of railway track open 1876 Alexander Bell sends first voice message along a telegraph line 1878 Joseph Swan makes successful light bulb
ARTS	1811–18 Publication of Jane Austen's six novels. 1813 Founding of Philharmonic Society of London. 1822 Royal Academy of Music founded in London.	1830 William Cobbett writes *Rural Rides* 1835 Charles Dickens writes *Sketches by Boz* 1838 National Gallery opens	1859 Charles Darwin writes *Origin of Species* 1860 George Eliot writes *The Mill on the Floss* 1865 Lewis Carroll writes *Alice in Wonderland*	1883 Royal College of Music founded in London 1883 Robert Louis Stevenson writes *Treasure Island* 1895 Beginning of Promenade Concerts in London
RELIGION	1801 Church Missionary Society founded 1804 British and Foreign Bible Society formed in London 1807 Clapham Sect formed to campaign on social issues	1827 John Nelson Darby founds Plymouth Brethren 1829 Catholic Emancipation Act – Catholics allowed to sit in parliament	1860 Bishop Wilberforce attacks Darwin's theory of evolution 1865 William Booth founds Salvation Army	1890 James Frazer writes *The Golden Bough: A Study in Magic and Religion* 1895 Construction of Catholic cathedral at Westminster begins
DAILY LIFE	1807 Britain ends slave trade 1811 Beginning of Luddite disturbances 1813 Elizabeth Fry begins prison reform 1819 'Peterloo Massacre' in Manchester 1824 Repeal of Combination Act	1840 Introduction of the Penny Post 1840–54 Second Highland Clearances 1844 'Ragged Schools' set up for poorest children 1845–49 Failure of potato crop in Ireland 1848 Public Health Act to set up boards of health 1854–56 Crimean War	1850 Factory Act establishes standard working day 1851 Great Exhibition held in Crystal Palace, Hyde Park, London 1868 First Trades Union Congress (TUC) in Manchester 1870 Education Act sets up School Boards	1875 Public Health Act sets up authorities to oversee housing, sanitation etc 1880 Education Act makes school compulsory for children aged 5–10 1887 Queen Victoria celebrates her Diamond Jubilee

POLITICS

1900–1925	1925–1950	1950–1975	1975–TODAY
1901 Death of Queen Victoria. Succeeded by Edward VII 1909 Lloyd George's 'People's Budget' rejected by House of Lords 1910 Death of Edward VII. Succeeded by George V 1914–18 World War I 1916 Easter Uprising in Dublin	1926 General strike 1929 New York Stock Exchange crash and start of Great Depression 1939–45 World War II 1945 Labour wins general election 1948 *Empire Windrush* arrives with 492 Jamaican immigrants on board	1952 Death of George VI. He is succeeded by Elizabeth II 1973 Britain becomes a member of EEC	1979 Margaret Thatcher becomes Britain's first woman prime minister 1997 Labour win the general election 1998 Northern Ireland peace agreement 2003 Britain aids US in Iraq War

EXPLORATION

1900–1925	1925–1950	1950–1975	1975–TODAY
1907–09 Expedition in Antarctica of Ernest Shackleton 1910–12 Robert Falcon Scott's attempt to reach the South Pole ends in disaster, with death of all five members of the expedition	1933 Wilfred Thesiger crosses Danakil in Ethiopia	1953 Edmund Hillary and Norgay Tenzing become first people to climb Mount Everest. Vivien Fuchs makes first crossing of Antarctica 1969 US astronaut Neil Armstrong becomes first man on the Moon	1981–82 Ranulph Fiennes' Transglobe expedition circumnavigates world around the poles 2003 *Beagle* spacecraft is lost while descending to the Martian surface.

TECHNOLOGY

1900–1925	1925–1950	1950–1975	1975–TODAY
1917 Ernest Rutherford splits the atom 1920 First public broadcasting service opens in Britain	1926 John Logie Baird invents television 1928 Alexander Fleming discovers penicillin 1937 Frank Whittle builds first jet engine	1957 First atomic bomb exploded by Britain in the Pacific	1978 Louise Brown, first test-tube baby, is born 1994 Completion of the Channel Tunnel 2000 Mobile phones, internet, DVDs, satellite TV are commonplace

ARTS

1900–1925	1925–1950	1950–1975	1975–TODAY
1909 Vaughan Williams composes *Fantasy on a Theme by Tallis* 1913 D. H. Lawrence writes *Sons and Lovers* 1914 Charlie Chaplin creates film character *The Tramp*	1926 AA Milne writes *Winnie the Pooh* 1935 TS Eliot writes *Murder in the Cathedral*	1956 Bill Haley's hit 'Rock Around the Clock'. 1963 'Please Please Me' becomes Beatles' first number 1 hit	1985 'Live Aid' rock concert raises money for famine relief 1998 Museum of Pop Music opens in Sheffield 2005 'Live Eight' concerts held around the world to raise awareness of global poverty

RELIGION

1900–1925	1925–1950	1950–1975	1975–TODAY
1917 Balfour Declaration: Britain backs homeland for Jews in Palestine 1920 Disestablishment of Anglican Church in Wales	1929 Presbyterian churches in Scotland unite	1968–69 Civil Rights marches in Northern Ireland 1970 Completion of New English Bible	1982 Pope John Paul II visits Britain 1994 First women priests ordained in the Church of England 1995 Opening of Hindu temple in Neasden 2005 Pope John Paul II dies. Succeeded by Pope Benedict XVI

DAILY LIFE

1900–1925	1925–1950	1950–1975	1975–TODAY
1906 Education Act to provide free school meals for poor 1908 Coal Mines Act fixes working day to eight hours 1912 Sinking of the *Titanic* 1918 Vote given to women over 30 if they are ratepayers or wives of ratepayers	1928 Vote given to all women over 21 1931–2 Almost 3 million people (22 per cent of workforce) unemployed 1936 Jarrow Crusade 1940 'Blitz' in London 1948 Start of National Health Service	1951 Festival of Britain 1958 Formation of Campaign for Nuclear Disarmament (CND) 1967 Abortion Act makes termination of pregnancies legal 1969 Divorce Reform Act	1975 Equal Opportunities Act introduced 1999 House of Lords reform 1999 Scottish parliament and Welsh Assembly set up 2005 Terrorist attacks on London kill 56 people in four separate explosions

Kings and Queens

ENGLAND

Boudicca (Iceni tribe leader) led revolt against Romans in AD 60

King Arthur thought to have defeated Saxons in AD 500

Ethelbald of Mercia proclaims himself king of all Saxon kingdoms AD 736

Offa is first proper English king 757–96

The Viking King Cnut rules England 1017–35

Edward 'the Confessor' 1042–66

Harold 1066 (killed at Battle of Hastings)

William 'the Conqueror' (William I) 1066–87

William II (William Rufus) 1087–1100

ENGLAND, SCOTLAND AND WALES

Henry I 1100–35

David I (Scotland) 1124–53

Stephen 1135–54

Malcolm IV (Scotland) 1153–65

Henry II 1154–89

William I (Scotland) 1165–1214

Richard I 1189–99

John 1199–1216

Alexander II (Scotland) 1214–49 (Britain ruled by council 1216–32)

Henry III 1216–72

Llywelyn I 'the Great' (Wales) 1219–40

Llywelyn II 'the Last' (Wales) 1240–83

Alexander III (Scotland) 1249–1306

Edward I 1272–1307

Prince Edward (son of Edward I) crowned Prince of Wales 1301

Robert Bruce (Scotland) 1306–29

Edward II 1307–27

Edward III 1327–77

Richard II 1377–99

Henry IV 1399–1413

Owain Glyn Dwr is made Prince of Wales 1400

Henry V 1413–22

HOUSE OF LANCASTER

Henry VI 1422–53 (declared insane and York is appointed protector) – 1455 King recovers – 1461 deposed

HOUSE OF YORK

Edward of York 1461–70

HOUSE OF LANCASTER

Henry IV reinstated 1470–71

HOUSE OF YORK

Edward V 1471–83

Richard III 1483–85

THE TUDORS

Henry VII (Henry Tudor) 1485–1509

Henry VIII 1509–47

Edward VI 1547–53

Jane Grey 1553 (nine days)

Mary 1553–58

Elizabeth I 1558–1603

HOUSE OF STUART (UNITED KINGDOM)

James I (James VI of Scotland) 1603–25

Charles I 1625–49 (executed)

Republicans rule 1649–60

Charles II (The Restoration) 1660–85

James II 1685–88

William of Orange and Mary (Glorious Revolution)1688–1702

Anne 1702–14

HOUSE OF HANOVER

George I 1714–27

George II 1727–60

George III 1760–1820

George IV (Prince Regent 1811–20) 1820–30

William IV 1830–37

Victoria 1837–1901

HOUSE OF SAXE-COBURG-GOTHA (WINDSOR AFTER 1917)

Edward VII 1901–10

George V 1910–36

Edward VIII 1936 (abdicated)

George VI 1936–52

Elizabeth II 1952–

Battles in British History

500 BC Many hillforts are constructed, and civil wars break out

55 BC First Roman expedition to Britain by Julius Caesar

AD 43 Successful Roman invasion of Britain under Claudius (advance throughout country continued for next 20 years)

367 Roman Britain is raided by Picts, Scots, Saxons and Irish

407 Saxons move into Roman Britain, after the Romans leave

c. 500 Celtic Briton victory over Anglo-Saxons at Mount Badon, led by King Arthur

789 First of the major Viking raids

793 Sacking of the monastery at Lindisfarne

878 Defeat of Danes at Edington in Wiltshire

1066 Battle of Stamford Bridge

1066 Battle of Hastings

1096 The First Crusade; Jerusalem retaken

1139 Civil War

1147 Second Crusade

1189–91 Third Crusade

1202–54 Four more crusades

1264 Civil War

1271 Eighth crusade

1314 Battle of Bannockburn

1337–1453 Hundred Years' War

1346 Battle of Crécy

1356 Battle of Poitiers

1381 Peasants' Revolt

1415 Battle of Agincourt

1455 Civil war (Wars of the Roses) begins

1485 Battle of Bosworth Field

1513 Battle of Flodden (England–Scotland)

1534 The Reformation

1536 England united with Wales

1585 War between England and Spain

1588 Defeat of Spanish Armada (invasion averted)

1594 Start of Nine Years' War between England and Ireland

1603 Irish starved into surrender

1624–30 War with Spain

1626–29 War with France

1642–26, 1648 Civil Wars

1690 Battle of the Boyne

1701–13 War of the Spanish Succession

1704 Battle of Blenheim

1715 and 1745 Jacobite Rebellions

1740–48 War of the Austrian Succession

1746 Battle of Culloden

1756–63 Seven Years' War

1775–83 War of American Independence

1793–1815 Wars with France

1805 Battle of Trafalgar

1815 Battle of Waterloo

1839–42 First Opium War

1845–46, 1848–49 Sikh Wars

1854–55 Crimean War

1856–60 Second Opium War

1857–58 Indian Mutiny and First War of Independence

1878–79 Zulu War

1880–81 First South African War

1899–1902 Boer War

1914–18 World War I

1916 Battle of the Somme, Battle of Jutland

1916–21 Anglo-Irish conflict

1917 Battle of Passchendaele

1939–45 World War II

1940 Battle of Britain

1942 Battle of El Alamein

1944 D-Day invasion

1956 Suez Crisis

1969–98 Northern Ireland troubles

1982 Falklands War

1990-91 Gulf War

2001 Invasion of Afghanistan

2003 Iraq War

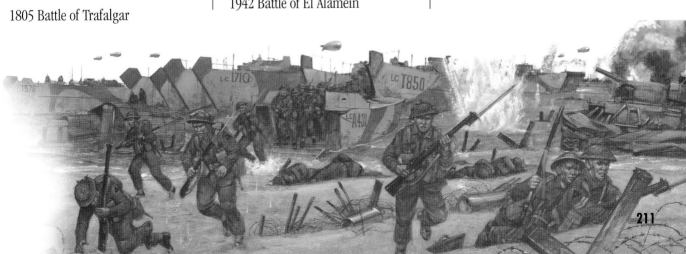

Glossary

ABDICATION When a ruler chooses to give up his or her throne.

AD (ANNO DOMINI) Indicates dates after the birth of Christ. It means 'in the year of our Lord'.

AGRICULTURAL REVOLUTION The changing of farming methods during the 18th and 19th centuries which saw a large increase in the amount of food produced.

ANGLO-SAXON A person who originally came from what is today western Germany and settled in Britain during the fifth century AD.

ANTISEPTIC Something that destroys bacteria.

ASSASSINATION The killing of a person.

ASTRONOMER A person who studies stars.

BARON A nobleman who was granted an area of land by the king.

BARROW An ancient tomb that was covered with a large mound of earth.

BC (BEFORE CHRIST) Indicates dates before the birth of Christ.

BLACK DEATH Another name for the bubonic plague.

BLITZ Short for 'blitzkrieg' which is German for 'lightning war', it describes the German aerial bombardment of British cities in 1940.

BODICE The upper part of a dress which was pulled together tightly over a blouse.

BOERS Descendents of Dutch farmers who settled in South Africa.

CELT A person who lived in Britain, Gaul (France) and Spain before the arrival of the Romans.

CHIEFTAIN The leader of a tribe.

CHIVALRY The code that described how a knight should behave. It demanded courage, fighting skill, loyalty, generosity and courtesy, especially towards women.

CHOLERA A disease which affects the intestines, causing cramps, vomiting and diarrhoea. It is caused by eating and drinking infected food and water and it can be fatal if untreated.

CIVIL WAR A war that is fought between two groups of people who live in the same country.

COAT OF ARMS A system of symbols used to show to which family a noble man or woman belonged.

COLD WAR The period during the last half of the 20th century when there was a stand-off between western countries and communist countries.

COMMONWEALTH The countries that used to make up the British empire which have now joined together to form an economic organization.

CORONATION When a king or queen is crowned.

CRUSADES A series of campaigns by Christian armies to capture and control the Holy Land in the Middle East.

CURTAIN WALL A low wall surrounding a castle which acted as the first line of defence.

DREADNOUGHT A type of very large battleship built towards the end of the 19th century and the start of the 20th century.

DROVER A person who drives sheep or cattle to and from market.

DRUIDS Celtic priests.

DRY-STONE WALL A type of wall that is put together without using cement.

EMANCIPATION To free a group of people from a particular restraint.

EMIGRANT A person who leaves one country to go to live in another.

ENLIGHTENMENT A period during the 17th and 18th centuries that saw great advances in science, the arts and philosophy.

EUROPEAN UNION The economic organization formed by countries throughout Europe. Many of these countries replaced their old currencies with a single currency, the euro.

EXCOMMUNICATE To exclude someone from the Roman Catholic Church.

FEUDALISM The system under which medieval society was structured, with kings and lords granting land in return for military service or rent.

FORUM The central part of a Roman town which acted as its marketplace and the centre for business.

FOUNDRY A building where metals are melted in a furnace or large fire.

GARRISON A group of soldiers who guard a military base.

GAUL A part of Europe that is now modern-day France.

GRAVE GOODS Items placed inside a tomb that were intended for the dead person to use in the afterlife.

HENGE A circular structure that was built out of standing stones or wooden posts.

HIBERNIA The Roman name for Ireland.

ICE AGE A period in Earth's history when temperatures were cooler and large ice sheets covered much of Europe, Asia and North America.

INDUSTRIAL REVOLUTION A period during the 18th and 19th centuries when industry expanded greatly and people moved in large numbers to live and work in towns.

LEGIONARY A Roman soldier.

MACHINE GUN A type of gun which can fire a large number of bullets with a single squeeze of the trigger.

MARTYR A person who is killed because of his or her religious beliefs.

MIDDLE AGES A historical period lasting from the fall of the Roman empire in 476 AD to 1453 and the start of the Renaissance.

MILITANT Someone who holds extreme views and promotes them vigorously.

MOAT A large lake surrounding a castle.

MONASTERY A place where monks live and worship.

MOURNING To grieve for the death of someone.

NATURAL SELECTION The process by which living things adapt and change to suit the conditions in which they live.

NAVVIES A term used to describe labourers who worked on the railways in the 19th century.

NORMANS People who came from Normandy in what is modern France.

NEANDERTHALS A primitive form of human that evolved between 200,000 and 100,000 years ago.

OBSOLETE Out of date.

OPIUM A highly addictive drug.

OTTOMAN EMPIRE The Turkish empire which lasted from the 13th century until 1918 and the end of World War I.

PALE An area of Ireland around Dublin that England ruled during the 1400s.

PILGRIMS People who travel to sacred places. Also, a term used to describe a group of settlers who moved from Britain to North America in 1620.

PLANTAGENET The royal family of England from Henry II (1154) until Richard III (died 1485).

QUERN A handmill that was used to grind grain into flour.

REFORMATION A movement to reform the Catholic Church during the 16th century which led to the creation of the Protestant Church.

REGENT A person who governs a country while the king or queen is away, sick or too young to govern.

RENAISSANCE Literally 'rebirth'. A period during the 15th and 16th centuries which saw an outburst of creative ideas.

REPEAL To cancel a law or decision.

SELECTIVE BREEDING Choosing the best animals to breed and have young in order to improve gradually the quality and quantity of meat, milk or wool.

SOUP KITCHEN A place where free food is given to the poor.

STOCKADE A protective fence usually made from wooden posts.

STUART The royal family of Scotland from 1371 to 1714 which also ruled England from 1603 to 1714.

SUFFRAGE The right to cast a vote in an election.

SUFFRAGETTES Women who campaigned to get the vote at the start of the 20th century.

TALLY STICK A stick carried by a trader on which he would carve notches to record a deal.

TAPESTRY A large piece of cloth with a woven picture showing a scene or event.

TARTAN A type of checked, woven material. In Scotland the checked pattern of the tartan told people to which family you belonged.

TORC A necklace or armband that is made out of twisted metal.

TOURNAMENT An ancient tomb that was covered with a large mound of earth.

TRADE UNION An organization that campaigns to improve workers' rights and conditions.

TRANSPORTATION Sending criminals overseas to carry out their sentences.

TREBUCHET A large catapult.

TRILITHON A stone structure that is made up of two standing stones with a third stone placed across them.

TUDOR The royal family of England from Henry VII (1485) to the death of Elizabeth I (1603).

VASSAL A servant.

VIKING A person who came from Scandinavia (Denmark, Norway and Sweden) between the 8th and 11th centuries.

WELFARE STATE A system where the government gives money and support to the poor, elderly and sick.

WORKHOUSE A 19th-century building where poor people were put to work in return for food and accommodation instead of receiving a wage.

WEBSITES

http://www.bbc.co.uk/history/

http://www.channel4.com/history/

http://www.royal.gov.uk/

http://www.spartacus.schoolnet.co.uk/REVhistory.htm

http://www.historyonthenet.com/

http://www.activehistory.co.uk/

http://www.nationalarchives.gov.uk/museum/

http://www.thehistorychannel.co.uk/site/home/

Index

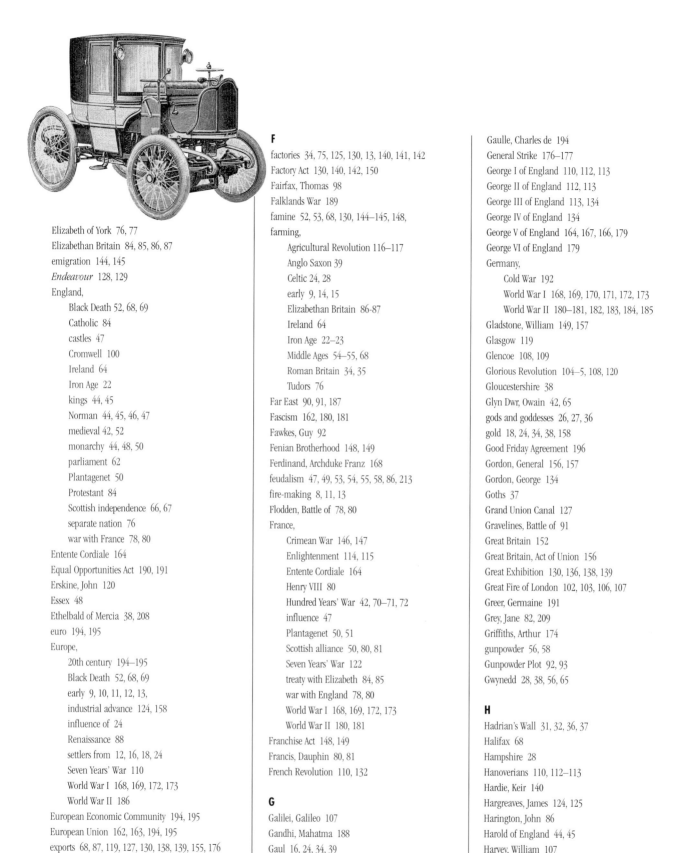

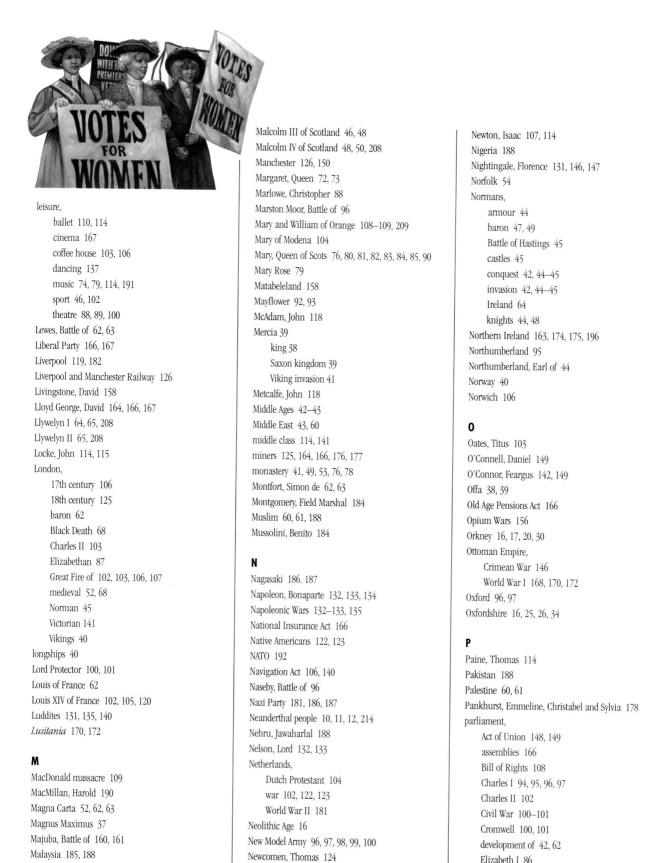

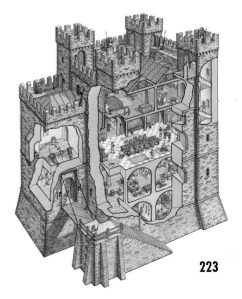

Acknowledgements

The publishers wish to thank the following artists who have contributed to this book:

Richard Hook, Vanessa Card, Peter Sarson, Mike White, James Field,
Mike Taylor, Stephen Sweet, Alison Winfield, Mel Pickering, Stephan Chabluk,
Theodore Rowland-Entwistle, Mike Lacey, Sue Stitt, Roger Kent, Roger Payne,
Martin Sanders, Rob Sheffield, David Ashby, Chris Forsey, Simon Girling Associates, Linden Artists,
Maltings Partnership and Temple Rogers Agency.

The publishers wish to thank the following for supplying photographs for this book:
16bl Dreamstime.com, 20–21 Dreamstime.com, 24br Dreamstime.com, 25tr Dreamstime.com/Matthew Collingwood,
31b Dreamstime.com, 32b Dreamstime.com, 47br Dreamstime.com, 51r istockphoto.com,
56bl Dreamstime.com/Violet Star, 62b Dreamstime.com, 76c Dreamstime.com, 85tr istockphoto.com,
85br Dreamstime.com, 89b Dreamstime.com, 157b Dreamstime.com/Christine Dedman,
162br and 190c Dreamstime.com/Paul Butchard, 166b ITN archive, 167br ITN archive, 175b stock.xchng.com,
179tr ITN archive, 182bl and br ITN archive, 183tl Dreamstime.com, 186bl Dreamstime.com/Mark Nedzbala, 187br ITN archive,
188bl Dreamstime.com, 191tl and tr Dreamstime.com, 192tl Dreamstime.com/Daniel Gale, 192br Dreamstime.com,
193b Dreamstime.com/Adam Booth, 194b courtesy of Eurostar, 196b stock.xchng.com, 197t Dreamstime.com,
197c ITN archive, 198tl Dreamstime.com, 198b Dreamstime.com, 199t Digital Vision, 199c Dreamstime.com/Franz Pfuegl,
199b Dreamstime.com/Gordon Ball

Cover images:
Front: br David Hunter/Robert Harding World Imagery/CORBIS, bc The Gallery Collection/CORBIS,
bl Richard T. Nowitz/CORBIS, c Angelo Hornak/CORBIS, tr Archivo Iconografico, S.A./CORBIS,
tc Barry Lewis/Corbis, tl Dave Bartruff/CORBIS.
Back: bl RoyalPress A. Nieboer/dpa/CORBIS, bc Malcom Fife/zefa/CORBIS,
tl Paul Seheult/Eye Ubiquitous/CORBIS, tr Skyscan/CORBIS.
Spine: Tim Graham/CORBIS.